THIRTEEN
COPTIC
ACROSTIC HYMNS

GRIFFITH INSTITUTE PUBLICATIONS

EDITOR JOHN BAINES

THIRTEEN
COPTIC
ACROSTIC HYMNS
FROM MANUSCRIPT M574 OF THE
PIERPONT MORGAN LIBRARY

EDITED BY
K. H. KUHN AND W. J. TAIT

GRIFFITH INSTITUTE
ASHMOLEAN MUSEUM
OXFORD · 1996

© The Griffith Institute 1996

ISBN 0 900416 66 1

British Library Cataloguing-in-Publication Data:
A catalogue record for this book is available from the
British Library

Typeset in Monotype Imprint, Porson Greek,
and Coptic MT by Nigel Strudwick

Imageset at Oxford University Computing Service

Printed in England by The Alden Press, Oxford

CONTENTS

PREFACE

Our interest in this collection of Coptic hymns was first aroused by a brief description given by Hans Quecke in his magisterial work *Untersuchungen zum koptischen Stundengebet* (1970). The texts present many problems and, in spite of prolonged study of the material, the solutions offered must sometimes be tentative. Our chief aim has been to make the hymns accessible to a wider public.

It is our pleasant duty to record our thanks to the authorities of the Pierpont Morgan Library, New York, for having granted permission for the publication of the relevant section of M574, and to the Committee of the Griffith Institute for their generous support of this publication. We gratefully acknowledge a grant towards the cost of the plates received from the Caton-Thompson Fund of University College London. Finally, our thanks are due to John Baines for his kind scholarly and technical help during the production of this volume.

K. H. Kuhn
W. J. Tait
April 1994

ⲱ ⲛⲧⲱⲥ ⲡⲁⲅⲓⲟⲥ ⲙⲉⲣⲕⲟⲩⲣⲓⲟⲥ · ⲛ̄ⲧⲟⲩⲡⲉⲛ
ⲧⲁⲩⲕⲱⲧ ⲡⲉⲣⲥⲓⲥ · ⲁⲩⲡⲁⲧⲁⲥⲥⲉ ⲙ̄ⲡⲁⲛⲟ
ⲙⲟⲥ ⲁⲩⲙⲟⲩ · ⲁⲡⲣⲁⲛ ⲙ̄ⲡⲛⲟⲩⲧⲉ ⲭⲓ ⲧⲁⲓⲟ :—
ⲡⲁⲗ ⲫⲁ ⲃⲏ ⲧⲁ ⲙ̄ⲡⲁⲅⲓⲟⲥ ⲃⲓⲕⲧⲱⲣ ⲡⲉⲥⲧⲣⲁⲧⲉⲗⲁ
ⲗⲏ ⲑ ⲱⲥ ⲟⲩⲛ̄ⲟⲃ ⲡⲉ ⲡⲉⲕ ⲧⲁⲓⲟ · ⲙ̄ⲡ ⲉⲑⲟⲩ
ⲛ̄ⲧⲁ ⲡⲛⲟⲩⲧⲉ ⲧⲁⲁⲩ ⲛⲁⲕ · ⲉⲛⲧ ⲩⲏ ⲧⲉⲛⲛⲉⲙⲁϥ
ⲧⲏⲣⲟⲩ · ⲁⲡⲁ ⲃⲓⲕⲧⲱⲣ ⲡ̄ϣⲏⲣⲉⲛ̄ ϩⲣⲱⲙⲁⲛ ⲟⲥ
ⲃ ⲓⲟⲥ ⲛⲓⲙ ⲛ̄ⲣⲱⲙ ⲉⲛⲧⲁⲩⲙⲁⲥⲧ ⲩ · ⲱⲁⲩ ⲧⲟⲩ
ϩⲣ̄ⲱⲛ ⲉⲥⲟⲟⲩϩ ⲓ ⲭⲱϥ · ⲛ̄ⲧⲉⲣⲟⲩⲙⲓⲥⲉ ⲛⲁ
ⲡⲁ ⲃⲓⲕⲧⲱⲣ · ⲁⲩ ⲟⲩ ⲕⲟⲛⲟⲃⲓⲟⲛ ⲉⲛⲟⲩⲃⲉ ⲭⲱϥ
ⲅ ⲉⲅⲁⲣⲁ ⲧⲉⲩⲙⲁⲁⲩ ⲫⲟⲣ ⲙⲙⲟⲩ · ⲁⲥ ⲟⲩⲕⲟ
ⲛⲟⲃⲓⲟⲛ ⲛ̄ⲛⲟⲩⲃ ⲉ ⲓ ⲭⲱϥ · ⲁⲥ ⲙⲟⲩ ⲣ ⲉⲣⲟϥ
ⲛ̄ⲙ ⲥⲁⲗ ⲃ̄ · ⲁⲥ ⲭⲟⲟⲩ ⲉ ⲡ ⲡⲁⲗⲗⲁⲧⲓ ⲟⲛ ⲱⲁⲡⲉⲣⲟ
ⲇ ⲉⲣⲉ ⲇⲓⲟⲕⲗⲏⲧⲓⲁⲛⲟⲥ ⲡ̄ⲣⲣⲟ · ⲛⲁⲩ ⲉⲡ ⲧⲁ ⲓ ⲟ
ⲟⲥ ⲁⲡⲁ ⲃⲓⲕⲧⲱⲣ · ⲉⲣⲉ ⲡⲕⲟⲛⲟⲃⲓⲟⲛ ⲛ̄ⲛⲟⲩⲃ
ⲉ ⲓ ⲭⲱϥ · ⲁϥⲙⲟⲩϩ ⲛ̄ϭⲱⲛⲧ ⲡ ⲉ ⲡ ⲉϩⲟⲩⲟ
ⲉⲓ ⲧⲁⲡⲉ ⲭⲁ ⲩ ⲛ̄ⲧⲉⲩⲙⲁⲁⲩ · ⲭⲉ ⲁ ⲙⲏ ⲧⲁ ⲙⲟⲓ
ⲱ ⲙⲁⲣⲑⲁ · ⲭⲉ ⲁ ⲛⲟⲕ ⲧⲉ ⲡ̄ⲣⲣⲟ · ⲭⲉ ⲃⲓⲕ
ⲧⲱⲣ ⲡⲟⲩ ϣⲏⲣⲉ ⲡⲉ · ⲍ ⲱ ⲧⲁ ⲙⲉⲙⲁⲣⲑⲁ
ⲉ ⲟϣ ⲁ ⲭⲉ ⲙⲉ ⲇⲓⲟⲕⲗⲏⲧⲓ ⲁ ⲛⲟⲥ ⲡ̄ⲣⲣⲟ · ⲭⲉ ⲡ̄ⲣ
ⲣⲟ ⲟⲩⲛ̄ϩ ⲱ ⲁ ⲉ ⲛⲉ ϩ · ⲕⲉⲗⲉⲩⲉ ⲛ̄ⲁ ⲓ ⲧⲁⲱⲁ ⲭⲉ
ⲏ ⲧⲁ ⲡⲉ ⲭⲉ ⲡ̄ⲣⲣⲟ ⲛⲁⲥ · ⲭⲉ ⲑ ⲉ ⲣⲟⲩ ⲉ ⲱ ⲱⲁ ⲭⲉ
ⲙ̄ⲡ̄ⲣ̄ⲣ̄ϭⲱ ⲧⲉ · ⲡⲉ ⲭⲁ ⲥ ⲛⲁⲩ ⲭⲉ ⲛ̄ⲧⲟⲕ ⲡⲉ ⲡ̄ⲣ̄ⲣⲟ
ⲁⲩⲱ ⲃⲓⲕⲧⲱⲣ ⲧⲉ ⲡⲉ ⲕ ϣⲏⲣⲉ · ⲑ ⲏ ⲛ̄ⲧⲁ ⲓ ⲣ̄
ⲣ ⲟ ⲥ ⲱ ⲧⲙ̄ ⲉⲡⲁ ⲓ · ⲁϥ ⲟⲩ ⲕⲟⲛⲟⲃⲓⲟⲛ ⲛ̄ⲛⲟⲩⲃ
ⲉ ⲓ ⲭⲱϥ · ⲁϥⲙⲟⲩ ⲣ ⲙ̄ⲙⲟϥ ⲛ̄ⲟⲩ ⲙⲟⲩ ⲥ̄ ⲛ̄ⲛⲟⲩⲃ ·
ⲁⲩ ⲇ ⲁⲩ ⲛ̄ ⲙⲉ ϣ ⲱⲙ ⲧ ⲉ ⲡ̄ⲡⲁⲗⲗⲁⲧⲓⲟⲛ
ⲓ ⲱ ⲛⲱ ⲡ ϣⲏⲣⲉ ⲙ̄ ⲡⲉⲕⲕⲟⲛⲟⲃⲓⲟⲛ ⲛ̄ⲛⲟⲩⲃ ·
ⲛ̄ⲧⲁⲩ ϣ ⲱⲡⲉⲛ ⲑ ⲉ ⲛⲟⲩ ⲁ ⲉ ⲧⲟⲥ · ϩⲛ̄ ⲛⲉ ⲃⲓ ⲭ
ⲛ̄ ⲇⲓ ⲟⲕⲗ ⲏ ⲧⲓ ⲁ ⲛⲟⲥ · ⲁϥ ⲡ ⲓ ⲱ ⲧⲉ ⲡ ⲭⲓ ⲥ ⲉ ⲉⲩ ⲃ ⲱ
ⲱⲧ ⲛ̄ⲥⲱϥ · ⲕⲉⲅⲁⲣ ⲁ ⲩ ϥ ⲱⲛ̄ ⲛ̄ⲧ ⲛ̄ ⲅⲓ ⲡ̄ⲣⲣⲟ
ⲗ ⲁ ⲩ̄ϥ ⲣ̄ ⲟⲩ ⲥⲱⲛ̄ ϩⲛ̄ ⲁⲡⲁ ⲃⲓⲕⲧⲱⲣ · ⲁϥ ⲭⲟⲟⲩϥ

ⲙⲁⲁⲩ

ⲗ ⲉⲣⲁⲧϥ ⲉⲍⲣⲱⲙⲁⲛⲟⲥ· ⲁϥⲡⲱⲧ ⲉϩⲟⲩⲛ ϣⲁⲧⲉϥ
ⲗⲉϣⲓⲛ ⲏⲙⲁⲣ ⲑⲁⲧⲁ ⲙⲁⲁⲩ· ⲙⲁⲛⲁⲩ ⲭⲓⲙⲙⲟⲓ
ⲉϩⲣⲁⲓ ⲉ ⲕ ⲏⲗⲓⲉ· ⲧⲁⲙⲟⲩ ⲍⲓ ⲭⲙⲡ ⲣⲁⲛⲛⲓⲥ·
ϣⲱⲡⲉ ⲛⲛⲁⲏⲧ ⲙⲙⲁⲓ ⲁ ⲅ ⲁⲡⲏ

ⲙ ⲛⲛⲥⲁⲛⲁⲩ ⲭⲓⲛⲁⲡⲁ ⲃⲓⲕⲧⲱⲣ· ⲉⲡⲕⲁⲥⲧⲣⲟⲛ
ⲛⲁⲛⲧⲓⲛⲱⲟⲩ· ⲁⲡ ϣⲏ ⲣⲉ ⲙ ⲡⲛⲟⲩⲧⲉ ⲡⲱⲧ
ϣⲁⲣⲟϥ· ⲁϥⲥⲉ ⲗ ⲥⲱ ⲗ ϩⲛ ⲛⲉϥ ϩⲓⲥⲉ

ⲛ ⲧⲉⲣⲉ ⲁⲡⲁ ⲃⲓⲕⲧⲱⲣ ⲛⲁⲩ ⲉⲡ ⲥⲱⲣ· ⲁϥⲣⲁϣⲉ
ⲙⲙⲁⲧⲉ ⲁϥ ⲧⲉ ⲗ ⲏ ⲗ· ⲭⲉⲛⲧⲉⲣⲓⲛ ⲁⲩ ⲡⲉⲕ
ⲍⲟⲡⲁ ⲥⲟⲛ· ⲁⲓ ⲣ ⲑⲉ ⲉⲱ ⲭⲉⲓⲛⲁⲩ ⲉⲓⲥ

ⲝ ⲁ ⲟⲩ ⲛ ⲉ ⲍ ⲣⲱⲙⲁⲛⲟⲥ ⲡⲁⲓⲱⲧ· ⲡⲉ ⲭⲉⲡ ⲥⲱⲣ
ⲛ ⲁⲡⲁ ⲃⲓⲕⲧⲱⲣ· ⲭⲉ ϯ ⲥ ⲟⲟⲩ ⲛ ⲉ ⲍ ⲣⲱⲙⲁⲛⲟⲥ
ⲡⲉ ⲕ ⲓⲱ ⲧ· ⲁⲩ ⲱ ⲙⲁⲣ ⲑⲁ ⲧ ⲉ ⲧⲉⲕ ⲙⲁⲁⲩ

ⲟ ⲩⲁⲛ ⲟⲉⲓ ⲕ ⲍ ⲁ ⲧⲏ ⲕ ⲧⲁ ⲟⲩ ⲱ ⲙ ⲛ ⲙ ⲙⲁ ⲕ· ⲡⲉ ⲭⲉ
ⲡ ⲥ ⲱⲣ ⲛ ⲁ ⲡⲁ ⲃⲓⲕ ⲧⲱⲣ· ⲡⲉ ⲭⲁ ⲩ ⲭⲉ ϥ ⲟⲛ ⲍ
ⲛ ⲟ ⲓ ⲡⲁ ⲟ ⲥ· ⲡⲁ ⲭ ⲟⲩ ⲧ ⲉ ⲛ ⲟ ⲟ ⲩ ⲥ ⲡ ⲟ ⲟ ⲩ ⲙ ⲡ ⲟ ⲩ ⲉⲙ
ⲟ ⲉ ⲓ ⲕ· ⲡⲉ ⲭⲉ ⲡ ⲥⲱⲣ ⲛ ⲁ ⲡⲁ ⲃⲓⲕ ⲧⲱⲣ· ⲭⲉ

ⲡ ⲕ ⲍ ⲙ ⲟ ⲟⲥ ⲉ ⲕ ⲣⲟⲩ ⲍ ⲓ ⲡⲉ ⲓ ⲙⲁ· ⲉ ⲣ ⲉ ⲛ ⲉ ⲓ ⲡ ⲱ ⲁ ⲍ
ⲍ ⲓ ⲡ ⲉ ⲕ ⲥ ⲱ ⲙⲁ· ⲉ ⲧ ⲉ ⲙ ⲛ ⲗ ⲁ ⲁ ⲩ ⲛ ⲣ ⲱ ⲙ ⲉ ⲍ ⲁ ⲧⲏ ⲕ

ⲣ ⲁ ⲁ ⲩ ⲙ ⲡ ⲱ ⲗ ⲍ ⲉ ⲧ ⲍ ⲓ ⲡⲁ ⲥ ⲱ ⲙⲁ· ⲁ ⲓ ⲉ ⲙ ⲡ ϣ ⲁ
ⲙ ⲙ ⲟ ⲟ ⲩ ⲍ ⲁ ⲛ ⲁ ⲛ ⲟ ⲃⲉ· ⲁ ⲗ ⲗ ⲁ ϣ ⲁ ⲓ ϣ ⲁ ⲛ ⲉ ⲙ ⲟ ⲧ
ⲛ ⲧ ⲟ ⲟ ⲧ ⲩ ⲙ ⲡ ⲛ ⲟ ⲩ ⲧ ⲉ· ⲭⲉ ⲙ ⲡ ⲱ ⲁ ⲁ ⲩ ⲥ ⲟ ⲩ ⲧ ⲍ ⲩ ⲥ

ⲥ ⲟ ⲩ ⲱ ⲛ ⲧ ⲛ ⲁ ⲕ ⲱ ⲡⲁ ⲥ ⲱ ⲧ ⲡ ⲃⲓ ⲕ ⲧ ⲱ ⲣ· ⲭⲉ ⲁ ⲛ ⲟ ⲕ
ⲡ ⲉ ⲧ ⲡ ⲉ ⲕ ⲣ ⲣ ⲟ· ⲁ ⲛ ⲟ ⲕ ⲡ ⲉ ϥ ϣ ⲟ ⲟ ⲡ ⲛ ⲙ ⲙ ⲁ ⲕ· ⲍ ⲓ
ⲙ ⲁ ⲛ ⲓ ⲙ ϣ ⲁ ⲩ ⲭ ⲓ ⲧ ⲕ ⲉ ⲣ ⲟ ⲩ· ϯ ⲓ ⲱ ⲣ ⲕ ⲛ ⲁ ⲕ

ⲱ ⲡⲁ ⲥ ⲱ ⲧ ⲡ ⲃ ⲓ ⲕ ⲧ ⲱ ⲣ· ⲭⲉ ⲉ ⲓ ϣ ⲁ ⲛ ϯ ⲉ ⲟ ⲟ ⲩ ⲛ ⲟ ⲩ
ⲙ ⲁ ⲣ ⲧ ⲩ ⲣ ⲟ ⲥ· ϣ ⲁ ⲛ ⲭ ⲟ ⲟ ⲥ ⲛ ⲁ ϥ· ⲭⲉ ⲛ ⲁ ϯ ⲉ ⲟ ⲟ ⲩ
ⲛ ⲁ ⲕ· ⲛ ⲑ ⲉ ⲛ ⲃ ⲓ ⲕ ⲧ ⲱ ⲣ ⲡ ϣ ⲏ ⲣ ⲉ ⲛ ⲍ ⲣ ⲱ ⲙ ⲁ ⲛ ⲟ ⲥ

ⲩ ⲙ ⲡ ⲁ ⲓ ⲥ ⲉ ⲡ ⲣ ⲉ ⲓ ⲡ ⲟ ⲩ ⲥ ⲓ ⲣ ⲉ· ⲛ ⲧ ⲉ ⲣ ⲟ ⲩ ⲭ ⲓ ⲧ ϥ ⲉ ϩ ⲣ ⲁ ⲓ
ⲉ ⲛ ⲉ ⲡ ⲏ ⲩ ⲉ· ⲁ ⲩ ⲧ ⲁ ⲙ ⲓ ⲟ ⲩ ⲉ ⲡ ⲏ ⲓ ⲛ ⲁ ⲡⲁ ⲃ ⲓ ⲕ ⲧ ⲱ ⲣ
ⲉ ϥ ⲕ ⲱ ⲧ ⲉ ⲛ ⲟ ⲩ ⲃ ⲍ ⲓ ⲱ ⲛ ⲉ ⲙ ⲙ ⲉ

Page ⲣⲛⲉ: Hymn III, 10/3–20/4

INTRODUCTION

These thirteen Sahidic hymns, hitherto unedited, are taken from a ninth century manuscript belonging to the Pierpont Morgan Library, M574, pp. p̄n̄–p̄oⲥ̄, line 13. The text is available in the photographic edition, *Bybliothecae Pierpont Morgan codices coptici photographice expressi* (Rome 1922), volume 13, plates 154–80. A description of the manuscript and its contents is to be found in H. Hyvernat, *A Check List of Coptic Manuscripts in the Pierpont Morgan Library* (New York 1919), 5, No. IX. Hyvernat stated that the codex consists of 91 leaves, measuring 280 mm (height) by 220 mm (width), and the text is written in one column of 26–28 lines.[1] According to a supplementary description of the manuscript by H. Quecke,[2] the codex actually consists of 90 leaves, the colophon being written on the inside of the back cover. The content of the whole codex is liturgical in character and is fully analysed by Quecke.[3] A further description of the manuscript and a summary of its contents have appeared in L. Depuydt's catalogue of the Pierpont Morgan Coptic manuscripts.[4] Each hymn is an alphabetic acrostic,[5] consisting normally of 24 stanzas[6] and using the 24 letters

---

[1] The number of lines in the hymns here edited actually varies between 29 and 36.

[2] *Untersuchungen zum koptischen Stundengebet* (Publications de l'Institut orientaliste de Louvain 3, Louvain 1970), 91–6. [Hereafter *Stundengebet.*]

[3] *Stundengebet*, 97–104. For remarks on the alphabetic acrostic hymns, see p. 101, and on their language, see pp. 388–9.

[4] *Catalogue of Coptic Manuscripts in the Pierpont Morgan Library* (Corpus of Illuminated Manuscripts 4–5: Oriental Series 1–2; 2 vols., Louvain 1993): for the manuscript (No. 59), see I, 113–21; for the summary of the contents of the alphabetic acrostic hymns, see there section IV, pp. 118–19.

[5] The manuscript uses the term ⲁⲗⲫⲁⲃⲏⲧⲁ; in our translation we have rendered this by 'alphabetic acrostic'.

[6] It should be noted that in the terminology adopted here each hymn is composed of *stanzas*, which are in turn composed of *verses*. References to hymn, stanza, and verse are given in the form XIII,24/4.

of the Greek alphabet in sequence at the beginning of each stanza.[1] In Hymn IV, alone, the letters are used in reverse order. Quecke draws attention to the fact that the later Bohairic Psali are constructed in the same way, and that it has been conjectured that our hymns represent an earlier form of the same genre.[2] The hymns are in praise of the Virgin Mary, the apostles, and a number of saints particularly popular in the Coptic Church, and it may be assumed that they were used on the appropriate saint's day, while the two hymns which have for their subject the resurrection and the ascension, and baptism may have been appointed for the relevant seasons in the ecclesiastical year. Although the group of hymns clearly forms a separate unit within the manuscript M574, it is not divided off by a title from the preceding section. Each hymn, however, has its own heading, stating its subject. The hymns are numbered from one to thirteen, and this numeral stands in the left-hand margin, normally preceding each heading directly. Hymns I–IX are called in their headings ⲁⲗⲫⲁⲃⲏⲧⲁ, while in Hymns X–XIII the format of the heading changes: they are characterized only by their subject matter and the term ⲁⲗⲫⲁⲃⲏⲧⲁ is not included. The colophon of the manuscript contains a date, expressed in terms of the era of the Martyrs, which was read by Hyvernat in his *Check List* as either year 611 or year 614 (i.e. either AD 894/5 or AD 897/8); this view went unchallenged[3] until Depuydt recently stated—surely correctly, to judge from the plate in the photographic edition—that only the reading 614 (AD 897/8) is possible.[4]

---

[1] It should be stressed that it was the scribe's aim that each stanza should begin with the correct written letter, rather than sound. As discussed below, he would resort to unorthodox spellings in order to place the desired letter at the beginning of a stanza. He would not use correct spellings that have an appropriate pronunciation, but the wrong initial letter: thus ⲁⲁⲁ would not begin a stanza where ⲧ was required.

[2] *Stundengebet*, 101. Cf. Yassa 'Abd al-Masih, 'A Greco-Arabic Psali', *Bulletin de l'Institut des Études Coptes* [single issue, unnumbered] (1958), 77–100 (see especially pp. 87–8 and 98).

[3] E.g. by A. van Lantschoot, *Recueil des colophons des manuscrits chrétiens d'Égypte* 1: *Les colophons coptes des manuscrits sahidiques* (Bibliothèque du Muséon 1, Louvain 1929), fasc. 1, 41–2, No. xxiii; and by Quecke, *Stundengebet*, 95 (esp. n. 2).

[4] *Catalogue of Coptic Manuscripts* 1, 119 (esp. n. 4).

Contents

A brief summary of the content of each hymn may now be given.

Hymn I is in praise of the Virgin Mary. It is a mosaic of biblical proof texts designed to celebrate her honour and preeminence. The references to the Old Testament are of particular interest and may strike the modern reader as bizarre and inappropriate. They bear witness to the allegorical interpretation of the Bible in the tradition of the Church. They are not the invention of the hymnographer and many of them can be paralleled in patristic and liturgical writings.[1] The hymn ends with an invitation to all the peoples of the world to join in the celebration of the feast of the Mother of God.

Hymn II is in praise of St Mercurius,[2] one of the most popular soldier saints in the Egyptian Church, who suffered martyrdom for his faith. The hymn describes Mercurius' valiant deeds as a soldier of the emperor Decius. He was given encouragement by the vision and the words of angels. The emperor conferred great honours upon him but, as he refused to sacrifice to the emperor's gods, he was beheaded. He was buried and a martyr's shrine was built over his grave at which great miracles occurred. Many years later Mercurius was credited with having miraculously brought about the death of Julian the Apostate.

Hymn III is in praise of St Victor,[3] the general, another soldier saint and martyr revered in the Coptic Church. The hymn describes how Victor, the son of Romanus and Martha, was brought clothed in gold into the presence of the emperor Diocletian by his mother. The emperor at first resented the presumption

---

[1]   See H. Graef, *Mary: a History of Doctrine and Devotion* 1 (London 1963). See also e.g. R. Hillier, 'Joseph the Hymnographer and Mary the Gate', *Journal of Theological Studies* 36 (1985), 311–20. Some of the biblical images also occur in the Graeco-Arabic Psali mentioned in p. 2 n. 2 above.

[2]   See the relevant article by M. van Esbroeck in A. S. Atiya (editor in chief), *The Coptic Encyclopedia* (New York 1991) V, 1592–4 [hereafter *Copt. Enc.*]. See also De L. O'Leary, *The Saints of Egypt* (London 1937), 201–2. For some other hymns on St Mercurius, see M. Cramer, *Koptische Hymnologie in deutscher Übersetzung* (Wiesbaden 1969), 4–12.

[3]   See the relevant article by M. van Esbroeck and Khalil Samir *Copt. Enc.* VII, 2303–8. See also O'Leary, *The Saints of Egypt*, 278–81. An encomium on St Victor appears in the Pierpont Morgan manuscript M591: see the photographic edition, *Bybliothecae Pierpont Morgan codices coptici photographice expressi* (Rome 1922) 28, plates 68–98; A. B. Scott has published an edition and English translation of this text in L. Depuydt (general editor), *Encomiastica from the Pierpont Morgan Library* (Corpus Scriptorum Christianorum Orientalium 544–5/Copt. 47–8, Louvain 1993) I, 133–52; II, 103–18.

implied by Victor's dress of gold but, after having been appeased by Martha, he honoured him by appointing him third in his palace. Later Diocletian changed his policy and began to persecute the Christians and Victor announced to his mother that he must die for the name of Jesus. He was taken to Antinoe where he was vouchsafed a vision of Christ who conversed with him, promising him a glorious reward in heaven.

Hymn IV is in praise of St Claudius, the general, another soldier saint and martyr, who is honoured in this hymn together with St Victor.[1] In contrast to the preceding hymn, the one on Claudius contains few biographical details. It is, rather, a more generalized panegyric supported by many biblical quotations and allusions. The friendship of Victor and Claudius is compared to that of David and Jonathan, and we are told that the two saints performed many healing miracles. Finally their martyrdoms are briefly recounted.

Hymn V is in praise of St Theodore,[2] the general, another soldier saint and martyr of the Coptic Church. After an introductory passage in praise of the saint, there follows an account of his visit to the city of Euchaites. A woman whose children were in the clutches of a dragon came to meet him and to enlist his support. Theodore slew the dragon and freed the children. He is revered as a miracle worker and as a helper in distress. Another specific feat of the saint is mentioned: he is said to have saved a woman who, on a visit to the baths, was in danger of being ravished. His renown is recorded everywhere and he is glorified for having been given the power to cast out demons.

Hymn VI is in praise of Severus,[3] the patriarch of Antioch (AD 512–518), who spent some years of his life in Egypt and was a champion of the Monophysite cause. In this hymn he is celebrated as a learned teacher and as the destroyer of the heretics. There is then a reference to an audience with the empress Theodora which Severus had at the imperial court in Constantinople. During this, a

[1] On Claudius, see O'Leary, *The Saints of Egypt*, 111. For other hymnic material on St Claudius and St Victor, see Cramer, *Koptische Hymnologie*, 17–21.

[2] See the relevant article by T. Orlandi in *Copt. Enc.* VII, 2237–8. See also O'Leary, *The Saints of Egypt*, 262–5. For other hymnic material on St Theodore, see Cramer, *Koptische Hymnologie*, 12–17. H. Junker, *Koptische Poesie des 10. Jahrhunderts*, 2 vols. (Berlin 1908–11), includes poems praising or briefly mentioning the same saints celebrated in these acrostic hymns: e.g. for St Theodore, see II, 200–7.

[3] See the relevant article by L. Knezevich in *Copt. Enc.* VII, 2123–5. See also O'Leary, *The Saints of Egypt*, 249–50.

eunuch attending the empress had a vision of Christ conversing with Severus and warning him not to stay there, as it was a place of unbelief. This may be a veiled reference to the political situation in Constantinople for, while the empress favoured the Monophysites, the emperor, Justinian I, supported those who adhered to the decisions of the Council of Chalcedon. In this hymn Severus is depicted as putting to shame the bishops of Chalcedon, and everyone is exhorted to honour his memory. The hymn ends with a request to Severus to intercede with God on behalf of all sinners.

Hymn VII breaks new ground. It has for its subject the resurrection and ascension, and the hymnographer is concerned to show by biblical quotations that both the Old and the New Testaments bear witness to these two doctrines. The incarnation is described as a wonder but a greater wonder still is the resurrection and ascension. Mention of the coming of the Holy Spirit leads the writer to end the hymn with a paean to the Holy Trinity.

Hymn VIII is in praise of the Archangel Michael.[1] A reference to the feast of St Michael at the beginning of the hymn shows clearly that these hymns had their proper place in the liturgy of the Coptic church and were used on the appropriate saint's day. Again the hymnographer combs the Bible for proof texts which are meant to demonstrate Michael's aid and protection for various biblical personages. In most of these biblical passages, Michael is not mentioned by name but the reference is simply to an unnamed angel—the exception is VIII,4, with its reference to Daniel 10.21. In the final stanzas of the hymn all gifts of healing and all forgiveness are said to come from heaven through Michael's prayers, and all the peoples of the world are asked to pray to Michael for his intercession.

Hymn IX is in praise of the twelve apostles. It is a mosaic of biblical quotations and allusions. Christ chose poor men to be his apostles. They are his friends and brothers, and they will be rewarded for their labours. They will take part in the final judgement of the world. In the later stanzas the apostles are mentioned by name and brief remarks on each one are added. Surprisingly, instead of Simon the Cananaean, the list includes Simon of Cyrene.

---

[1] See the relevant article by M. van Esbroeck in *Copt. Enc.* v, 1616–20. See also O'Leary, *The Saints of Egypt*, 203. For other hymns on the archangels Michael and Gabriel, see Cramer, *Koptische Hymnologie*, 92–103, and G. M. Browne, *Michigan Coptic Texts* (Papyrologica castroctaviana, studia et textus 7, Barcelona 1979), 34–41.

Judas Iscariot is, of course, omitted, and mention is made of St Paul the apostle and, additionally, Luke the apostle and Mark the evangelist. All the information on the apostles is taken from the New Testament except in the case of Andrew, where it is taken apparently from a tradition recorded in the apocryphal Acts of Andrew and Matthias.[1]

Hymn X, like Hymn VII, has for its subject a fundamental tenet of the Christian Church, baptism. The recurring theme of the hymn is Christ's baptism in the Jordan. It leads on to the baptism of all Christians with the Holy Spirit and water for the forgiveness of sins. Philip's baptism of the Ethiopian eunuch is also mentioned.

Hymn XI, like Hymn VI, is in praise of Severus of Antioch. The patriarch is depicted as having received from God the same authority as that which was given by Christ to St Peter. He is compared to Elijah in his zealous defence of the right faith, to St Peter, the faithful shepherd, in his teaching, and to Moses in his law-giving. Severus is hailed as an apostolic teacher of true doctrine, knowledgeable in the scriptures, a fighter for the faith of the perfect Trinity. He is asked to intercede with God for the forgiveness of the sins of the people.

Hymn XII is in praise of St Antony.[2] He is revered for having chosen to embrace the monastic life, the perfect way to follow the Lord Jesus. The fathers in the desert lived in fear of demons who tempted them with many delusions, but with the Saviour's help the demons were defeated. By his virtuous life, Antony became a guide for many, and his way of life was much admired. The desert fathers had as their forerunners Elijah, Elisha, and John the Baptist who were their exemplars. They lived a life of solitude and prayer and God granted them every gift of healing. In the final stanza, Antony is asked to intercede with God for mercy and the forgiveness of sins.

---

[1]   See the Acts of Andrew and Matthias (M. R. James, *The Apocryphal New Testament* (Oxford 1924 and corr. repr. 1953), 453-8, and J. K. Elliott, *The Apocryphal New Testament* (Oxford 1993), 240–2 and 283–99). Cf. E. Lucchesi et J.-M. Prieur, 'Fragments coptes des Actes d'André et Matthias et d'André et Barthélemy', *Analecta Bollandiana* 96 (1978), 339-50. See also D. R. MacDonald, *The Acts of Andrew and the Acts of Andrew and Matthias in the City of the Cannibals* (Texts and Translations 33, Christian Apocrypha 1, Atlanta 1990) and J.-M. Prieur, *Acta Andreae* (Corpus Christianorum, Series Apocryphorum 5–6, Turnhout 1989).

[2]   See the relevant article by A. Guillaumont, *Copt. Enc.* I, 149–51. See also O'Leary, *The Saints of Egypt*, 76–9. For other hymns on St Antony, see Cramer, *Koptische Hymnologie*, 31–4.

Hymn XIII is in praise of Apa Shenoute.[1] Shenoute, who was the abbot of the White Monastery in the fifth century, held the ecclesiastical rank of archimandrite. He is compared at length to Moses. Like Moses, he had visions of God who conversed with him. He was called to be a prophet while still in his mother's womb, as Moses was called to his mission by God out of the burning bush. Like Moses, he became the leader of his people, the monks, whose life under his guidance became like that of the holy angels. Like Moses, he disciplined his followers. Moses built the tabernacle; Shenoute laid the foundation of the monastery's church. Moses was covered by a cloud until God gave him the law; Shenoute was taken on a cloud from his monastery to the palace of Theodosius II (AD 408–450) for an interview with the emperor. At the end of the hymn, Shenoute is asked to intercede with God for the forgiveness of sins.

As can be seen from this summary of the contents of the thirteen hymns, the most prominent source on which the hymnographer relied was the Bible. Quotations from and allusions to the Old and the New Testaments abound. In addition, the author drew upon the legends and stories surrounding the saints celebrated in the hymns. These hagiographic traditions must have been well known to the users of this collection of hymns, for the author's handling of his material is often very allusive. This is a general feature of the hymns. Although it is obviously due in part to the problems of presenting the material within the constraints of four-verse stanzas, it is clearly not entirely a technical problem. A particularly striking example is that of the allusion, in II,21–4, to the tradition that St Mercurius miraculously brought about the death of Julian the Apostate, and that an icon of the saint bore witness to this; four stanzas are devoted to the topic, but the passage could hardly be intelligible to anyone ignorant of the legend.

Structure

It is now desirable to look a little more closely at the form and structure of these hymns.[2] First, it must be made clear that in the

---

[1] See the relevant article by K. H. Kuhn, *Copt. Enc.* VII, 2131–3. See also O'Leary, *The Saints of Egypt*, 251–5. For other hymns on Apa Shenoute, see Junker, *Koptische Poesie des 10. Jahrhunderts* II, 214–19; Cramer, *Koptische Hymnologie*, 51–5; and the six Bohairic alphabetic hymns edited by J. Leipoldt, *Sinuthii Archimandritae Vita et Opera Omnia* III (CSCO 42/Copt. 2, Louvain 1908), 226–42.

[2] For a collection of source material for the history of hymnology in

manuscript the hymns are not set out as formal poetry. The text is written continuously, but paragraph marks and punctuation have enabled us to define the structure of every hymn. The beginning of each stanza is indicated by a paragraph mark (*diplé*, >) and an enlarged, partly coloured,[1] and (in the case of some letters) slightly ornate initial letter, protruding into the left-hand margin. If the new stanza begins in the middle of a manuscript line, the paragraph mark and the enlarged letter appear at the beginning of the next manuscript line. This follows normal practice for signalling the start of new sections of text in Coptic literary manuscripts, but it has the curious consequence that a proportion (in several hymns, over a half)[2] of the enlarged letters are *not* the first letters of stanzas, and thus do *not* highlight the alphabetic sequence around which the acrostic is constructed. Indeed, even fewer of the enlarged letters would have belonged to this alphabet if the scribe had not occasionally compressed his material or left spaces, in order to be able to start a new stanza on a new line. Sometimes, the first letter of a stanza, when not at the beginning of a manuscript line, is made just a little larger than normal, although never of a size to rival the regular enlarged letters.[3] The first three verses of each four-verse stanza are terminated by a stop at roughly mid-height; the fourth verse has at its end as punctuation mark two short slanting parallel lines (⸗).[4] In our edition the hymns are set out in stanzas and the normal

antiquity, see M. Lattke, *Hymnus: Materialien zu einer Geschichte der antiken Hymnologie* (Novum Testamentum et Orbis Antiquus 19, Freiburg and Göttingen 1991). For a summary account of Coptic poetry, and bibliography, see the article by K. H. Kuhn in *Copt. Enc.* VI, 1985–6.

[1] We are grateful to Sarah Clackson for examining the relevant portion of M574, and ascertaining that, wherever the manuscript employs coloured ink (that is, in enlarged letters, regularly in the letter ϕ, in punctuation, in *diplés*, and in lines over *nomina sacra*, page-numbers, and other numerals), the colour is red, used in conjunction with the normal brownish ink of the text. An exception is the elaborate *diplé* at the commencement of Hymn XIII (p. $\overline{\text{ρολ}}$), where red, yellow, and a distinctive black or dark blue are used.

[2] In the case of Hymn XI, only seven of the enlarged letters match the acrostic scheme, and in Hymn XIII, only five.

[3] E.g. II,3/1, 21/1 (although ϕ is usually rather large and partly coloured); at stanza 15 of Hymns I, X, and XIII and at stanza 10 of Hymn IV (the hymn with reverse alphabetic arrangement), the initial ο has within it the dot typical of the enlarged letters in the manuscript, and the ε at Hymn VII, stanza 5 is decorated by two dots.

[4] The punctuation of the first three verses is generally either reinforced or accompanied by a second, red dot; the two strokes at the end of stanzas are reinforced in red. The punctuation at the end of an entire hymn takes the form :-.

punctuation marks of the manuscript are included regularly throughout; only in rare cases can the expected punctuation not be seen on the photographs of the manuscript, and it may be surmised that some of those missing have been damaged rather than omitted; they are supplied in the transcription, normally without comment.[1] In the few instances where there is any doubt about the structure of a stanza, attention is drawn to the problem in the footnotes to the Coptic text.

As in the case of other Coptic poetry, the arrangement of these hymns is not strictly speaking metrical but rather rhythmical. Each hymn consists of 24 stanzas. There is one exception: Hymn VIII has 25 stanzas, the reason being that VIII,4 introduces the prophet Daniel—the first verse of the stanza begins with the letter ⲁ in accordance with the scheme of the alphabetic acrostic—and the following stanza, VIII,5, continues to deal with the subject of Daniel but lies outside the alphabetic scheme, as is confirmed by the fact that the scribe did not provide stanza 5 with an enlarged initial letter. Normally, each stanza consists of four verses, but again there are exceptions. In II,1 there are only three verses. Of course it is possible that this irregularity is due to a scribal error that has crept in somewhere along the line of transmission, for it must be assumed that the version of the hymns here edited is a copy that has come down to us by chance. There are also some stanzas of five verses. In three cases (III,24; IV,24; IX,24) the hymn ends with ϭⲟⲡⲥ ⲉⲡϭⲥ, 'Pray to the Lord', but both structure and punctuation make it clear that this final verse did not form part of the original hymn. It was probably added by some pious scribe.[2] The case is different in V,17, where the fifth verse clearly is part of the stanza and where the punctuation in the manuscript confirms that the stanza has five

---

[1] Possible cases of the omission of punctuation marks are rarer in the middle of a manuscript line than at the end (where the punctuation might have been regarded as less necessary). However, at V,14/3–4, VII,8/4–5, and VIII,1/3–4, for example, the spacing of the text makes it certain that the expected punctuation in the middle of a manuscript line has been omitted rather than damaged. The final punctuation marks of stanzas are never lacking.

[2] In each instance, the phrase conveniently fills a small blank space at the end of a manuscript line; in Hymns IV and IX, this occurs at the end of a manuscript page.

verses.[1] Similarly, VII,8 also has five verses.[2] Finally, there is one stanza, V,24, which consists of six verses.[3]

The hymnographer faced a number of problems in accommodating the hymns within the framework of the alphabetic acrostic scheme.[4] Some of the Greek letters are used relatively rarely in Coptic and, in order to follow the scheme, he found it necessary to adopt special devices in spelling. The scheme also influenced his choice of vocabulary. Some examples may be given. ⲃⲱⲱ occurs for ϥⲱⲱ (e.g. I,2); ⲃⲓ for ϥⲓ (VII,2); ⲃⲉⲣⲙⲉⲛⲧⲣⲉ for ϥ- (IX,2). The introduction of the Greek exclamation ⲃⲁⲃⲁⲓ (XIII,2) is particularly noteworthy. The spellings ⲅⲉⲕⲁⲣ (e.g. I,3), ⲅⲉⲣⲁⲣ (e.g. II,3), and ⲅⲁⲓⲅⲁⲣ (XIII,3) for ⲕⲁⲓⲅⲁⲣ (e.g. XI,10) and ⲕⲉⲅⲁⲣ (e.g. III,10), which are also used within the scheme, should be noted. ⲇ for ⲧ occurs in ⲇⲱⲟⲩⲛ (II,4), in ⲇⲉⲣⲉ- for (ⲛ)ⲧⲉⲣⲉ- (III,4), and in ⲇⲁⲓ (IX,4). ⲍ stands for ⲥ in ⲍⲱⲧⲙ (e.g. III,6), in ⲍⲉⲉⲣⲙⲉⲛⲧⲣⲉ (IV,19), in ⲍⲩⲙⲁⲛⲉ (σημαίνειν, VII,6), and in ⲍⲩⲛⲏⲇⲏⲥⲓⲥ (XII,6). ⲏ stands for ⲉⲓ in ⲏⲥ (e.g. II,7), and in ⲏⲧⲇ (εἶτα, e.g. III,7). The use of the initial ⲓ threw up two problems. ⲓⲱ (III,9) is either the Greek exclamation ἰώ, or possibly a variant spelling of ϩⲁⲉⲓⲟ; ⲓⲉⲥ (IV,16) stands probably for ⲉⲓⲥ. Of special interest is the use of ⲗ within the acrostic. In III,11 there occurs the Fayyumic ⲗⲉⲱⲓ for ⲣⲁⲱⲉ.[5] Quecke deduces from this last usage that at least Hymn III originated in the Fayyum and he considers the possibility that the whole collection of hymns represents a local Fayyumic tradition. He finds support for this idea in the fact that he has so far been

---

[1]   There seems to be no firm ground for suggesting any particular emendation to this stanza.

[2]   In VII,8, the fourth verse lacks a mark of punctuation. The fourth verse represents the relevant gospel text, while the fifth verse interprets it. Thus it would be possible to argue that the stanza may originally have consisted of the regular four verses, and either the fourth or fifth may have been added as a gloss.

[3]   In V,24, no obvious emendation suggests itself. The last two verses could be deleted, but they match the sentiments of the closing verses of several of the hymns. The stanza commences with a triple invocation of martyrs, apostles, and prophets; the martyrs (alone) are mentioned in stanza 23, and conceivably the second and third verses might be deleted from stanza 24.

[4]   On the subject of alphabetic acrostics, see the recent bibliography in W. Brashear and H. Satzinger, 'Ein akrostichischer griechischer Hymnus mit koptischer Übersetzung (Wagner-Museum K 1003)', *Journal of Coptic Studies* 1 (1990), 37–58 (see pp. 40–1). See also H. Quecke, 'Eine koptische alphabetische Akrostichis', *Orientalia* 61 (1992), 1–9.

[5]   The only occurrence of ⲗ for ⲣ in the hymns apart from this instance demanded by the alphabetic acrostic scheme is in VI,9/1, ⲉⲗⲉⲧⲓⲛ.

unable to find any parallels to our hymns in later Bohairic texts of the same genre.[1] The origin of our hymns will be considered once more below in connection with a brief analysis of their language. But at this point reference must be made to an irregular use of the letter ⲣ within the alphabetic acrostic. In the same hymn (III,17) there occurs ⲣⲁⲁⲩ for ⲗⲁⲁⲩ, a spelling that is inexplicable as any natural dialect form. The author of the hymns perhaps simply invented this spelling because of his need for a word beginning with ⲣ in III,17, encouraged by his awareness that Fayyumic ⲗ so frequently stands for a Sahidic ⲣ, a situation which he thought it might be permissible to reverse mechanically.

Next we must consider the use of ϫ in the alphabetic acrostic scheme. This is used for ⲕⲥ in a number of instances: ϫⲱⲕ (e.g. XII,14), ϫⲁⲟⲩⲛ (e.g. II,14), ϫⲁⲟⲩⲛⲁⲙ for ⲕ(ⲛ)ⲥⲁ- (VII,14), ϫⲱⲧⲡ (IX,14), ϫⲩⲙⲁⲛⲉ (X,14), and, with the ⲥ duplicated, ϫⲥⲙⲁⲙⲁⲁⲧ (IV,11; V,14). The letter ⲧ for ⲇ occurs in the names ⲧⲉⲕⲓⲟⲥ (II,19) and ⲧⲁⲅⲉⲓⲇ (IV,6). The use of the letter ⲩ in the acrostic presented special problems. It is used in Greek loan-words where ϩ is normally expected as the initial letter: ⲩⲙⲛⲉⲩⲉ (e.g. I,20), ⲩⲡⲟⲙⲟⲛⲏ (VI,20). ⲩ is substituted for ⲛ in ⲩⲧⲁϥ for ⲛⲧⲟϥ (II,20). There also occur ⲩⲓ, presumably for ⲟⲩⲏⲓ (e.g. III,20), and ⲩⲓⲥ, presumably for ⲉⲓⲥ (V,20). The letter ⲩ also occurs in Greek loan-words beginning with ἥ or ἤ ⲩⲗⲏⲕⲓⲇ (XI,20), ⲩ, presumably for ἤ (XIII,20), and ⲩⲗⲓⲁⲥ, Elijah (XII,20). In order to maintain the alphabetic acrostic, the hymnographer also used ⲫⲱⲥⲟⲛ for ἐφ᾽ ὅσον (XIII,21), and ⲱⲛⲧⲱⲥ for ὄντως (e.g. II,24). It should be noted that many of the devices adopted here in an effort to observe the rules of the alphabetic acrostic arrangement are also to be found in the later Bohairic Psali which follow the same pattern.[2]

Language and date

The language of the manuscript M574 has been analysed in considerable detail by Quecke,[3] but he explicitly omits from his enquiry the particular section which contains our hymns. Nevertheless, some of his remarks bear upon the language of the hymns and will serve as a convenient starting point for a brief description. The

---

[1]   *Stundengebet*, 388–9.
[2]   Cf. the relevant material in R. Tuki, ⲡⲓϫⲱⲙ ⲛⲧⲉ ⲛⲓⲑⲉⲟⲧⲟⲕⲓⲁ ⲛⲉⲙ ⲕⲁⲧⲁ ⲧⲁϫⲓⲥ ⲛⲧⲉ ⲡⲓⲁⲃⲟⲧ ⲭⲟⲓⲁⲕ (Rome 1764).
[3]   See *Stundengebet*, 350–89, and also the description of similar material by G. M. Browne, *Michigan Coptic Texts*, 35 (cf. p. 52).

hymns are written in Sahidic with a strong admixture of Fayyumic forms.[1] This is a common feature of many Pierpont Morgan manuscripts and can be explained by the fact that these manuscripts were written for the Monastery of the Archangel St Michael at Hamouli in the Fayyum. It is assumed on this evidence that a Fayyumic-speaking scribe must have contaminated a Sahidic exemplar with dialect forms which he was accustomed to using in his own speech. Quecke observes that the number of Fayyumic forms increases in the section of M574 which contains the hymns, and he draws special attention to the frequent use of ε- for ⲛ- in expressing the genitive (e.g. I,15/1; I,22/3, /4), and the related usage of ϩε- for ϩⲛ- (e.g. II,23/4) and ⲙε- for ⲙⲛ- (e.g. III,6/2).[2] The use of εⲥⲱⲟⲩ for ⲛⲥⲱⲟⲩ (II,22/2) belongs in the same category.

Some further examples of non-Sahidic forms may now be given in order to characterize the language of the hymns. The Fayyumic features, ⲃ for ϥ and ⲗ for ⲣ have already been mentioned in the preceding section. In some instances the supralinear stroke replaces a full vowel: ϩⲛ̄- for ϩεⲛ- (e.g. I,10/3); but the opposite is also to be observed: ϩεⲛ- for ϩⲛ̄- (e.g. I,1/2); ⲙεⲛ for ⲙⲛ̄, 'not to be' (e.g. IV,13/1); ⲟⲩⲁⲛ for ⲟⲩⲛ̄- (e.g. III,15/1); ⲛεⲙⲁⲩ for ⲛⲙ̄ⲙⲁⲩ (e.g. VIII,14/2). Instead of the plural definite article ⲛ̄- there stands occasionally the full form ⲛε- (e.g. I,1/3; II,1/1, /3); there also occurs the plural form ⲛⲙ̄- in ⲛⲙ̄ⲡⲏⲩε (e.g. VII,12/3).[3] The following Fayyumic conjugational prefixes occur: Second Present, e.g. ⲁⲧεⲧⲛ- (VIII,14/3); ⲁⲩⲛⲏⲩ (VIII,23/3); Causative Infinitive, ⲁϥⲧⲣⲟⲩ- (III,10/2). Occasionally the Second Perfect is used with the meaning of the Temporalis, a common Fayyumic usage (e.g. II,23/2; IV,18/3). The non-Sahidic *nomina sacra* ⲡⲟ̄ⲥ (e.g. I,19/2) and ⲫ̄ϯ (e.g. VI,12/4) frequently occur. The Fayyumic preference for the use of the letter ⲏ is apparent in many spellings, e.g. ⲛⲏ for ⲛε, the dative form (e.g. I,17/1); ⲑⲏ for ⲑε (e.g. II,8/1); ⲥⲁⲃⲏ for ⲥⲁⲃε (IX,5/3); ⲧⲏⲛⲁϩ for ⲧⲛϩ (XII,7/4); ϩⲁⲙϣⲏ for ϩⲁⲙϣε

---

[1] Junker, *Koptische Poesie des 10. Jahrhunderts* I, 85–93, in analysing the language of similar material, expressed the matter somewhat differently, for example writing of 'Unregelmässigkeiten' (p. 85)—which was perhaps the general approach until the intensification of work upon Coptic dialects in recent decades. Junker's view was that his texts had been composed in good Sahidic, but corrupted both by oral tradition and the shortcomings of the eventual scribe or scribes.

[2] *Stundengebet*, 388, and p. 372 with n. 94.

[3] On this form, see *Stundengebet*, 373–4.

(VIII,10/1); ϫιϭΗΗΟΥϵ for ϫιϭϵϵΥϵ (II,11/3). The vocalic change ⲁ for Sahidic ⲟ is to be observed often. A few examples will suffice: ⲥⲁⲟⲩⲛ for ⲥⲟⲟⲩⲛ (III,14/1); ϫⲁⲁⲓ for ϫⲟⲉ (II,23/4); ⲡⲉⲑⲁⲩ for ⲡⲉⲑⲟⲟⲩ (V,19/4); ⲙⲁⲩ for ⲙⲟⲟⲩ (X,4/2); ⲁⲛ for ⲟⲛ (VII,11/1). Occasionally, verbs end in ⲓ for ⲉ, e.g. ⲗⲉϣⲓ for ⲣⲁϣⲉ (III,11/1); ϣⲓⲛⲓ for ϣⲓⲛⲉ (VIII,20/3). The letter ⲓ also sometimes stands for ⲉⲓ, as in ϭⲓⲛⲓ for ϭⲓⲛⲉⲓ (V,8/1) and ⲓⲉⲡ- for ⲉⲓⲉⲡ- from ⲉⲓⲟⲡⲉ (I,4/3). Mention should also be made of the use of Greek verbs with the prefix ⲣ-, ⲉⲣ-, or ⲉⲗ-, the construct form of ⲉⲓⲣⲉ:- ⲣⲃⲟⲏⲑⲓ (V,10/3); ⲉⲣⲃⲟⲏⲑⲓ (V,17/5); and ⲉⲗⲉⲧⲓⲛ (VI,9/1).

The above examples, it is hoped, give some idea how heavily the language of our hymns is influenced by Fayyumic usage. It should be noticed, however, that quite often Sahidic and Fayyumic forms stand side by side. The frequency with which Fayyumic forms occur may lend some colour to Quecke's tentative hypothesis that our collection of hymns represents a local Fayyumic tradition, but the evidence is not fully conclusive.

The date of the composition of the hymns, or of the making of this collection, cannot be determined. The manuscript which contains them was written in AD 897/8, but, as already mentioned, it may be assumed that it is a later copy or compilation. The subject-matter provides little evidence as to date, except that the two hymns on Severus of Antioch (c. AD 465–538) are not likely to have been written until after his death.

Editorial conventions

Something has already been said about the arrangement of the Coptic text in this edition. Little more of a technical nature need be added. The hymns contain many scribal abbreviations, and these are typical of the manuscript as a whole. The commonest *nomina sacra* have been retained in the transcription, but other abbreviations have been expanded there. They are of a routine nature, and do not, we believe, in themselves raise any problems for the understanding of the text. Therefore, details of them have been relegated to a separate series of notes on pp. 147–53, where a few other matters of palaeography are also discussed. Abbreviations (apart from *nomina sacra*) are especially common at or towards the ends of manuscript lines, as the scribe evidently felt some disinclination to allow just a few letters at the end of a metrical verse to spill over into the following manuscript line, and, as already mentioned, occasionally sought to ensure that a new stanza began a new manuscript line.

(pp. ρ̄π̄-ρ̄π̄ᾱ)

ᾱ ⲡⲁⲗⲫⲁⲃⲏⲧⲁ ⲛ̄ⲧ̄ⲡⲁⲣⲑⲉⲛⲟⲥ:-

1 ⲁⲡⲉⲡⲛ̄ⲁ̄ ⲉ̄ⲧⲟⲩⲁⲁⲃ ϣⲁⲭⲉ·
ϩⲉⲛⲧⲧⲁⲡⲣⲟ ⲛ̄ⲛⲉⲧⲟⲩⲁ̄ⲁⲃ ⲧⲏⲣⲟⲩ·
ⲉⲧⲃⲉⲛⲉⲧⲁⲓⲟ̄ ⲙ̄ⲙⲁⲣⲓⲁ ⲧ̄ⲣ̄ⲣⲱ·
ⲧⲉⲑⲉⲱ̄ⲇⲱⲕⲟⲥ ⲉ̄ⲧⲟⲩⲁⲁⲃⸯ

2 ⲃⲱϣ ⲉ̄ⲃⲟⲗ ⲛ̄ϭⲓⲇ̄ⲁ̄ⲇ̄·
ⲭⲉⲥⲱⲧ̄ⲙ̄ ⲧⲁϣⲉⲉ̄ⲣⲉ ⲛ̄ⲧⲉⲛⲁⲩ·
ⲛ̄ⲧⲉⲣ̄ⲡⲱⲃϣ̄ ⲉ̄ⲡⲟⲩⲗⲁⲟⲥ·
ⲙⲛ̄ⲛⲁⲡⲏⲓ ⲙ̄ⲡⲟⲩⲓⲱⲧⸯ

3 ⲅⲉⲕⲁⲣ ⲙⲱⲩⲥⲏⲥ ⲡⲉⲡⲣⲟⲫⲏⲧⲏⲥ·
ⲭⲱ ⲙ̄ⲡⲧⲁⲓⲟ̄ ⲙ̄ⲙⲁⲣⲓⲁ̄ ⲧⲉⲣⲱ·
ⲉϥⲑⲉⲱⲣⲓ ⲙ̄ⲡ̄ⲃⲁⲧⲟⲥ ⲉϥⲙⲟⲩϩ·
ϩⲛ̄ⲟⲩⲕⲱϩⲧ ⲁⲩⲱ̄ ⲛ̄ϥ̄ⲣⲟⲕϩ̄ ⲁⲛⸯ

4 ⲇ̄ⲁ̄ⲇ̄ ⲯⲁⲗⲗⲓ ⲉ̄ⲣⲟϥ ⲉϥⲭⲱ ⲙ̄ⲙⲟⲥ·
ⲭⲉⲁ̄ⲧⲉⲣⲱ ⲁ̄ϩⲉⲣⲁⲧⲥ̄ ϩⲓⲟⲩⲛⲁⲙ ⲙ̄ⲡ̄ⲣ̄ⲣⲟ·
ϩⲛ̄ⲟⲩϩ̄ⲃⲥⲱ ⲉ̄ⲥⲟ ⲛⲓⲉⲡⲛ̄ⲟⲩⲃ·
ⲉⲥⲃⲟⲟⲗⲉ ⲉ̄ⲥⲟ ⲛⲁⲅⲉⲓ ⲁⲩⲁⲛⸯ

The alphabetic acrostic on the Virgin

1   The Holy Spirit has spoken
    by the mouth of all the saints
    about the honours of Mary, the queen,
    the holy mother of God.

2   David proclaims:
    Hearken, my daughter, and see,
    and forget your people
    and those of your father's house.[1]

3   For also Moses, the prophet,
    tells of the honour of Mary, the queen,
    when he beholds the bush, as it burns
    with fire and is not consumed.[2]

4   David sings about it, saying:
    The queen stood at the king's right hand
    in a garment worked with gold,
    being clothed in various colours.[3]

---

[1]   Cf. Ps. 44.11.
[2]   Cf. Ex. 3.2.
[3]   Cf. Ps. 44.10.

5   ⲉϥⲉⲣⲙⲛ̄ⲧⲣⲉ ⲟⲛ ⲉϥϫⲱ ⲙ̄ⲙⲟⲥ·
    ⲛ̄ϭⲓⲡⲉⲓⲡⲣⲟⲫⲏⲧⲏⲥ ⲛⲟⲩⲱⲧ·
    ϫⲉⲥⲉⲛⲁⲣ̄ⲡⲙⲉⲉⲩⲉ̄ ⲙ̄ⲡⲟⲩⲣⲁⲛ·
    ϩⲓⲅⲉⲛⲉⲁ ⲛⲓⲙ ϩⲓⲅⲉⲛⲉⲁ⸗

6   ⲍⲁⲭⲁⲣⲓⲁⲥ ⲡⲉⲡⲣⲟⲫⲏⲧⲏⲥ·
    ϫⲱ ⲙ̄ⲡⲧⲁⲓⲟ ⲙ̄ⲙⲁⲣⲓⲁ ⲧⲉⲣⲱ·
    ⲉⲧⲃⲉⲧ̄ⲗⲩⲭⲛⲓⲁ ⲛ̄ⲛⲟⲩⲃ·
    ⲛ̄ⲧⲁϥⲛⲁⲩ ⲉ̄ⲣⲟⲥ ϩⲙ̄ⲡⲙⲁ ⲉ̄ⲧⲟⲩⲁⲁⲃ⸗

7   ⲏⲥⲁⲓⲁⲥ ⲡⲉⲡⲣⲟⲫⲏⲧⲏⲥ·
    ϫⲱ ⲙ̄ⲡⲧⲁⲓⲟ̄ ⲙ̄ⲙⲁⲣⲓⲁ̄ ⲧⲉⲣⲱ·
    ϫⲉⲉⲓⲥ ⲧ̄ⲡⲁⲣⲑⲉⲛⲟⲥ ⲛⲁⲱ̄ ⲛ̄ⲥ̄ϫ̄ⲡⲟ ⲛⲟⲩϣⲏⲣⲉ·
    ⲙⲟⲩⲧⲉ ⲉ̄ⲡⲉϥⲣⲁⲛ ϫⲉⲉⲙⲙⲁⲛⲟⲩⲏⲗ⸗

8   ⲑⲉⲱ̄ⲣⲓ ⲛⲏⲥⲁⲓⲁⲥ·
    ⲉϥⲱϣ ⲉ̄ⲃⲟⲗ ⲉϥϫⲱ ⲙ̄ⲙⲟⲥ·
    ϫⲉⲥⲉⲛⲁϯ ⲙ̄ⲡ̄ϫⲱⲱⲙⲉ ⲉⲧⲧⲟⲟⲃⲉ·
    ⲉ̄ⲧⲟⲟⲧϥ̄ ⲛⲟⲩⲣⲱⲙⲉ ⲉϥⲥⲟⲟⲩⲛ̄ ⲛ̄ⲥ̄ϩⲁⲓ⸗

9   ⲓⲁⲕⲱⲃ ⲡ̄ⲡⲁⲧⲣⲓⲁⲣⲭⲏⲥ·
    ϫⲱ ⲙ̄ⲡⲧⲁⲓⲟ̄ ⲙ̄ⲙⲁⲣⲓⲁ̄ ⲧⲉⲣⲱ·
    ⲉϥⲑⲉⲱ̄ⲣⲓ ⲛ̄ⲧⲉⲃⲗⲟⲟ̄ϭⲉ·
    ⲉ̄ⲣⲉⲡⲛⲟⲩⲧⲉ ϩ̄ⲙⲟⲟⲥ ϩⲓϫⲱⲥ⸗

5   He also testifies, saying
    —this same prophet—:
    Your name will be remembered
    in all generations.[1]

6   Zechariah, the prophet,
    tells of the honour of Mary, the queen,
    (when speaking) about the golden candlestick
    which he saw in the holy place.[2]

7   Isaiah, the prophet,
    tells of the honour of Mary, the queen:
    Behold, the Virgin shall conceive and bear a son.
    Call his name Immanuel.[3]

8   Consider Isaiah,
    when he proclaims, saying:
    They shall give the book that is sealed
    to a man who is literate.[4]

9   Jacob, the patriarch,
    tells of the honour of Mary, the queen,
    as he beholds the ladder,
    on which God sits.[5]

---

[1] Cf. Ps. 44.18.
[2] Cf. Zech. 4.2.
[3] Cf. Is. 7.14.
[4] Cf. Is. 29.11.
[5] Cf. Gen. 28.12–13.

10 ⲕⲁⲗⲱⲥ ⲁϥϫⲟⲟⲥ ⲛ̄ϭⲓⲇⲁ̄ⲇ̄·
ϩ̄ⲙ̄ⲡⲉⲯⲁⲗⲧⲏⲣⲓⲟⲛ ⲉⲧⲧⲁⲓⲏⲩ·
ϫⲉⲁⲩϫⲱ ⲛ̄ϩ̄ⲛ̄ⲧⲁⲓⲟ ⲉⲧⲃⲏⲧⲉ·
ⲧ̄ⲡⲟⲗⲓⲥ ⲙ̄ⲡⲉⲛⲛⲟⲩⲧⲉ ⲉ̄ⲧⲟⲩⲁⲁⲃ⁑

11 ⲗⲟⲩⲕⲁⲥ ⲡⲉⲩⲁⲅⲅⲉⲗⲓⲥⲧⲏⲥ·
ϫⲉϩⲣⲁⲓ ϩ̄ⲙ̄ⲡ̄ⲙⲉϩⲥⲟⲟⲩ ⲛⲉⲃⲟⲧ·
ⲁⲩϫⲟⲟⲩ ⲙ̄ⲡⲁⲣⲭⲁⲅⲅⲉⲗⲟⲥ·
ⲱ̣ⲁⲧⲡⲁⲣⲑⲉⲛⲟⲥ ⲉⲧⲟⲩⲁⲁⲃ ⲙⲁⲣⲓⲁ⁑

12 ⲙⲁⲑⲉⲟⲥ ⲡⲉⲩⲁⲅⲅⲉⲗⲓⲥⲧⲏⲥ·
ϫⲱ ⲙ̄ⲡ̄|ⲧⲁⲓⲟ̄[1] ⲙ̄ⲙⲁⲣⲓⲁ̄ ⲧⲉⲣⲱ·
ϫⲉⲛⲧⲟⲡⲉ ⲡⲁϩⲟ ⲉⲧϩⲏⲡ ϩ̄ⲛ̄ⲧ̄ⲥⲱⲱ̣ⲉ·
ⲛ̄ⲧⲁⲩϩⲉ ⲉⲡⲙⲁⲣⲕⲁⲣⲓⲧⲏⲥ ⲛ̄ϩⲏⲧϥ̄⁑

13 ⲛⲉⲣⲱⲟⲩ ⲧⲏⲣⲟⲩ ⲙ̄ⲡⲉⲓⲕⲟⲥⲙⲟⲥ·
ⲛⲁⲙⲟⲟⲱ̣ⲉ ⲉ̄ⲃⲟⲗ ϩ̄ⲙ̄ⲡⲟⲩⲟ̄ⲉⲓⲛ·[2]
ⲁⲩⲱ̄ ⲛ̄ϩⲉⲑⲛⲟⲥ ϩ̄ⲙ̄ⲡⲟⲩⲡⲓⲣⲉ·
ⲧⲉⲑⲉⲱⲇⲱⲕⲟⲥ ⲙⲁⲣⲓⲁ⁑

14 ϫ̄ⲱⲕ ⲙ̄ⲙⲁⲛ ⲉ̄ϯⲑⲉⲱ̄ⲣⲓⲁ·
ⲱ̄ ⲉ̄ⲍⲉⲕⲓⲏⲗ ⲡⲉⲡⲣⲟⲫⲏⲧⲏⲥ·
ⲉⲧⲃⲉⲧⲡⲩⲗⲏ ⲉⲧⲱ̣ⲁⲧ̄ⲙ ⲉ̄ⲡⲁⲣⲭⲱⲛ·
ⲛ̄ⲧⲁϥⲟⲩⲱⲙ ⲙ̄ⲡⲉϥⲟⲉⲓⲕ ⲛ̄ϩⲏⲧⲥ̄⁑

---

[1] Page ⲣ̄ⲛ̄ⲇ̄ begins.
[2] For ϩⲙⲡⲟⲩⲟⲩⲟⲉⲓⲛ.

10   David spoke well
     in the precious psalter:
     Excellent things of you were spoken,
     O city of our holy God.[1]

11   Luke, the evangelist, says:
     In the sixth month
     the archangel was sent
     to the holy Virgin Mary.[2]

12   Matthew, the evangelist,
     tells of the honour of Mary, the queen:
     You are the treasure hidden in the field,
     in which the pearl was found.[3]

13   All the kings of this world
     shall go forth in your light,
     and the nations in your brilliance,[4]
     O mother of God, Mary.

14   You draw us to the contemplation,
     O Ezekiel, the prophet,
     of the gate that is shut to the ruler,
     where he ate his bread.[5]

---

[1]   Cf. Ps. 86.3.
[2]   Cf. Lk. 1.26–7.
[3]   Cf. Mt. 13.44–6. The meaning is: You, Mary, are the treasure
… in which the pearl, Jesus, was found.
[4]   Cf. Is. 60.3.
[5]   Cf. Ez. 44.1–3.

15 ογπε πβωλ ετπγλη ετϣατεμ·
ⲛ̄ⲥⲁⲧⲉⲑⲉϢⲇⲟⲕⲟⲥ·
ⲧⲉⲛⲧⲁⲥⲭⲡⲟ ⲛⲁⲛ ⲉⲡⲣ̄ⲣⲟ ⲙ̄ⲡⲉⲟⲟⲩ·
ⲉ̄ⲣⲉⲧⲉⲥⲡⲁⲣⲑⲉⲛⲓⲁ̄ ⲧⲟⲟ̄ⲃⲉ⸓

16 ⲡⲁⲓⲡⲉ ⲡⲱⲛⲉ ⲛ̄ⲧⲁⲇⲁⲛⲓⲏⲗ ⲛⲁⲩ ⲉ̄ⲣⲟϥ·
ⲉ̄ⲁⲩϣⲁⲁⲧϥ ⲉⲃⲟⲗ ⲁⲭⲛ̄ϭⲓⲭ·
ⲉ̄ⲧⲉⲡⲁⲓⲡⲉ ⲡⲉⲭ̅ⲥ̅·
ⲛ̄ⲧⲁⲧⲡⲁⲣⲑⲉⲛⲟⲥ ⲙⲓⲥⲉ ⲙ̄ⲙⲟϥ⸓

17 ⲣⲁϣⲉ ⲛⲏ ⲧ̅ϣⲉⲉⲣⲉ ⲛ̄ⲥⲓⲱⲛ·
ϫⲉⲉⲓⲥ ⲡⲟⲩⲣ̄ⲣⲟ ⲛⲏⲩ ⲛⲉ·
ⲉ̄ⲧⲉⲡⲁⲓⲡⲉ ⲉⲙⲙⲁⲛⲟⲩⲏⲗ·
ⲉ̄ⲣⲉⲧⲡⲁⲣⲑⲉⲛⲟⲥ ⲧⲱⲟⲩⲛ ⲙ̄ⲙⲟϥ⸓

18 ⲥⲱⲧⲙ̄ ⲉ̄ⲡⲉⲩⲁⲅⲅⲉⲗⲓⲥⲧⲏⲥ·
ϫⲉⲁ̄ⲙⲁⲣⲓⲁ̄ ⲧⲱⲟⲩⲛ ϩⲛ̄ⲛⲉⲓϩⲟⲟⲩ·
ⲁⲥⲃⲱⲕ ⲉϩⲣⲁⲓ ⲉ̄ⲧⲱⲣⲓⲛⲏ·
ⲁⲥⲁⲥⲡⲁⲍⲉ ⲛⲉⲗⲓⲥⲁⲃⲉⲧ⸓

19 ⲧⲟⲧⲉ ⲡⲉϫⲁⲥ ⲛ̄ϭⲓⲙⲁⲣⲓⲁ·
ϫⲉⲁ̄ⲧⲁⲯⲩⲭⲏ ϫⲓⲥⲉ ⲙ̄ⲡϭ̅ⲥ̅·
ⲁⲩⲱ̅ ⲁ̄ⲡⲁⲡⲛ̅ⲁ̅ ⲧⲉⲗⲏⲗ·
ⲉ̄ϫⲙ̄ⲡ̅ⲛⲟⲩⲧⲉ ⲡⲁⲥⲱ̅ⲣ̅⸓

15 What is the interpretation of the gate that is shut
except the mother of God,
who bore to us the king of glory
with her virginity sealed?

16 This is the stone which Daniel saw,
that was cut out without hands,[1]
which is Christ,
whom the Virgin brought forth.

17 Rejoice, O daughter of Zion,
for behold your king is coming to you,[2]
which is Immanuel,
whom the Virgin bore.

18 Listen to the evangelist:
Mary arose in these days
and went up into the hill country.
She saluted Elisabeth.[3]

19 Then Mary said:
My soul has magnified the Lord,
and my spirit has rejoiced
in God, my Saviour.[4]

---

[1] Cf. Dan. 2.34.
[2] Cf. Zech. 9.9.
[3] Cf. Lk. 1.39–40.
[4] Lk. 1.46–7.

20 ϩⲩⲙⲛⲉⲩⲉ̄ ⲉ̄ⲧⲉⲑⲉⲱⲇⲱⲕⲟⲥ·
ⲱ̄ ⲛⲉⲫⲩⲗⲏ ⲧⲏⲣⲟⲩ ⲛ̄ⲧⲉⲡⲕⲁϩ·
ⲙⲛ̄ⲛⲉⲗⲁⲟⲥ ⲙ̄ⲡⲓⲥⲧⲟⲥ·
ⲙⲛ̄ⲛⲉⲧⲁⲅⲙⲁ ⲛⲁⲅⲅⲉⲗⲓⲕⲟⲛ⳹

21 ⲫⲓⲥⲓⲱⲗⲱⲅⲟⲥ[1] ⲥⲟⲗⲟⲙⲱⲛ·
ϫⲱ ⲙ̄ⲡ̄ⲧⲁⲓⲟ̄ ⲙⲙⲁⲣⲓⲁ̄ ⲧⲉⲣⲱ·
ϫⲉⲧⲁⲥⲱⲛⲉ ⲧⲁϣⲉⲗⲉⲉⲧ·
ⲧⲁϭⲣⲟⲙⲡⲉ ⲉⲧϫⲏⲕ ⲉ̄ⲃⲟⲗ⳹

22 ⲭⲉⲣⲉ ⲙⲁⲣⲓⲁ̄ ⲧⲉⲣⲱ·
ⲭⲉⲣⲉ ⲧ̄ⲡⲁⲣⲑⲉⲛⲟⲥ ⲉ̄ⲧⲟⲩⲁⲁⲃ·
ⲭⲉⲣⲉ ⲧⲕⲓⲃⲱⲧⲟⲥ ⲉⲡⲣⲁϣⲉ·
ⲭⲉⲣⲉ ⲡ̄ⲙⲁ ⲛⲙ̄ⲧⲟⲛ ⲉⲡⲛⲟⲩⲧⲉ⳹

23 ⲯⲁⲗⲗⲓ ⲉ̄ⲡⲉⲛⲛⲟⲩⲧⲉ ⲯⲁⲗⲗⲉⲓ·
ⲯⲁⲗⲓ ⲉ̄ⲡⲉⲛⲉⲣⲟ ⲯⲁⲗⲓ·
ϫⲉⲁϥⲃⲱⲕ ⲉϩⲣⲁⲓ ⲉ̄ⲛⲙⲡⲏⲩⲉ̄·
ⲁϥϫⲓ ⲛ̄ⲧⲉϥⲙⲁⲁⲩ ⲉⲡϫⲓⲥⲉ ⲛ̄ⲙⲙⲁϥ⳹

24 ⲱ̄ ⲛⲉⲗⲁⲟⲥ ⲧⲏⲣⲟⲩ ⲙ̄ⲡ̄ⲕⲟⲥⲙⲟⲥ·
ⲙⲁⲣⲉⲛⲣ̄ⲡ̄ϣⲁ ⲛ̄ⲧⲉⲑⲉⲱ̄ⲇⲱⲕⲟⲥ·
ⲛ̄ⲥⲡⲁⲣⲁⲕⲁⲗⲓ ⲙⲡⲉⲥϣⲏⲣⲉ ϩⲁⲣⲟⲛ·
ⲛ̄ϥ̄ⲕⲁⲛⲉⲛⲛⲟⲃⲉ ⲛⲁⲛ ⲉ̄ⲃⲟⲗ:-

---

[1] The absence of the definite article is, no doubt, due to
the alphabetic arrangement of the hymn, which at this point
requires ⲫ.

20   Sing praises to the mother of God,
O all the tribes of the earth,
together with the faithful peoples
and the angelic ranks.

21   The natural philosopher[1] Solomon
tells of the honour of Mary, the queen:
My sister, my bride,
my perfect dove.[2]

22   Hail Mary, the queen.
Hail holy Virgin.
Hail ark of joy.
Hail God's resting-place.

23   Sing to our God, sing.
Sing to our king, sing,
for he has gone up to heaven,
he has taken his mother with him on high.

24   O all the peoples of the world,
let us celebrate the feast of the mother of God,
that she may beseech her son for us
to forgive us our sins.

---

[1]   'Physiologus': for the association of Solomon in the Coptic church with the Greek text *Physiologus*, see C. D. G. Müller, 'Physiologus', *Copt. Enc.* VI, 1965-6.

[2]   Cf. Song of Songs 5.1–2.

◄ HYMN TWO ►

(pp. $\overline{\text{PNB}}$-$\overline{\text{PN}\underline{\text{A}}}$, line 3)

$\overline{\text{B}}$ ⲡⲁⲗⲫⲁⲃⲏⲧⲁ ⲙ̄ⲡ̄ϩⲁⲅⲓⲟⲥ ⲙⲉⲣⲕⲟⲩⲣⲓⲟⲥ:-

1 ⲁⲡⲟⲩⲟⲉⲓⲛ ϣⲁ ⲛ̄ⲛⲉⲇⲓⲕⲁⲓⲟⲥ·
   ⲁⲡⲟⲩⲛⲟϥ ⲧⲁϩⲟ ⲛ̄ⲛⲉⲧⲥⲟⲩⲧⲱⲛ·
   ⲡⲟⲩⲛⲟϥ ⲉ̄ⲛⲉⲇⲓⲕⲉⲟⲥⲡⲉ ⲡ̄ϭⲥ⳽[1]

2 ⲃⲱϣ ⲉⲃⲟⲗ ⲛ̄ϭⲓⲡⲉⲛⲥⲱ̄ⲣ̄·
   ϩⲛ̄ⲛⲉⲩⲁⲅⲅⲉⲗⲓⲟⲛ ⲉⲧⲧⲁⲓⲏⲩ·
   ϫⲉⲛⲉⲇⲓⲕⲁⲓⲟⲥ ⲛⲁⲣ̄ⲟⲩⲟⲉⲓⲛ ⲛ̄ⲑⲉ ⲙ̄ⲡ̄ⲣⲏ·
   ϩⲛ̄ⲧⲙⲉⲧⲉⲣⲟ ⲙ̄ⲡⲉⲩⲉⲓⲱⲧ⳽

3 ⲅⲉⲅⲁⲣ ⲁⲡϩⲁⲅⲓⲟⲥ ⲙⲉⲣⲕⲟⲩⲣⲓⲟⲥ·
   ⲛⲁⲩ ⲉ̄ⲡⲟⲩⲟ̄ⲉⲓⲛ ⲛ̄ϫⲓⲛⲉϥⲟ ⲛⲕⲟⲩⲓ·
   ϩⲙ̄ⲡ̄ⲡⲟⲗⲉⲙⲟⲥ ⲛ̄ⲛⲉⲃⲁⲣⲃⲁⲣⲟⲥ·
   ⲉ̄ⲣⲉⲡⲁⲅⲅⲉⲗⲟⲥ ϣⲁϫⲉ ⲛⲙ̄ⲙⲁϥ⳽

4 ⲇⲱⲟⲩⲛ̄ ⲉϩⲣⲁⲓ ⲙⲉⲣⲕⲟⲩⲣⲓⲟⲥ·
   ϫⲓ ⲛⲁⲕ ⲉ̄ⲧⲥⲏⲃⲉ ⲉⲧϩⲛ̄ⲧⲁϭⲓϫ·
   ⲧ̄ⲡⲉⲕⲟⲩⲟⲓ ⲉ̄ⲛⲉⲃⲁⲣⲃⲁⲣⲟⲥ·
   ϭⲟϫϭⲉϫ ⲙ̄ⲙⲟⲟⲩ ϩⲛ̄ⲧⲉⲕϭⲟⲙ⳽

---

[1] The first stanza clearly consists of only three verses.

26

The alphabetic acrostic on St Mercurius

1   Light has risen for the righteous.
       Joy has been established for the upright.
       The joy of the righteous is the Lord.[1]

2   Our Saviour proclaims
       in the precious gospels:
       The righteous shall shine as the sun
       in the kingdom of their Father.[2]

3   For also St Mercurius
       saw the light, while he was still young,
       in the war against the barbarians,
       when the angel spoke with him:

4   Arise, Mercurius,
       take this sword, which is in my hand,
       advance against the barbarians,
       smite them with your strength.

---

[1]   Cf. Ps. 96.11–12.
[2]   Mt. 13.43.

5 ⲉ̄ϣⲱⲡⲉ ⲉⲕϣⲁⲛϫⲓⲡⲉϭⲣⲟ·
ⲙ̄ⲡⲣ̄ⲣ̄ⲡⲱⲃϢ̄ ⲉ̄ⲡϫⲟⲉⲓⲥ ⲡⲉⲕⲛⲟⲩⲧⲉ·
ⲡⲓⲥⲧⲉⲩⲉ̄ ⲉ̄ⲡⲉⲭ̄ⲥ̄ ⲓ̄ⲥ̄·
ⲛ̄ⲅ̄ⲙⲓϣⲉ ⲉ̄ϫⲛ̄ⲧⲉϥⲡⲓⲥⲧⲓⲥ⚏

6 ⲍⲱⲅⲣⲁⲫⲓ ⲛⲁⲛ ⲉⲡⲉⲕⲃⲓⲟⲥ ⲉ̄ⲧⲟⲩⲁ̄ⲁⲃ·
ⲱ̄ ⲡ̄ϩⲁⲅⲓⲟⲥ ⲙⲉⲣⲕⲟⲩⲣⲓⲟⲥ·
ⲛ̄ϫⲓⲛⲉⲕⲟ̄ ⲛ̄ⲕⲟⲩⲓ ϩⲙ̄ⲡⲏⲓ ⲛ̄ⲛⲉⲕⲉⲓⲟⲧⲉ·
ⲁⲩ†ⲡⲉⲕⲣⲁⲛ ϫⲉⲫⲓⲗⲱⲡⲁⲧⲏⲣ⚏

7 ⲏ̄ⲥ[1] ⲇⲉⲕⲓⲟⲥ ⲡⲉⲣⲣⲟ·
ⲙⲛ̄ⲟⲩⲁⲗⲗⲏⲣⲓⲁ̄ⲛⲟⲥ ⲡⲉⲧⲥⲟⲟϥ·
ⲁⲩϫⲟⲟⲩⲕ̄ ⲉⲡⲡⲟⲗⲉⲙⲟⲥ·
ⲉⲧⲣⲉⲕⲙⲓϣⲉ ⲙ̄ⲛ̄ⲛⲉⲩϫⲁϫⲉ⚏

8 ⲑⲏ ⲛ̄ⲧⲁⲕⲡⲱⲧ ⲉⲡⲡⲟⲗⲉⲙⲟⲥ·
ⲁⲕⲛⲁⲩ ⲉ̄ⲡⲁⲣⲭⲁⲅⲅⲉⲗⲟⲥ·
ⲉ̄ⲣⲉⲧⲉϥⲥⲏⲃⲉ ⲧⲟⲕⲙ̄ ϩⲛ̄ⲧⲉϥϭⲓϫ·
ⲁϥⲥⲟⲟⲩⲧⲛ̄ ⲙ̄ⲙⲟⲥ ⲉ̄ⲣⲟⲕ ⲉϥⲣⲁϣⲉ⚏

9 ⲓⲏⲥⲟⲩ ⲡ̄ϣⲏⲣⲉ ⲛ̄ⲛⲁⲩⲏ̄·
ⲁ̄ⲙⲓⲭⲁⲏⲗ ⲁϩⲉⲣⲁⲧϥ̄ ⲉ̄ⲣⲟϥ·
ⲁϥⲡⲁⲧⲁⲥⲥⲉ ⲛ̄·ⲕⲑ̄·ⲛ̄ⲣ̄ⲣⲟ·
ⲛⲟⲩⲟⲩⲛⲟⲩ ⲛⲟⲩⲱⲧ ϩⲛ̄ⲟⲩⲃⲉⲡⲏ⚏

---

[1] Almost certainly for ⲉⲓⲥ; cf. IV,18/1.

5   If you gain the victory,
do not forget the Lord your God.
Believe in Christ Jesus
and fight for his faith.[1]

6   Describe for us your holy life,
O St Mercurius.
While you were still little in the house of your parents,
you were given the name Philopater.

7   Behold, Decius,[2] the emperor,
and the abominable Valerian[3]
sent you into the war
to fight with their enemies.

8   As you went into the war,
you saw the archangel
with his sword drawn in his hand.
He extended it to you, rejoicing.

9   Joshua, the son of Nun
—Michael stood before him—
he smote twenty-nine kings
in one single hour, quickly.[4]

---

[1] Cf. Jude 3.
[2] AD 249–251.
[3] AD 253–260.
[4] Cf. Josh. 12.7–24.

10 ⲕⲁⲗⲱⲥ ⲁϥϫⲟⲟⲥ ⲛ̄ϭⲓⲇⲁ̄ⲇ̄·
ϩⲙ̄ⲡⲉⲯⲁⲗⲧⲏⲣⲓⲟⲛ ⲉⲧⲧⲁⲓⲏⲩ·
ϫⲉⲁⲩⲱ̄ ⲛ̄ⲑⲉ ⲛ̄ϩⲛ̄ⲥⲟⲧⲉ·
ϩⲛ̄ⲛⲉϭⲓϫ ⲙ̄ⲡⲇⲩⲛⲁⲧⲟⲥ⸕

11 ⲗⲟⲓⲡⲟⲛ ⲁ̄ⲡⲉⲧⲥⲏϩ ϫⲱⲕ ⲉ̄ⲃⲟⲗ ⲉ̄ϫⲱⲕ·
ϫⲉⲁⲕⲙⲟⲣ̄ⲧ ⲛⲟⲩϭⲟⲙ ϩⲙ̄ⲡⲡⲟⲗⲉⲙⲟⲥ·
ⲁⲕⲧⲁϩⲟⲓ ⲉ̄ⲣⲁⲧ ⲉ̄ϫⲛ̄ⲛⲁϫⲓⲥⲛ̄ⲛⲟⲩⲉ̄·
ⲁⲕⲧ̄ⲥⲁⲃⲟ ⲛ̄ⲛⲁϭⲓϫ ⲉⲩⲡⲟⲗⲉⲙⲟⲥ⸕

12 ⲙⲛ̄ⲛⲥⲁⲧⲣⲉⲕⲡⲱⲧ ⲉⲡⲡⲟⲗⲩⲙⲟⲥ·
ⲱ̄ ⲡ̄ϩⲁⲅⲓⲟⲥ ⲙⲉⲣⲕⲟⲩⲣⲓⲟⲥ·
ⲁⲕⲃⲟϫⲃⲉϫ ⲛ̄ⲥⲁⲛⲉⲃⲁⲣⲃⲁⲣⲟⲥ·
|ϣⲁⲛⲧⲉⲧⲥⲛⲃⲉ[1] ⲱ̄ϭⲉⲣ ϩⲉⲧⲉⲕϭⲓϫ⸕

13 ⲛ̄ⲧⲉⲣⲉⲡⲣ̄ⲣⲟ ⲛⲁⲩ ⲉ̄ⲡⲉⲛⲧⲁϥϣⲱⲡⲉ·
ⲁϥⲣⲁϣⲉ ⲉ̄ⲙⲁⲧⲉ ⲁϥⲧⲉⲗⲏⲗ·
ⲁϥⲧ̄ ⲛⲁⲕ ⲉ̄ϩⲛ̄ⲛⲟϭ ⲛ̄ⲧⲁⲓⲟ̄·
ⲁϥⲁⲁⲕ ⲛ̄ⲛⲟϭ ⲉⲡⲁⲣⲓⲑⲙⲟⲥ⸕

14 ϫⲁⲟⲩⲛ̄ ⲱ̄ ⲙⲉⲣⲕⲟⲩⲣⲓⲟⲥ·
ϫⲉⲁⲓⲧ̄ ⲛⲁⲕ ⲉ̄ϩⲛ̄ⲛⲟϭ ⲉ̄ⲧⲁⲓⲟ̄·
ⲁⲙⲟⲩ ⲛ̄ⲅ̄ⲑⲩⲥⲓⲁ̄ⲍⲉ ⲛ̄ⲛⲁⲛⲟⲩⲧⲉ·
ⲛ̄ⲅ̄ⲃⲱⲕ ⲉⲡⲙⲁ ⲛ̄ⲛⲉⲕϣⲃⲏⲣⲙⲁⲧⲟⲓ⸕

---

[1] Page ⲣ̄ⲛ̄ⲅ̄ begins.

10   David spoke well
     in the precious psalter:
     And it was as arrows
     in the hands of the mighty man.[1]

11   Then that which is written was fulfilled in you:
     You have girded me with strength in the war.
     You have set me upon my high places.
     You have instructed my hands for war.[2]

12   After you went into the war,
     O St Mercurius,
     you smote the barbarians
     until the sword stiffened in your hand.

13   When the emperor saw what had happened,
     he rejoiced greatly and was glad.
     He conferred great honours upon you.
     He appointed you commander of the forces.

14   You know, O Mercurius,
     that I have conferred great honours upon you.
     Come and sacrifice to my gods
     and join your fellow soldiers.

---

[1]   Ps. 126.4.
[2]   Cf. Ps. 17.33–5.

15 ⲟⲩⲙⲛ̄ⲧⲙⲁⲧⲟⲓ ⲛ̄ⲧⲉⲡⲓⲕⲟⲥⲙⲟⲥ·
ⲙⲛ̄ϩⲉⲛⲭⲣⲏⲙⲁ ⲛ̄ϣⲁⲩⲧⲁⲕⲟ·
ⲛ̄ϯⲉⲣⲭⲣⲓⲁ̄ ⲙ̄ⲙⲟⲟⲩ ⲁⲛ ⲱ̄ ⲡⲣⲣⲟ·
ⲁ̄ⲛⲟⲕ ⲟⲩϩⲙ̄ϩⲁⲗ ⲛⲧⲉⲡⲉⲭ̅ⲥ̅⳥

16 ⲡⲉⲭⲉⲡⲣ̄ⲣⲟ ⲛ̄ⲛⲉⲙⲁⲧⲟⲓ·
ϫⲉⲙⲉⲣⲕⲟⲩⲣⲓⲟⲥ ⲡⲉⲛⲧⲁⲓϫⲁⲥⲧ̄ϥ·
ϫⲓⲧ̄ϥ ⲉⲧⲕⲁⲡⲡⲁⲇⲟⲕⲓⲁ̄·
ϥⲓ ⲛ̄ⲧⲉϥⲁ̄ⲡⲉ ϩⲙ̄ⲡⲙⲁ ⲉ̄ⲧⲙ̄ⲙⲁⲩ⳥

17 ⲣⲱⲙⲉ ⲥ̄ⲛⲁⲩ ⲛ̄ⲥⲡⲟⲩⲇⲉⲟⲥ·
ⲁⲩⲕⲱⲱⲥ ⲙ̄ⲡⲉϥⲥⲱⲙⲁ ⲕⲁⲗⲱⲥ·
ⲁⲩⲕⲱⲧ ⲛⲟⲩⲙⲁⲣⲧⲩⲣⲓⲟⲛ ⲉ̄ⲣⲟϥ·
ⲁϩⲛ̄ⲛⲟϭ ⲛ̄ϭⲟⲙ ϣⲱⲡⲉ ⲛϩⲏⲧ̄ϥ⳥

18 ⲥⲉⲥⲩⲙⲁⲛⲉ ⲛⲁⲛ ϩⲛ̄ⲧⲙⲉϩⲙⲏⲧⲉ·
ⲙⲛ̄ⲧⲙⲉϩⲙⲛ̄ⲧⲟⲩⲉ̄ ⲛ̄ϩⲓⲥⲧⲱⲣⲓⲁ̄·
ⲛ̄ϭⲓ ·ⲃ̄· ⲛⲉⲡⲓⲥⲕⲟⲡⲟⲥ·
ⲉ̄ⲛⲉϭⲟⲙ ⲛ̄ⲧⲁⲕⲉⲓⲣⲉ ⲙ̄ⲙⲟⲟⲩ⳥

19 ⲧⲉⲕⲓⲟⲥ ⲇⲉ ⲛ̄ⲧⲉⲣⲉϥⲙⲟⲩ·
ⲁ̄ⲇⲓⲟⲕⲗⲏⲧⲓⲁ̄ⲛⲟⲥ ⲣ̄ⲣ̄ⲣⲟ ⲉ̄ⲡⲉϥⲙⲁ·
ⲁϥϩⲱⲧⲃ̄ ⲛⲟⲩⲙⲏⲏϣⲉ ⲙ̄ⲙⲁⲣⲧⲩⲣⲟⲥ·
ⲙⲛ̄ⲥⲱϥ ⲁ̄ⲕⲱⲥⲧⲁⲛⲧⲓⲛⲟⲥ ⲣ̄ⲣ̄ⲣⲟ⳥

15   This world's soldiering
      and possessions that perish
      I do not need, O emperor.
      I am a servant of Christ.

16   The emperor said to the soldiers:
      Mercurius, whom I exalted,
      take to Cappadocia,
      and behead him there.[1]

17   Two zealous men
      buried his body fittingly.
      They built a martyr's shrine for him,
      wherein great miracles occurred.

18   They declare to us in the tenth
      and the eleventh (chapter) of the history (of the
          Church)
      —(these) two bishops—
      the miracles which you performed.[2]

19   Now, when Decius died,
      Diocletian[3] became emperor in his stead.
      He killed many martyrs.
      After him Constantine[4] became emperor.

---

[1]   Cf. T. Orlandi (ed.), *Passione e miracoli di S. Mercurio* (Milan 1976), 38–9.
[2]   Cf. T. Orlandi (ed.), *Passione e miracoli di S. Mercurio*, 54-5; see also T. Orlandi (ed.), *Storia della Chiesa di Alessandria* I (Milan 1967), 48–50, 67–8, 98–100.
[3]   AD 284–305.
[4]   AD 306–337.

20 n̄taq¹ πενταqϭωλп̄ ε̄βολ·
м̄πεϲ†ос ν̄ιϲ·
аqκωτ νογмннϣε м̄мартнριον·
ā2ν̄νοϭ ν̄ϭομ ϣωπε ν2нт̄q⸗

21 φιλωπатнρ мερκογριοϲ·
αγzωγραφι м̄πεqλιмнν·²
2ν̄†πολιϲ м̄π̄νοϭ βαϲιλιοϲ·
ē ρειογλιανοϲ ō νερο⸗

22 χρнма νιм ν̄τετεκλнϲια·
аqχοογ ēϲωογ αqqιτογ·
ετβε̄τλοιϭε νογā πολογιā·
ν̄ταβαϲιλιοϲ тαаϲ ē π̄ρρο⸗

23 ψει νιē πιϲκοποϲ·³
ν̄ταγναγ επ2αγιοϲ мερκογριοϲ·
ερεπεqκονλαριον λαλнγ ēϲνοq·
2επεq2το εqταλнγ ετχααι⸗

24 | ωντωϲ⁴ π̄2αγιοϲ мερκογριοϲ·
ν̄τοq πενταqκωτ̄περϲιϲ·
аqπαταϲϲε м̄πανομοϲ αqмογ·
απραν м̄π̄νογτε χιταιō:-

---

¹ Almost certainly for ntаq (S. ntoq).
² On the etymology of this word, which also occurs in IV,12/3, see G. Godron, 'λιμнν, "portrait", "image"', BSAC 25 (1983), 1–52, and idem, 'A nouveau λιμнν (compléments)', BSAC 29 (1990), 43–7. It is not included in the Index of Loan-Words.
³ Read ννιεπιϲκοποϲ.
⁴ Page p̄n̄λ begins (see Plate 1).

20 It was he who revealed
    the cross of Jesus.
    He built many martyrs' shrines,
    wherein great miracles occurred.

21 Philopater Mercurius'
    portrait was painted
    in the city of Basil the Great,[1]
    while Julian[2] was emperor.

22 All the possessions of the Church
    he[3] sent for and took
    on account of a reply,
    which Basil had given to the emperor.[4]

23 O the satisfaction of these bishops!,
    when they saw St Mercurius,
    with his spear stained with blood
    upon his horse (in an icon) put up on the wall.[5]

24 Truly, it was St Mercurius,
    who had gone to Persia;
    he smote the lawless one and he died.
    The name of God was honoured.

---

[1] Basil of Caesarea (c. AD 330–379).
[2] AD 361–363.
[3] i.e. Julian.
[4] Cf. T. Orlandi (ed.), *Passione e miracoli di S. Mercurio*, 54–5.
[5] Cf. T. Orlandi (ed.), *Passione e miracoli di S. Mercurio*, 58–61.

◄ HYMN THREE ►

(pp. $\overline{\text{PN}\Delta}$, line 4 – $\overline{\text{PN}\varsigma}$, line 12)

Γ̄ ΠΑΛΦΑΒΗΤΑ Μ̄Π̄ϨΑΓΙΟС ΒΙΚΤΩΡ ΠΕСΤΡΑΤΕΛΑΤΗС:-

1 ΑΛΗΘΩС ΟΥΝΟΟ͠ΒΠΕ ΠΕΚΤΑΙΟ·
   Μ̄Π̄ΕΟΟΥ Ν̄ΤΑΠ̄ΝΟΥΤΕ ΤΑΑϤ ΝΑΚ·
   ϨΝ̄Τ̄ΜΗΤΕ Ν̄ΝΕΜΑΡΤΥΡΟС ΤΗΡΟΥ·
   ΑΠΑ ΒΙΚΤΩΡ Π̄ϢΗΡΕ Ν̄ϨΡΩΜΑΝΟС⸗

2 ΒΙΟС ΝΙΜ Ν̄ΡΩΜΕ Ν̄ΤΑΥΜΑСΤϤ̄·
   ϢΑΥ†ΟΥϨ̄Β̄СΩ ΝΕСΟΟΥ ϨΙΧΩϤ·
   Ν̄ΤΕΡΟΥΜΙСΕ ΝΑΠΑ ΒΙΚΤΩΡ·
   ΑΥ†ΟΥΚΟΝΟΒΙΟΝ Ε̄ΝΟΥΒ̄ Ε̄ΧΩϤ⸗

3 ΓΕΓΑΡ Ᾱ ΤΕϤΜΑΑΥ ΦΟΡΙ Μ̄ΜΟϤ·
   ΑС†ΟΥΚΟΝ ΩΒΙΟΝ Ν̄ΝΟΥΒ ϨΙΧΩϤ·
   ΑСΜΟΥⲢ̄ ΕΡΟϤ Ν̄ϨΜ̄ϨΑΛ ·Β̄·
   ΑСΧΟΟΥϤ ΕΠΠΑΛΛΑΤΙΟΝ ϢΑΠΕΡΟ⸗

4 ΔΕΡΕΔΙΟΚΛΗΤΙᾹΝΟС[1] Π̄Ρ̄ΡΟ·
   ΝΑΥ ΕΠϨΑΓΙΟС ᾹΠΑ ΒΙΚΤΩΡ·
   Ε̄ΡΕΠΚΟΝΟΒΙΟΝ Ν̄ΝΟΥΒ̄ ϨΙΧΩϤ·
   ΑϤΜΟΥϨ̄ Ν̄ϬΩΝ̄Τ̄ Ε̄ΠΕϨΟΥΟ⸗

---

[1] For ΝΤΕΡΕ-.

36

◄ HYMN THREE ►

The alphabetic acrostic on St Victor, the general

1 Truly, great is your honour
   and the glory which God has given you
   among all the martyrs,
   Apa Victor, the son of Romanus.

2 Every human life that has been born
   has a covering of sheep's wool put upon it.
   When Apa Victor was born,
   a garment[1] of gold was put upon him.

3 For his mother carried him
   and put a garment of gold upon him.
   She assigned two servants to him
   and sent him to the palace to the emperor.

4 When Diocletian, the emperor,
   saw the holy Apa Victor
   with the garment of gold upon him,
   he was greatly filled with wrath.

---

[1] Lit.: 'couch with mosquito curtains', 'canopy'. W. Till, *Koptische Heiligen- und Martyrerlegenden* 1 (Orientalia Christiana Analecta 102, Rome 1935), 54, nn. 1–3, suggests that the word in this legend signifies a garment or headgear.

5 ЄΙΤΑ ΠЄΧΑϤ ΝΤЄϤΜΑΑΥ·
ΧЄΑΜΗ ΤΑΜΟΙ ⲱ ΜΑΡΘΑ·
ΧЄⲀΝΟΚΤЄ¹ ⲠⲢⲢΟ·
ΧЄⲂΙΚΤⲰΡ ΠΟΥϢΗΡЄΠЄⳅ

6 ⳤⲰΤⲘ ⲈΜΑΡΘΑ·
ЄⲤϢΑΧЄ ΜЄⲆΙΟΚΛΗΤΙΑΝΟⳕ ⲠⲢⲢΟ·
ΧЄⲠⲢⲢΟ ⲱΝⳍ ϢΑⲈΝЄⳍ·
ΚЄΛЄⲅⲈ ΝΑΙ ΤΑϢΑΧЄⳅ

7 ⲚΤΑ ΠЄΧЄⲠⲢⲢΟ ΝΑⳕ·
ΧЄΘΗ ЄΡΟΥЄϢϢΑΧЄ ⲘⲠⲢⲢⳍΟΤЄ·
ΠЄΧΑⳕ ΝΑϤ ΧЄΝΤΟΚΠЄ ⲠⲢⲢΟ·
ΑΥⲱ ⲂΙΚΤⲰΡΤЄ¹ ΠЄΚϢΗΡЄⳅ

8 ΘΗ ⲚΤΑⲠⲢⲢΟ ⳕⲰΤⲘ ⲈΠΑΙ·
ΑϤ†ΟΥΚΟΝΟⲂΙΟΝ ⲚΝΟΥⲂ ⳍΙΧⲰϤ·
ΑϤΜΟΥⲢ ⲘΜΟϤ ΝΟΥΜΟΥⳕ ⲚΝΟΥⲂ·
ΑϤⲀΑϤ ⲘΜЄⳍϢΟΜⲦ ⳍⲘⲠⲠΑΛΛΑΤΙΟΝⳅ

9 ΙⲰ² Ν⳥ⲠΗΡЄ ΜΠЄΚΚΟΝΟⲂΙΟΝ ⲚΝΟΥⲂ·
ⲚΤΑϤϢⲰΠЄ ⲚΘЄ ΝΟΥⲀⲈΤΟⳕ·
ⳍⲚΝЄ⳪ΙΧ ⲚⲆΙΟΚΛΗΤΙⲀΝΟⳕ·
ΑϤΠⲰΤ ЄΠΧΙⳕЄ ЄΥ⳪ⲰϢΤ ⲚⳕⲰϤⳅ

---

¹ For -ⲡⲉ. Note the same irregular use in III,7/4, III,24/3,
and VIII,16/3.
² ιⲱ stands perhaps for the Greek exclamatory particle ἰώ
(note in this connection the use of the Greek exclamation βαβαί in
XIII,2/1), or alternatively for ⳍⲁ(ⲉ)ιⲟ, ⲁιⲱ: see W. E. Crum, *A
Coptic Dictionary* (Oxford 1939), 636b.

5 Then he said to his[1] mother:
Come, tell me, O Martha,
whether I am the emperor,
or whether Victor your son is.

6 Listen to Martha,
speaking to the emperor Diocletian:
O Emperor, live for ever.
Command me and I shall speak.

7 Then the emperor said to her:
As you wish to speak, do not be afraid.
She said to him: You are the emperor
and Victor is your son.[2]

8 As the emperor heard this,
he put the garment of gold upon him
and girded him with a golden girdle.
He appointed him to be the third in the palace.

9 Yea, the marvels of your garment of gold
which became as an eagle
in the hands of Diocletian.
It went aloft while they were looking after it.[3]

---

[1] i.e. Victor's.

[2] The outline of the story in stanzas 4–7 seems to be that Diocletian resents the presumption implied by the golden garment and is appeased only when Martha acknowledges his supremacy and Victor's subordination to him.

[3] In the Ethiopic version of the legend, summarized by E.A. Wallis Budge, *Coptic Martyrdoms etc in the Dialect of Upper Egypt* (London 1914), xxiv, an angel snatched the cloth of gold away, when Diocletian attempted to steal it, and flew up into the air with it.

10 ⲕⲉⲅⲁⲣ ⲁϥϭⲱⲛⲧ̄ ⲛ̄ϭⲓⲡⲣ̄ⲣⲟ·
ⲁϥⲧ̄ⲣⲟⲩⲥⲱⲛⲅ̄ ⲛⲁⲡⲁ ⲃⲓⲕⲧⲱⲣ·
ⲁϥϫⲟⲟⲩ ⲓ ⲉ̄ⲣⲁⲧϥ̄[1] ⲉ̄ⲣⲱⲙⲁⲛⲟⲥ·
ⲁϥⲡⲱⲧ ⲉ̄ϩⲟⲩⲛ̄ ϣⲁⲧⲉϥⲙⲁⲁⲩ⳾

11 ⲗⲉϣⲓ ⲛⲏ ⲙⲁⲣⲑⲁ ⲧⲁⲙⲁⲁⲩ·
ⲙⲁⲛ ⲁⲩϫⲓ ⲙ̄ⲙⲟⲓ ⲉϩⲣⲁⲓ ⲉ̄ⲕⲏⲙⲉ·
ⲧⲁⲙⲟⲩ ϩⲓϫⲙ̄ⲡ̄ⲣⲁⲛ ⲛⲓ̄ⲥ̄·
ϣⲱⲡⲉ ⲛ̄ⲛⲁⲏⲧ ⲙ̄ⲙⲁⲓⲁ̄ⲅⲁⲡⲏ⳾

12 ⲙⲛ̄ⲛⲥⲁⲛⲁⲓ ⲁⲩϫⲓ ⲛⲁⲡⲁ ⲃⲓⲕⲧⲱⲣ·
ⲉⲡⲕⲁⲥⲧⲣⲟⲛ ⲛⲁⲛⲧⲓⲛⲱⲟⲩ·
ⲁⲡϣⲏⲣⲉ ⲙ̄ⲡⲛⲟⲩⲧⲉ ⲡⲱⲧ ϣⲁⲣⲟϥ·
ⲁϥⲥⲉⲗⲥⲱⲗϥ̄ ϩⲛ̄ⲛⲉϥϩⲓⲥⲉ⳾

13 ⲛ̄ⲧⲉⲣⲉⲁⲡⲁ ⲃⲓⲕⲧⲱⲣ ⲛⲁⲩ ⲉⲡⲥⲱⲣ·
ⲁϥⲣⲁϣⲉ ⲙ̄ⲙⲁⲧⲉ ⲁϥⲧⲉⲗⲏⲗ·
ϫⲉⲛⲧⲉⲣⲓⲛⲁⲩ ⲉ̄ⲡⲉⲕϩⲟ ⲡⲁⲥⲟⲛ·
ⲁⲓⲣ̄ⲑⲉ ⲉϣϫⲉ ⲁⲓⲛⲁⲩ ⲉ̄ⲓ̄ⲥ̄⳾

14 ϫⲁⲟⲩⲛ̄ ⲉϩⲣⲱⲙⲁⲛⲟⲥ ⲡⲁⲓⲱⲧ·
ⲡⲉϫⲉⲡⲥⲱⲣ ⲛⲁⲡⲁ ⲃⲓⲕⲧⲱⲣ·
ϫⲉϯⲥⲟⲟⲩⲛ̄ ⲉϩⲣⲱⲙⲁⲛⲟⲥ ⲡⲉⲕⲓⲱⲧ·
ⲁⲩⲱ̄ ⲙⲁⲣⲑⲁⲧⲉ ⲧⲉⲕⲙⲁⲁⲩ⳾

---

[1] Page ⲣ̄ⲛ̄ⲉ̄ begins (see Plate 2).

40

10   Then[1] the emperor was wroth;
           he had them bind Apa Victor
           and sent him to Romanus.
           He went to his mother.

11   Rejoice, Martha, my mother,
           for they have taken me down to Egypt
           that I may die for the name of Jesus.
           Be merciful, loving charity.

12   Afterwards they took Apa Victor
           to the fortress of Antinoe.
           The Son of God came to him
           and comforted him in his sufferings.

13   When Apa Victor saw the Saviour,
           he rejoiced greatly and was glad,
           saying: When I saw your face, my brother,
           it was as if I had seen Jesus.

14   Do you know Romanus, my father?
           The Saviour said to Apa Victor:
           I know Romanus, your father,
           and Martha is your mother.

---

[1]   Lit.: 'for'.

15 ΟΥⲀⲚ ΟⲈΙΚ ⲌⲀⲦΗΚ ⲦⲀΟΥⲰⲘ ⲚⲘ̄ⲘⲀΚ·
   ⲡⲈⲭⲈⲡ̄ⲥⲰ̄ⲣ̄ ⲚⲀⲡⲀ ΒΙΚⲦⲰⲣ·
   ⲡⲈⲭⲀϥ ⲭⲈϥΟⲚ̄Ⳅ Ⲛ̄ϬΙ Ῑⲥ̄ ⲡⲀϬ̄ⲥ̄·
   ⲡⲀⲭΟΥⲦⲤⲚΟΟΥⲤ̄ ⲡΟΟΥ Ⲙ̄ⲡΙΟΥⲈⲘⲞⲈΙΚ⳹

16 ⲡⲈⲭⲈⲡ̄ⲥ̄Ⲱ̄ⲣ̄ ⲚⲀⲡⲀ ΒΙΚⲦⲰⲣ·
   ⲭⲈⲈΚⳄⲘΟΟⲤ ⲈΚⲣΟΥ ⳘⲘ̄ⲡⲈΙⲘⲀ·
   Ⲉ̄ⲣⲈⲚⲈΙⲡⲰⳆⳄ ⳘⲘ̄ⲡⲈΚⲤⲰⲘⲀ·
   Ⲉ̄ⲦⲈⲘⲚ̄ⲖⲀⲀΥ Ⲛ̄ⲣⲰⲘⲈ ⳄⲀⲦΗΚ⳹

17 ⲣⲀⲀΥ Ⲙ̄ⲡⲰⳆⳄ ⲈⲦⳄⲘ̄ⲡⲀⲤⲰⲘⲀ·
   ⲀΙⲈⲘⲡ̄ⲱⲀ ⲘⲘΟΟΥ ⳄⲀⲚⲀⲚΟΒⲈ·
   ⲀⲖⲖⲀ ⲱⲀΙⲱⲀⲡⳄⲘΟⲦ Ⲛ̄ⲦΟΟⲦ̄ϥ Ⲙ̄ⲡⲚΟΥⲦⲈ·
   ⲭⲈⲀΙⲘⲡ̄ⲱⲀ ⲀΥⲤΟⲱⳅ̄ ⳄⲀῙⲥ̄⳹

18 ⲤΟΥⲰⲚⲦ̄ ⲚⲀΚ ⲱ̄ ⲡⲀⲤⲰⲦⲡ̄ ΒΙΚⲦⲰⲣ·
   ⲭⲈⲀ̄ⲚΟΚⲡⲈ Ῑⲥ̄ ⲡⲈΚⲣ̄ⲣΟ·
   Ⲁ̄ⲚΟΚ ⲡⲈⲦ⳿ⲱΟΟⲡ ⲚⲘ̄ⲘⲀΚ·
   ⳄⲘ̄ⲘⲀ ⲚΙⲘ Ⲛ̄ⲱⲀΥⲭΙⲦ̄Κ Ⲉ̄ⲣΟϥ⳹

19 ⲦΙⲰⲣⲕ̄ ⲚⲀΚ ⲱ̄ ⲡⲀⲤⲰⲦⲡ̄ ΒΙΚⲦⲰⲣ·
   ⲭⲈⲈΙⲱⲀⲚ⳿Ⲧ⳿Ⲉ̄ΟΟΥ ⲚΟΥⲘⲀⲣⲦΥⲣΟⲤ·
   ⲱⲀΙⲭΟΟⲤ ⲚⲀϥ· ⲭⲈⳆⲚⲀ⳿Ⲧ⳿Ⲉ̄ΟΟ̄Υ ⲚⲀΚ·
   Ⲛ̄ⲐⲈ Ⲛ̄ΒΙΚⲦⲰⲣ ⲡ̄ⲱΗⲣⲈ Ⲛ̄ⳆⲣⲰⲘⲀⲚΟⲤ⳹

15   Have you bread with you that I may eat with you?,
      said the Saviour to Apa Victor.
      He said: As Jesus, my Lord, lives,
      today is the twenty-second day I have not eaten bread.

16   The Saviour said to Apa Victor:
      What are you doing sitting in this place,
      with these wounds on your body,
      where no man is with you?

17   Of any wound which is on my body
      I was worthy for my sins,
      but I give thanks to God
      that I was worthy to be struck for Jesus.

18   Know me, O my chosen, Victor,
      for I am Jesus, your king.
      I am with you
      wherever they take you.

19   I swear to you, O my chosen, Victor,
      if I glorify a martyr,
      I shall say to him: I shall glorify you
      like Victor, the son of Romanus.

20 ϩⲓ¹ ⲡⲁⲏⲥⲉ ⲡ̄ⲣⲉⲙⲡⲟⲩⲥⲓⲣⲉ·
ⲛ̄ⲧⲉⲣⲟⲩϫⲓⲧϥ̄ ⲉϩⲣⲁⲓ ⲉⲛⲉⲡⲏⲩⲉ̄·
ⲁⲩⲧⲁⲙⲟϥ ⲉ̄ⲡⲏⲓ ⲛⲁⲡⲁ ⲃⲓⲕⲧⲱⲣ·
ⲉϥⲕⲱⲧ ⲉ̄ⲛⲟⲩⲃ̄ ϩⲓⲱ̄ⲛⲉ ⲙ̄ⲙⲉ⧸

21 ⲓ ϥⲱⲃ² ⲉ̄ⲡⲏⲓ ⲡⲁⲡ̄ⲣ̄ⲣⲟⲡⲉ·
ⲡⲉϫⲉⲡⲁⲏⲥⲉ ⲙ̄ⲡⲁⲅⲅⲉⲗⲟⲥ·
ⲡⲉϫⲁϥ ϫⲉⲡⲉ³ ⲡⲏⲓ ⲛⲁⲡⲁ ⲃⲓⲕⲧⲱⲣ·
ⲛ̄ⲧⲁⲩⲕⲟⲧϥ̄ ⲉϩⲣⲁⲓ ϩⲉⲛⲉⲡⲏⲩⲉ⧸

22 ⲭⲁⲣⲓⲍⲉ ⲛⲁⲕ ⲉ̄ⲡⲏⲓ ϩⲱⲱⲕ·
ⲡⲉϫⲉⲡⲁⲅⲅⲉⲗⲟⲥ ⲉ̄ⲡⲁⲏⲥⲉ·
ⲡⲉϫⲁϥ ϫⲉⲁⲕⲉⲣⲡⲁⲙⲉⲉⲩⲉ̄ ⲡⲁⲃ̄ⲥ̄·
ⲁⲗⲗⲁ ⲟⲩⲕⲟⲩⲓⲡⲉ ⲙ̄ⲡⲁⲣⲁⲡϣⲟⲣⲡ̄⧸

23 ⲯⲉⲓ ⲉ̄ⲡⲉⲓⲛⲟϭ ⲛ̄ⲧⲁⲓⲟ̄·
ⲛ̄ⲧⲁⲓ̄ⲥ̄ ⲧⲁⲁϥ ⲛⲁⲡⲁ ⲃⲓⲕⲧⲱⲣ·
ⲡⲉϫⲉⲡⲁⲏⲥⲉ ⲙ̄ⲡⲁⲅⲅⲉⲗⲟⲥ·
ϫⲉⲁⲓⲟⲩⲉϣⲡⲱⲓ ϩⲱⲱⲧ ⲉϥⲟ̄ ⲛ̄ⲑⲉ ⲙ̄ⲡⲁⲓ⧸

24 ⲱⲛⲧⲱⲥ ⲟⲩⲁⲧ ⲡⲏⲓ ⲙ̄ⲡⲣ̄ⲣⲟ·
ⲁⲩⲱ̄ ⲟⲩⲁⲧ ⲡⲏⲓ ⲙ̄ⲡⲁⲣⲭⲱⲛ·
ⲡⲁⲓⲧⲉ⁴ ⲡⲏⲓ ⲛⲁⲡⲁ ⲃⲓⲕⲧⲱⲣ·
ⲙⲉⲟⲩⲟⲛ ⲉϥⲧⲛ̄ⲧⲱⲛ ⲉ̄ⲣⲟϥ:-
ⲥⲟⲡⲥ̄ ⲉ̄ⲡⲃ̄ⲥ̄⁵

---

¹ ϩⲓ, which also occurs in IV,5/1 and IX,20/1, perhaps stands for ⲟⲩϩⲓ.
² Page ⲣ̄ⲛ̄ⲋ̄ begins.
³ Note the irregular position of -ⲡⲉ.
⁴ See n. 1 on p. 38. above.
⁵ The last verse is clearly not part of the hymn, but was added by the scribe; it was perhaps intended as a prayer, to fill out the line in the manuscript (see p. 9).

20 Truly, Paese[1] of Busiris,[2]
    when taken up to heaven,
    was shown the house of Apa Victor,
    built of gold and precious stones.

21 This kind of house is the king's,
    said Paese to the angel.
    He said: It is the house of Apa Victor
    which was built in heaven.

22 Bestow this (other) house on yourself,
    said the angel to Paese.
    He said: You have remembered me, my lord,
    but it is smaller than the first.

23 O the abundance of this great honour,
    which Jesus gave to Apa Victor!
    Paese said to the angel:
    I wanted my own to be like this.

24 Indeed, the house of the king is different,
    and the house of the ruler is different.
    This is the house of Apa Victor,
    there is none like it.
    Pray to the Lord.[3]

---

[1] For this martyr, see De Lacy O'Leary, *The Saints of Egypt*
(London 1937), 211.
[2] The Busiris (Abusir) near Ashmunein in Middle Egypt.
[3] The last verse is clearly not part of the hymn, but a later
scribal addition (see p. 9).

◄ HYMN FOUR ►

(pp. p̄n̄ϛ, line 13 – p̄n̄н̄)

ā̄ ⲡⲁⲗⲫⲁⲃⲏⲧⲁ ⲛⲁⲡⲁ ⲕⲗⲁⲩⲇⲓⲟⲥ ⲡⲉⲥ̄ⲧⲣⲁⲧⲉⲗⲁⲧⲏⲥ:-

1 ⲱ ⲧϭⲟⲧ ē̄ⲡⲉⲇⲟⲩ ⲙ̄ⲡ̄ⲧⲁⲓⲟ·
ⲛ̄ⲧⲁⲡⲉⲛⲥ̄ⲱ̄ⲣ ⲛⲁⲅⲁⲑⲟⲥ·
ⲭⲁⲣⲓⲍⲉ ⲙ̄ⲙⲟϥ ⲛ̄ⲛⲉϥⲡⲉⲧⲟⲩⲁⲁⲃ·
ⲁ̄ⲡⲁ ⲃⲓⲕⲧⲱⲣ ⲙ̄ⲕ̄ⲗⲁⲩⲇⲓⲟⲥ⳱

2 ⲯⲱⲧⲏⲣ ⲱ̄ϣ ē̄ⲃⲟⲗ ⲉϥⲭⲱ ⲙ̄ⲙⲟⲥ·
ϫⲉⲛⲁⲓⲁⲧⲟⲩ ⲛ̄ⲛⲉⲛⲧⲁⲩⲡⲱⲧ ⲛ̄ⲥⲱⲟⲩ·
ⲉⲧⲃⲉⲧⲇⲓⲕⲁⲓⲟⲥⲩⲛⲏ·
ϫⲉⲧⲱⲟⲩⲧⲉ ⲧⲙ̄ⲛ̄ⲧⲉⲣⲟ ⲛ̄ⲙ̄ⲡⲏⲩē̄⳱

3 ⲭⲉⲣⲉ ⲛⲉⲙⲁⲣⲧⲩⲣⲟⲥ ē̄ⲧⲟⲩ̄ⲁ̄ⲁⲃ·
ⲭⲉⲣⲉ ⲛⲁⲑⲗⲏⲧⲏⲥ ⲛ̄ϫⲱ̄ⲱ̄ⲣⲉ·
ⲭⲉⲣⲉ ⲛⲉⲛⲧⲁⲩϫⲓ ⲛ̄ⲧⲉⲕⲗⲏⲣⲟⲛⲟⲙⲓⲁ̄·
ⲛ̄ⲧ̄ⲙ̄ⲛ̄ⲧⲉⲣⲟ ⲛ̄ⲙ̄ⲡⲏⲩē̄⳱

4 ⲫⲓē̄ⲣⲉⲩⲥ̄ ⲛⲁⲡⲟⲥⲧⲟⲗⲟⲥ ⲡⲁⲩⲗⲟⲥ·
ⲱ̄ϣ ē̄ⲃⲟⲗ ⲉϥⲭⲱ ⲙ̄ⲙⲟⲥ·
ϫⲉⲛⲉϩⲟⲡⲗⲟⲛ ⲛ̄ⲧⲙ̄ⲛ̄ⲧⲙⲁⲧⲟⲓ·
ⲛ̄ϩⲉⲛⲥⲁⲣⲕⲓⲕⲟⲛ ⲁⲛⲛⲉ⳱

46

➤ HYMN FOUR ➤

The alphabetic acrostic on Apa Claudius, the general

1   O the greatness of the glory and the honour
    which our good Saviour
    conferred upon his saints
    Apa Victor and Claudius.

2   The Saviour proclaims, saying:
    Blessed are they that have been persecuted
    for righteousness' sake,
    for theirs is the kingdom of heaven.[1]

3   Hail, holy martyrs.
    Hail, mighty champions.
    Hail to those who received the inheritance
    of the kingdom of heaven.

4   The apostolic priest Paul
    proclaims, saying:
    The weapons of warfare
    are not of the flesh.[2]

---

[1]   Mt. 5.10.
[2]   Cf. II Cor. 10.4.

47

5 ϭΙ[^1] ΠΕΤСΗϨ ΑϤϪⲰΚ ⲈΒΟⲗ ⲈϪⲰⲦⲚ·
   Ⲱ ⲀⲡⲀ ΒΙΚⲦⲰⲢ ⲘⲚ̅ⲔⲗⲀⲨⲆΙΟС·
   ϪⲈΟⲨⲚΟⲨⲈΙⲰⲦ ⲚⲀⲡⲀⲢⲀⲆΙⲆΟⲨ Ⲙ̅ΠⲈϤϢΗⲢⲈ·
   ⲀⲨⲰ ΟⲨСΟⲚ Ⲙ̅ΠⲈϤСΟⲚ⸗

6 ⲦⲀϬⲈΙⲆ ⲠⲢ̅ⲢΟ ⲰϢ ⲈΒΟⲗ·
   ϨⲈΠⲈⲮⲀⲗⲦΗⲢΙΟⲚ ⲈϤϪⲰ Ⲙ̅ΜΟС·
   ϪⲈⲀⲠⲀΙⲰⲦ | ΜⲈⲦⲀΜⲀⲀⲨ[^2] ⲔⲀⲀⲦ Ⲛ̅СⲰΟⲨ·
   ⲠϬ̅С ⲆⲈ ΠⲈⲚⲦⲀϤϢⲞⲠⲦ̅ ⲈⲢΟϤ⸗

7 СⲈⲈⲢⲘ̅Ⲛ̅ⲦⲢⲈ ⲄⲀⲢ ϨⲀⲢΟΚ·
   Ⲱ ⲠΠⲈⲦΟⲨⲀ̅ⲀⲂ ⲀⲠⲀ ΒΙΚⲦⲰⲢ·
   ϪⲈΠⲈΚΙⲰⲦ ⲀϤⲠⲀⲢⲀⲆΙⲆΟⲨ Ⲙ̅ΜΟΚ·
   Ⲉ̅ⲆΙΟΚⲗΗ†Ⲁ̅ⲚΟС ΠⲢ̅ⲢΟ⸗

8 ⲢⲰΜⲈ ⲚΙⲘ ⲚⲀⲚⲦΙΟⲬⲈⲨⲤ̅·
   СⲈ†Ⲉ̅ΟΟⲨ ⲚⲀΚ Ⲱ Ⲕ̅ⲗⲀⲨⲆΙΟС·
   ϪⲈⲀⲔϢⲰⲠⲈ Ⲛ̅ΘⲈ ⲚΙⲰⲂ Ⲙ̅ΠΙΟⲨⲞⲈΙϢ·
   ϨⲈⲚⲈⲘⲚ̅ⲦϢⲚ̅ϨⲦΗϤ Ⲉ̅ϨΟⲨⲚ Ⲉ̅ⲚⲈϨΗΚⲈ⸗

9 ⲠⲀⲨⲗΟС ⲠⲗⲀС Ⲉ̅ⲠⲈС†ⲚΟⲨΒⲈ·
   ⲰϢ Ⲉ̅ΒΟⲗ ⲈϤϪⲰ Ⲙ̅ΜΟС·
   ϪⲈ† ϨΙⲰⲦⲦΗⲨⲦⲚ̅ ⲚⲈⲦΟⲨⲀ̅ⲀⲂ Ⲙ̅ΜⲈⲢΙⲦ·
   Ⲛ̅ϨⲚ̅С̅Π̅ⲗⲀⲬⲚΟⲚ Ⲙ̅ΜⲚ̅ⲦϢⲀⲚ̅ϨⲦΗϤ⸗

---

[^1]: ϬΙ, which also occurs in III,20/1 and IX,20/1, perhaps stands for ΟⲨΗΙ.

[^2]: Page Ⲣ̅Ⲛ̅Ⲍ̅ begins.

5   Truly, that which is written has been fulfilled in you,
     O Apa Victor and Claudius:
     A father shall deliver up his son,
     and a brother his brother.[1]

6   King David proclaims
     in the psalter, saying:
     My father and my mother have forsaken me,
     but the Lord has received me.[2]

7   For it is testified of you,
     O holy Apa Victor,
     that your father delivered you up
     to the Emperor Diocletian.

8   All men of Antioch
     glorify you, O Claudius,
     for you were like Job in former times
     with compassion towards the poor.[3]

9   Paul, the perfumed tongue,
     proclaims, saying:
     Put on, beloved saints,
     hearts of compassion.[4]

---

[1]   Cf. Mt. 10.21; Mk. 13.12.
[2]   Ps. 26.10.
[3]   Cf. e.g. Job 29.12.
[4]   Cf. Col. 3.12.

10   ΟΥΚ̄¹ ΚΟΥΝΟϬ ⲱ Ⲕⲗⲁⲩⲇⲓⲟⲥ·
ⲟⲩⲛⲟϬⲡⲉ ⲡϣⲁϫⲉ ⲙⲡⲣ̄ⲣⲟ·
ⲕⲁⲧⲁⲡϣⲁϫⲉ ⲛ̄ⲥⲟⲗⲟⲙⲱⲛ·
ϫⲉⲟⲩⲕⲱ̄ϩⲧ̄ⲡⲉ ⲡϣⲁϫⲉ ⲙⲡⲣ̄ⲣⲟ⳥

11   ϩⲥ̄ⲙⲁⲙⲁⲁⲧ ⲛ̄ⲧⲟⲕ ⲱ ⲕ̄ⲗⲁⲩⲇⲓⲟⲥ·
ⲕ̄ⲧⲁⲓⲏⲩ ϩⲛ̄ⲛⲉⲕϩⲃⲏⲩⲉ̄ ⲧⲏⲣⲟⲩ·
ϫⲉⲁⲕⲕⲱ ⲙⲡⲉⲓⲕⲟⲥⲙⲟⲥ ⲛ̄ⲥⲱⲕ·
ⲁⲕⲃⲱⲕ ⲁⲕⲟⲩⲁϩⲕ̄ ⲛ̄ⲥⲁⲡⲥⲱ̄ⲣ⳥

12   ⲛⲉⲣⲱⲟⲩ ⲉⲧϩⲙ̄ⲡⲡⲁⲗⲗⲁⲧⲓⲟⲛ·
ⲁⲩⲉ̄ⲡⲓⲑⲩⲙⲓ ⲉ̄ⲡⲉⲕⲧⲁⲓⲟ̄·
ⲁⲩϩⲱⲅⲣⲁⲫⲓ ⲙ̄ⲡⲉⲕⲗⲓⲙⲏⲛ·²
ⲁⲩⲕⲁⲁϥ ⲉϥⲟ ⲛⲛⲁϣⲧⲉ ⲛⲁⲩ⳥

13   ⲙⲉⲛϣⲃⲏⲣ ⲉ̄ⲛⲁⲛⲟⲩϥ ϩⲉⲧⲉⲅⲣⲁⲫⲏ·
ⲛ̄ⲑⲉ ⲛⲇⲁ̄ⲇ̄ ⲙⲛ̄ⲓⲱⲛⲁⲑⲁⲛ·
ⲙⲛ̄ϣⲃⲏⲣ ⲉ̄ⲛⲁⲛⲟⲩϥ ϩⲉⲛⲉⲙⲁⲣⲧⲩⲣⲟⲥ·
ⲛ̄ⲑⲉ ⲛⲃⲓⲕⲧⲱⲣ ⲙⲛ̄ⲕ̄ⲗⲁⲩⲇⲓⲟⲥ⳥

14   ⲗⲁⲟⲥ ⲛⲓⲙ ⲉⲧϩⲓϫⲙ̄ⲡⲕⲁϩ·
ⲥⲉϯⲉ̄ⲟⲟⲩ ⲉ̄ⲛⲓⲙⲁⲣⲧⲩⲣⲟⲥ·
ⲉⲧⲃⲉⲛⲉⲓⲭⲁⲣⲓⲥⲙⲁ ⲛ̄ⲧⲁⲗϬⲟ·
ⲛ̄ⲧⲁⲡⲛⲟⲩⲧⲉ ⲭⲁⲣⲓⲍⲉ ⲙⲙⲟⲟⲩ ⲛⲁⲩ⳥

---

[1] Note the irregular use of ΟΥΚ. Perhaps ΟΥΚΟΥΝ was intended, which is not uncommon in Coptic. The Greek negative particle οὐ, οὐκ, does not appear to occur in Coptic except in Greek phrases, as e.g. ΟΥΚ ⲈϤⲈⲤⲦⲒ, ⲞⲨ ⲘⲞⲚⲞⲚ, ⲞⲨⲬ ⲞⲦⲒ, ⲞⲨ ⲄⲀⲢ, ⲞⲨ ⲠⲀⲚⲦⲰⲤ.

[2] On the etymology of this word, which also occurs in II,21/2, see G. Godron, 'ⲗⲓⲙⲏⲛ, "portrait", "image"', *BSAC* 25 (1983), 1–52, and idem, 'A nouveau ⲗⲓⲙⲏⲛ (compléments)', *BSAC* 29 (1990), 43–7. It is not included in the Index of Loan-Words.

10 Are you not great, O Claudius?
Great is the word of the king,
according to the word of Solomon:
The word of the king is a fire.[1]

11 You are blessed, O Claudius,
you are honoured in all your deeds,
for you have forsaken this world,
you went and followed the Saviour.

12 The kings who are in the palace
desired your honour.
They painted your portrait,
they set it up for their protection.

13 There is no friend as good in the scripture
as David and Jonathan.[2]
There is no friend as good among the martyrs
as Victor and Claudius.

14 All the peoples on earth
glorify these martyrs
because of these gifts of healing,
which God conferred upon them.

---

[1] Cf. perhaps Prov. 24.22.
[2] Cf. e.g. I Kg. 18.1.

15 ⲕⲉⲅⲁⲣ ⲛⲉϣⲏⲛ ⲛⲣⲉϥϯⲕⲁⲣⲡⲟⲥ·
ⲉⲩϣⲁⲛⲭⲓ ⲛ̄ϩⲛ̄ⲕⲗⲁⲇⲟⲥ ⲉ̄ⲃⲟⲗ ⲛ̄ϩⲏⲧⲟⲩ·
ⲛ̄ⲥⲉⲧⲱϭⲉ ⲙ̄ⲙⲟⲟⲩ ϩⲛ̄ⲟⲩⲕⲁϩ ⲛ̄ⲃ̄ⲣ̄ⲣⲉ·
ϣⲁⲩϯ ⲛⲟⲩⲕⲁⲣⲡⲟⲥ ⲉ̄ⲛⲁϣⲱϥ⳹

16 |ⲓⲉⲥ[1] ⲃⲓⲕⲧⲱⲣ ⲙⲛ̄ⲕⲗⲁⲩⲇⲓⲟⲥ·
ⲁⲩⲭⲓⲧⲟⲩ ⲉ̄ⲧⲁⲛⲧⲓⲟ̄ⲭⲓⲁ̄·
ⲁⲩⲉⲛⲧⲟⲩ ⲉ̄ⲧⲉⲭⲱⲣⲁ ⲛ̄ⲕⲏⲙⲉ·
ⲁⲩⲧⲁⲗϭⲟ ⲛⲟⲩⲟⲛ ⲛⲓⲙ ⲉⲧϣⲱⲛⲉ⳹

17 ⲑⲏ ⲙ̄ⲡⲉⲧⲣⲟⲥ ⲙⲛ̄ⲓⲱϩⲁⲛⲛⲏⲥ·
ⲉⲩⲧⲁⲗϭⲟ ⲛⲟⲩⲟⲛ ⲛⲓⲙ ⲉⲧϣⲱⲛⲉ·
ⲧⲁⲓⲧⲉ ⲑⲉ ⲛ̄ⲛⲓⲙⲁⲣⲧⲩⲣⲟⲥ·
ⲁⲡⲁ ⲃⲓⲕⲧⲱⲣ ⲙⲛ̄ⲕⲗⲁⲩⲇⲓⲟⲥ⳹

18 ⲏⲥ[2] ⲧⲉⲓⲛⲟϭ ⲛ̄ϣⲡⲏⲣⲉ ⲁⲥϣⲱⲡⲉ·
ϩⲛ̄ⲛⲓⲡⲉⲧⲟⲩⲁⲁⲃ ⲙ̄ⲙⲁⲣⲧⲩⲣⲟⲥ·
ⲛⲧⲁⲧⲧⲱⲧⲉ ⲛ̄ⲛⲉⲩⲭⲗⲁⲙⲩⲥ·
ⲧⲁⲗϭⲟ ⲛⲟⲩⲣⲱⲙⲉ ⲛ̄ⲕⲉⲗⲉⲫⲟⲥ⳹

19 ϩⲉⲉⲣⲙⲛ̄ⲧ̄ⲣⲉ ⲅⲁⲣ ϩⲁⲣⲟⲕ·
ⲱ̄ ⲡⲡⲉⲧⲟⲩⲁⲁⲃ ⲕⲗⲁⲩⲇⲓⲟⲥ·
ϫⲉⲙⲡⲉⲡϩⲏⲅⲉⲙⲱⲛ ⲉϥⲃⲁⲥⲁⲛⲓⲍⲉ ⲙ̄ⲙⲟⲕ·
ⲉⲧⲃⲉⲡⲉⲕⲛⲟϭ ⲛⲁⲝⲓⲱⲙⲁ⳹

---

[1] Page ⲣⲛ̄ⲏ̄, the last page of quire ⲓ̄, begins. ⲓⲉⲥ stands probably for ⲉⲓⲥ.

[2] Almost certainly for ⲉⲓⲥ; cf. II,7/1.

15 For when from fruit-bearing trees
    one takes away shoots
    and plants them in new earth,
    they will bear much fruit.

16 Behold, Victor and Claudius
    were taken to Antioch,
    and they were brought to the land of Egypt.
    They healed every one who was sick.

17 Even as Peter and John
    heal every one who is sick,[1]
    thus do these martyrs
    Apa Victor and Claudius.

18 Behold, this great miracle came to pass
    through these holy martyrs,
    when the fringe of their cloaks
    healed a leper.

19 For it is testified of you,
    O St Claudius,
    that the governor was not able to torture you
    because of your great reputation.

---

[1] Cf. Acts 3.1–10 and 5.12–16.

20 ЄΙС ⲠⲖⲀⲞⲤ ⲚⲚⲈⲢⲈⲘⲢⲀⲔⲞⲦⲈ·
    ⲀⲨⲦⲰⲞⲨⲚ ⲈⲌⲈⲚⲌⲀⲢⲘⲈⲚⲒⲞⲤ·
    ⲘⲠⲞⲨⲔⲀⲀⲨ ⲈⲌⲰⲦⲂ ⲚⲀⲠⲀ ⲂⲒⲔⲦⲰⲢ·
    ⲈⲦⲂⲈⲌⲢⲰⲘⲀⲚⲞⲤ ⲠⲈϤⲒⲰⲦ⳽

21 ⲆⲀⲚⲒⲎⲖ ⲞⲨⲔⲞⲨⲒⲠⲈ ⲌⲚⲐⲨⲖⲎⲔⲒⲀ·
    ⲀⲖⲖⲀ ⲞⲨⲚⲞϬⲠⲈ ⲌⲚⲦⲤⲞⲪⲒⲀ·
    ⲂⲒⲔⲦⲰⲢ ⲞⲨⲔⲞⲨⲒⲠⲈ ⲌⲚⲦⲈϤϬⲞⲦ·
    ⲀⲖⲖⲀ ⲠⲚⲞϬⲠⲈ ⲌⲚⲚⲈⲘⲀⲢⲦⲨⲢⲞⲤ⳽

22 ⲢⲈⲄⲀⲢ ⲆⲀⲆ ⲰϢ ⲈⲂⲞⲖ·
    ⲌⲈⲠⲈⲮⲀⲖⲦⲎⲢⲒⲞⲚ ⲈϤⲬⲰ ⲘⲘⲞⲤ·
    ⲬⲈⲠⲬⲞⲈⲒⲤ ⲚⲀⲌⲀⲢⲈⲌ ⲚⲦⲞϤ·
    ⲈⲦⲈⲮⲨⲬⲎ ⲚⲚⲈϤⲠⲈⲦⲞⲨⲀⲀⲂ⳽

23 ⲂⲒⲔⲦⲰⲢ ⲀⲨⲌⲰⲦⲂ ⲘⲘⲞϤ·
    ⲌⲒⲦⲚⲈⲨⲦⲨⲬⲒⲀⲚⲞⲤ ⲠⲖⲞⲨⳅ·
    ⲔⲖⲀⲨⲆⲒⲞⲤ ⲀⲨⲖⲞⲄⲬⲒⲌⲈ ⲘⲘⲞϤ·
    ⲌⲒⲦⲈⲚⲀⲢⲒⲀⲚⲞⲤ ⲠⲌⲎⲄⲈⲘⲰⲚ⳽

24 ⲀⲖⲎⲐⲰⲤ ⲀⲦⲈⲬⲰⲢⲀ ⲚⲔⲎⲘⲈ·
    ⲈⲘⲠϢⲀ ⲚⲞⲨⲚⲞϬ ⲚⲌⲘⲞⲦ·
    ⲈⲦⲂⲈⲠⲈⲤⲚⲞϤ ⲈⲚⲈⲒⲘⲀⲢⲦⲨⲢⲞⲤ·
    ⲀⲠⲀ ⲂⲒⲔⲦⲰⲢ ⲘⲚⲔⲖⲀⲨⲆⲒⲞⲤ:-
    ⲤⲞⲠⲤ ⲈⲠϬⲤ[1]

---

[1] The last verse is clearly not part of the hymn, but a later
scribal addition (see p. 9).

20 Behold, the people of Alexandria
    rose against Armenius.
    They did not allow Apa Victor to be killed
    because of Romanus, his father.

21 Daniel was young in age,
    but great in wisdom.[1]
    Victor was young in age,
    but the greatest among the martyrs.

22 For David proclaims
    in the psalter, saying:
    The Lord shall guard
    the souls of his saints.[2]

23 Victor was killed
    by Eutychianos, the military governor.
    Claudius was pierced with a spear
    by Arianus, the governor.

24 Truly, the land of Egypt
    was worthy of great grace
    because of the blood of these martyrs,
    Apa Victor and Claudius.
    Pray to the Lord.[3]

---

[1] Cf. perhaps Daniel 1.17.
[2] Cf. Ps. 96.10.
[3] The last verse is clearly not part of the hymn, but a later
scribal addition (see p. 9).

◄ HYMN FIVE ►

(pp. ϷΝΘ-Ϸ϶Ⳉ, line 6)

| ē¹ ⲡⲁⲗⲫⲁⲃⲏⲧⲁ ⲙ̄ⲡϩⲁⲅⲓⲟⲥ ⲑⲉⲱⲇⲱⲣⲟⲥ
ⲡⲉⲥⲧⲣⲁⲧⲉⲗⲁⲧⲏⲥ:-

1 ⲁⲗⲏⲑⲱⲥ ⲁ̄ⲕⲉⲙⲡ̄ⲱⲁ ⲛⲟⲩϩⲙⲟⲧ·
ⲙ̄ⲡⲙ̄ⲧⲟ ⲉ̄ⲃⲟⲗ ⲙ̄ⲡ̄ⲛⲟⲩⲧⲉ ⲛ̄ⲧⲡⲉ·
ⲱ ⲡⲉⲥ̄ⲧⲣⲁⲧⲉⲗⲁⲧⲏⲥ ⲉⲧⲧⲁⲓⲏⲩ·
ⲡ̄ϩⲁⲅⲓⲟⲥ ⲑⲉⲱⲇⲱⲣⲟⲥ⳦

2 ⲃⲱⲱⲯ ⲉ̄ⲃⲟⲗ ⲉ̄ⲣⲟⲕ ⲛ̄ϭⲓⲡⲉⲛⲥⲱ̄ⲣ·
ⲱ̄ ⲡⲉⲥ̄ⲧⲣⲁⲧⲉⲗⲁⲧⲏⲥ ⲉⲧⲧⲁⲓⲏⲩ·
ϫⲉⲟⲩⲟⲛ ⲛⲓⲙ ⲉⲧⲛⲁϯ̄ⲉ̄ⲟⲟⲩ ⲛⲁⲓ·
ⲁ̄ⲛⲟⲕ ϩⲱ ϯⲛⲁⲙⲉⲣⲓⲧ̄ϥ⳦

3 ⲅⲉⲅⲁⲣ ⲁϥϯ̄ⲉ̄ϫⲟⲩⲥⲓⲁ̄ ⲛⲁⲕ·
ⲱ̄ ⲡ̄ϩⲁⲅⲓⲟⲥ ⲑⲉⲱⲇⲱⲣⲟⲥ·
ⲉϩⲣⲁⲓ ⲉ̄ϫⲛ̄ⲛⲉⲇⲉⲙⲱⲛⲓⲟⲛ·
ⲁⲩⲱ̄ ⲁⲕⲛⲟϫⲟⲩ ⲉ̄ⲃⲟⲗ⳦

4 ⲁⲗⲁ̄ ⲡⲣ̄ⲣⲟ ⲱⲯ ⲉ̄ⲃⲟⲗ·
ϩⲙ̄ⲡⲉⲯⲁⲗⲧⲏⲣⲓⲟⲛ ⲉⲧⲧⲁⲓⲏⲩ·
ϫⲉⲡⲁⲓ ⲛⲁϫⲓ ⲛⲟⲩⲥ̄ⲙⲟⲩ ⲛ̄ⲧⲉⲡϭ̄ⲥ·
ⲟⲩⲙⲛ̄ⲧⲛⲁⲏⲧ ⲛ̄ⲧⲉⲡⲉϥⲥⲱⲧⲏⲣ⳦

---

¹ Page ϷΝΘ, the first page of quire ⲓⲁ, begins.

◄ HYMN FIVE ►

The alphabetic acrostic on St Theodore, the general

1   Truly, you were worthy of grace
before the God of heaven,
O renowned general,
St Theodore.

2   Our Saviour proclaims to you,
O renowned general:
Everyone who shall glorify me
I shall also love.[1]

3   For he gave you authority,
O St Theodore,
over the demons
and you cast them out.

4   King David proclaims
in the precious psalter:
This one shall receive blessing from the Lord
and compassion from his Saviour.[2]

---

[1]   Cf. perhaps John 14.21.
[2]   Cf. Ps. 23.5.

5 ⲉⲓⲛⲁϯ ⲙ̅ⲡⲁⲟⲩⲟⲓ ⲉ̅ⲛⲉⲕⲙⲛ̅ⲧ̅ϫⲱⲱ̅ⲣⲉ·
ⲱ̅ ⲡⲉⲥⲧⲣⲁⲧⲉⲗⲁⲧⲏⲥ ⲉⲧⲧⲁⲓⲏⲩ·
ⲙⲛ̅ⲛⲉϭⲟⲙ ⲙⲛ̅ⲛⲉϣ̅ⲡⲏⲣⲉ·
ⲛ̅ⲧⲁⲡ̅ⲛⲟⲩⲧⲉ ⲁ̅ⲁⲩ ⲉ̅ⲃⲟⲗ ϩⲓⲧⲟⲟⲧⲕ̅⸗

6 ⲍⲱⲅⲣⲁⲫⲓ ⲛⲁⲛ ⲉ̅ⲡⲉⲕⲧⲁⲓⲟ̅·
ⲙ̅ⲡ̅ⲛⲁⲩ ⲛ̅ⲧⲁⲕⲡⲱⲧ ⲉ̅ⲉⲩⲭⲏⲧⲟⲥ ⲧ̅ⲡⲟⲗⲓⲥ·
ⲁ̅ⲛⲉⲙⲏⲏ̅ϣⲉ ⲉⲓ ⲉ̅ⲃⲟⲗ ϩⲁϫⲱⲕ·
ⲉⲩⲣⲁϣⲉ ⲉⲩϯⲉⲟ̅ⲟⲩ ⲛⲁⲕ⸗

7 ⲏ̅ⲧⲁ ⲛ̅ⲧⲉⲣⲉϥⲡⲱⲧ ⲉ̅ⲉⲩⲭⲏⲧⲟⲥ ⲧ̅ⲡⲟⲗⲓⲥ·
ⲛ̅ϭⲓⲡⲉⲥⲧ̅ⲣⲁⲧⲉⲗⲁⲧⲏⲥ ⲉⲧⲧⲁⲓⲏⲩ·
ⲁⲩⲥ̅ϩⲓⲙⲉ ⲉⲓ ⲉ̅ⲃⲟⲗ ϩⲁϫⲱϥ·
ⲉ̅ⲥⲱϣ ⲉ̅ⲃⲟⲗ ⲉⲥϫⲱ ⲙ̅ⲙⲟⲥ⸗

8 ⲑⲓⲣⲏⲛⲏ ⲛ̅ⲧⲉⲕϭⲓⲛⲓ ϣⲁⲣⲟⲛ·
ⲱ̅ ⲡ̅ϩⲁⲅⲓⲟⲥ ⲑⲉⲱⲇⲱⲣⲟⲥ·
ϣⲁⲛ̅ϩⲧⲏⲕ ⲉ̅ϫⲱⲓ ⲙⲛ̅ⲛⲁϣⲏⲣⲉ·
ϫⲉⲁ̅ⲛⲟⲕ ⲟⲩⲭⲣⲏⲥⲧⲓⲁⲛⲟⲥ⸗

9 ⲓ̅ⲥ̅ ⲁϥⲧⲛ̅ⲛⲟⲟⲩ ⲛⲁⲛ·
ⲱ̅ ⲡⲉⲥⲧⲣⲁⲧⲉⲗⲁⲧⲏⲥ ⲉⲧⲧⲁⲓⲏⲩ·
ⲉⲧⲣⲉⲕⲣ̅ⲃⲟⲓⲑⲓ ⲉⲣⲟⲓ·
ϫⲉⲁ̅ⲛⲁⲧⲉⲓⲡⲟⲗⲓⲥ ϫⲓⲧ ⲛ̅ϭⲟⲛⲥ̅⸗

5   I shall proceed to your feats,
   O renowned general,
   and the mighty works and wonders
   which God performed through you.

6   Describe for us your renown
   at the time when you went to the city of Euchaites.
   The crowds came out to meet you,
   rejoicing and glorifying you.

7   Then, when there came to the city of Euchaites
   the renowned general,
   a woman came out to meet him,
   crying out and saying:

8   Peace be upon your visit to us,
   O St Theodore.
   Have mercy upon me and my children,
   for I am a Christian.

9   Jesus has sent to us,
   O renowned general,
   that you should help me,
   for the men of this city have treated me evilly.

10 ⲕⲁⲗⲱⲥ ⲁⲣϣⲁⲭⲉ ⲱ̅ ⲧⲉⲥϩⲓⲙⲉ·
ϩⲙ̅ⲡⲣⲁⲛ ⲉ̄ⲡⲉⲭ̅ⲥ̅·
ϥ̇ⲛⲁⲃ̄ⲃⲟⲏ̄ⲑⲓ ⲉ̄ⲣⲟ·
ⲁⲩⲱ̅ ⲛ̄ϥ̇†ϣⲓⲡⲉ ⲛⲛⲁⲧⲉⲓⲡⲟⲗⲓⲥ⸗

11 ⲗⲟⲓⲡⲟⲛ ⲧⲁⲙⲟⲓ ⲉⲡⲙⲁ ⲛ̄ⲛⲟⲩϣⲏⲣⲉ·
ⲛ̄ⲧⲁⲓⲉ̄ⲗⲉⲩⲑⲉⲣⲟⲩ[1] ⲙ̄ⲙⲟⲟⲩ·
ⲛ̄ⲧⲁⲡⲁⲧⲁⲥⲥⲉ ⲙ̄ⲡⲉⲇⲣⲁⲕⲱⲛ·
ⲧⲉⲡⲣⲁⲛ ⲉⲡⲛⲟⲩⲧⲉ ϫⲓⲧⲁⲓⲟ̄⸗

12 ⲙⲁⲣⲉⲛ†ⲉ̄ⲟⲟⲩ ⲉ̄ⲡⲉⲛⲥⲱ̅ⲣ̅·
ⲉϥ†ⲉ̄ⲟⲟⲩ ⲛ̄ⲛⲉϥⲡⲉⲧⲟⲩⲁ̄ⲁⲃ·
ϫⲉⲁⲩⲡⲉϩ̄ⲧⲡⲉⲩⲥ̄ⲛⲟϥ ⲉ̄ⲃⲟⲗ ϩⲁⲣⲟϥ·
ⲁϥⲡⲉϩ̄ⲧⲡⲱϥ ⲉ̄ⲃⲟⲗ ϩⲁⲡ̄ⲕⲟⲥⲙⲟⲥ ⲧⲏⲣϥ̇⸗

13 ⲛⲉⲙⲁⲧⲟⲓ ⲧⲏⲣⲟⲩ ⲉⲧϩⲓϫⲙ̄ⲡ̄ⲕⲁϩ·
ⲥⲉⲡⲏⲧ ϩⲓⲡⲉⲥⲗⲁⲇⲓⲟⲛ·
ⲁⲗⲗⲁ ⲟⲩⲁ̄ ⲛ̄ϩⲏⲧⲟⲩ ϣⲁϥϫⲓⲡⲉⲕⲗⲟⲙ·
ⲉ̄ⲧⲉⲛⲧⲟⲕⲡⲉ ⲱ̅ ⲡ̄ⲡⲉⲧⲟⲩⲁ̄ⲁⲃ ⲑⲉⲱⲇⲱⲣⲟⲥ⸗

14 ⳉⲥⲙⲁⲙⲁⲁⲧ ⲛ̄ⲧⲟⲕ ϩⲉⲛⲉⲙⲁⲣⲧⲩⲣⲟⲥ·
ⲱ̅ ⲡⲉⲥ̄ⲧⲣⲁⲧⲉⲗⲁⲧⲏⲥ ⲉⲧⲧⲁⲓⲏⲩ·
ⲉⲧⲃⲉⲛⲉⲃⲟⲙ ⲙⲛ̄ⲛⲉϣⲡⲏⲣⲉ·
ⲛ̄ⲧⲁⲡ̄ⲛⲟⲩⲧⲉ ⲭⲁⲣⲓⲍⲉ ⲙ̄ⲙⲟⲟⲩ ⲛⲁⲕ⸗

---

[1] Page ⲣ̅ⳅ̅ begins.

10   You have spoken well, O woman.
     In the name of Christ,
     he will help you
     and put to shame the men of this city.

11   Now tell me where your children are,
     and I shall free them
     and slay the dragon,
     that the name of God be honoured.

12   Let us glorify our Saviour,
     who glorifies his saints,
     for they shed their blood for him;
     he shed his for the whole world.

13   All soldiers who are on earth
     run the race,
     but one of them receives the crown,[1]
     namely you, O St Theodore.

14   You are blessed among the martyrs,
     O renowned general,
     because of the mighty works and wonders
     which God granted to you.

---

[1]   Cf. I Cor. 9.24.

15 ΟΥΛΛΟΣ ΕϥΟϢ ΝΗΥ Ε͞ΠΕΚΤΟΠΟΣ·
Ⲱ͞ Π͞ⲀⲄⲒⲞⲤ ⲐⲈⲰⲆⲰⲢⲞⲤ·
ⲈⲨⲐⲈⲰⲢⲒ Ⲛ͞ⲚⲈⲔⲘⲚ͞ⲦⲬⲰⲰ͞ⲢⲈ·
ⲈⲨⲈⲒⲚⲈ Ⲛ͞ⲚⲈⲨⲆⲰⲢⲞⲚ ⲚⲀⲔ⳽

16 ⲠⲈⲔⲢⲀⲚ ⳉⲞⲖⲆ͞ ⳉⲈⲚⲈⲘⲠⲎⲨⲈ͞·
ⳉⲚ͞ⲦⲦⲀⲠⲢⲞ Ⲛ͞ⲚⲈⲀⲄⲄⲈⲖⲞⲤ·
Ⲱ͞ ⲠⲈⲤ͞ⲦⲢⲀⲦⲈⲖⲀⲦⲎⲤ ⲈⲦⲦⲀⲒⲎⲨ·
Π͞ⲀⲄⲒⲞⲤ ⲐⲈⲰⲆⲰⲢⲞⲤ⳽

17 ⲢⲰⲘⲈ ⲚⲒⲘ ⲈⲦⳉⲒⳜⲘ͞Π͞ⲔⲀⳉ·
ⲈⲨϢⲀⲚⲠⲰⲦ ⳉⲚ͞ⲞⲨⲀ͞ⲚⲀⲄⲔⲎ·
ⲚⲤⲈⲢ͞ⲠⲘⲈⲈⲨⲈ͞ Ⲙ͞ⲠⲈⲔⲢⲀⲚ·
ϢⲀⲒⲠⲰⲦ Ⲛ͞ⲦⲈⲨⲚⲞⲨ·
ⲦⲀⲈⲢⲂⲞⲎ͞ⲐⲒ Ⲉ͞ⲢⲞⲞⲨ⳽[1]

18 ⲤⲰⲦⳜ Ⲉ͞ⲦⲈⲒⲔⲈⲚⲞⲃ ⲈϢⲠⲎⲢⲈ·
ⲈⲦⲠ͞ⲢⲈⲠⲒ Ⲙ͞ⲠⲈⲔⲈⲞⲞⲨ·
Ⲱ͞ ⲠⲈⲤ͞ⲦⲢⲀⲦⲈⲖⲀⲦⲎⲤ ⲈⲦⲦⲀⲒⲎⲨ·
Π͞ⲀⲄⲒⲞⲤ ⲐⲈⲰⲆⲰⲢⲞⲤ⳽

19 ⲦⲒⲚⲀⲨ ⲈⲨⲤ͞ⳉⲒⲘⲈ ⲈⲤⳉⲚ͞ⲦⲤⲒⲞ͞ⲞⲨⲚ͞·
Ⲛ͞ⲦⲈⲢⲞⲨⲰϢ[2] Ⲉ͞ⲬⲒⲦⲤ͞ Ⲉ͞ⲃⲞⲚⲤ͞·
ⲀⲤⲢ͞ⲠⲘⲈⲈⲨⲈ͞ Ⲙ͞ⲠⲈⲔⲢⲀⲚ·
ⲀⲔⲦⲞⲨⲬⲀⲤ Ⲙ͞ⲠⲈⲠⲈⲐⲀⲨ ⲦⲀⳉⲞⲤ⳽

---

[1] The punctuation in the manuscript confirms that this stanza has five verses.
[2] For ⲚⲦⲈⲢⲞⲨⲞⲨⲰϢ.

15 Many people come to your sanctuary,
    O St Theodore,
    contemplating your feats
    and bringing their gifts to you.

16 Your name is sweet in heaven
    in the mouth of the angels,
    O renowned general,
    St Theodore.

17 All men upon earth,
    if they run into distress
    and remember your name,
    I[1] shall go at once
    and help them.

18 Listen to this other great wonder,
    which is fitting to your glory,
    O renowned general,
    St Theodore.

19 I see a woman in the baths.
    When they wished to violate her,
    she remembered your name
    and you saved her; the evil did not befall her.[2]

---

[1] Note the abrupt change of person. The sense, however, is clear.

[2] For a narrative account of this incident, see ed. I.Balestri and H.Hyvernat, *Acta Martyrum* I (CSCO 43/Copt. 3=iii, 1, Louvain 1907) 186–7; Latin translation: CSCO 44/Copt. 4=iii, 1 (Louvain 1908) 115.

20 ϭⲓⲥ¹ ⲡⲉⲕⲣⲁⲛ ⳁⲱⲅⲣⲁⲫⲓ·
ⲱ̄ ⲡ̄ⲁⲅⲓⲟⲥ ⲑⲉⲱⲇⲱⲣⲟⲥ·
ϩⲛ̄ⲛⲉⲥⲓⲟ̄ⲟⲩⲛ ⲙⲛ̄ⲛⲉⲏⲓ·
ⲙⲛ̄ⲛⲉⲧⲉⲧⲣⲁⲡⲉⲗⲱⲛ ⲛ̄ⲛⲉⲡⲟⲗⲓⲥ⳾

21 ⲫⲱⲥⲧⲏⲣ ⲛⲓⲙ ⲉ̄ⲧⲣⲟⲩⲟ̄ⲉⲓⲛ·
ϩⲙ̄ⲡⲉⲥⲧⲉⲣⲉⲱⲙⲁ ⲛ̄ⲧⲡⲉ·
ⲥⲉϫⲱ ⲙ̄ⲡⲧⲁⲓⲟ̄ ⲛ̄ⲧⲉⲕⲙⲛ̄ⲧⲙⲁⲧⲟⲓ·
ⲱ̄ ⲡⲉⲥⲧ̄ⲣⲁⲧⲉⲗⲁⲧⲏⲥ ⲉⲧⲧⲁⲓⲏⲩ⳾

22 ⲭⲱⲣⲁ ⲛⲓⲙ ⲉⲧϩⲓϫⲙ̄ⲡⲕⲁϩ·
ⲥⲉⲧⲁϣⲉⲟ̄ⲉⲓϣ ⲉ̄ⲡⲉⲕⲧⲁⲓⲟ̄·
ⲙⲛ̄ⲡⲉⲟⲟⲩ ⲛ̄ⲧⲁⲡⲛⲟⲩⲧⲉ ⲧⲁⲁϥ ⲛⲁⲕ·
ⲉⲧⲃⲉⲛⲉⲇⲉⲙⲱⲛⲓⲟⲛ ⲛ̄ⲧⲁⲕⲛⲟϫⲟⲩ ⲉ̄ⲃⲟⲗ⳾

23 ⲓ ⲯⲁⲗⲓ² ⲉ̄ⲡⲉⲛⲛⲟⲩⲧⲉ ⲯⲁⲗⲓ·
ⲯⲁⲗⲗⲓ ⲉ̄ⲡⲉⲛⲉⲣⲟ ⲯⲁⲗⲗⲓ·
ϫⲉⲁϥϯⲉ̄ⲟⲟⲩ ⲉ̄ⲛⲉⲙⲁⲣⲧⲩⲣⲟⲥ·
ⲁϥϫⲓⲧⲟⲩ ⲉ̄ⲧⲉϥⲙⲉⲧⲉⲣⲟ⳾

24 ⲱ̄ ⲡⲉⲭⲱⲣⲟⲥ ⲉ̄ⲛⲉⲙⲁⲣⲧⲩⲣⲟⲥ·
ⲙⲉⲡⲉⲭⲟⲣⲟⲥ ⲛ̄ⲛⲁⲡⲟⲥⲧⲟⲗⲟⲥ·
ⲙⲛ̄ⲡⲉⲭⲟⲣⲟⲥ ⲉ̄ⲛⲉⲡⲣⲟⲫⲏⲧⲏⲥ·
ϯⲉ̄ⲟⲟⲩ ⲉ̄ⲡⲉⲭ̄ⲥ̄·
ϫⲉⲁⲩⲥ̄ⲧ̄ⲟⲩ ⲙ̄ⲙⲟϥ ϩⲁⲣⲟⲛ·
ϣⲁⲛⲧⲉϥⲥⲁⲧⲉⲛ ϩⲉⲛⲉⲛⲛⲟⲃⲉ:-³

---

¹ Presumably for ⲉⲓⲥ.
² Page ⲣ̄ⲝ̄ⲁ̄ begins.
³ The arrangement of this stanza in six verses is almost certainly correct (see p. 10, n. 3).

20 Behold, your name is depicted,
   O St Theodore,
   in the baths and in the houses
   and in the gateways of the cities.

21 All the luminaries which shine
   in the firmament of heaven
   speak of the renown of your warfare,
   O renowned general.

22 All the lands upon the earth
   proclaim your renown
   and the glory which God gave to you,
   because of the demons which you have cast out.

23 Sing to our God, sing.
   Sing to our King, sing,[1]
   for he has glorified the martyrs,
   he has taken them into his kingdom.

24 O the choir of the martyrs
   and the choir of the apostles
   and the choir of the prophets
   glorify Christ,
   for he was crucified for us
   to redeem us from our sins.

---

[1] Cf. Ps. 46.7.

◄ HYMN SIX ►

(pp. p̄ᴣ̄ᴀ, line 7 – p̄ᴣ̄ᴦ, line 4)

ⲋ̄ ⲡⲁⲗⲫⲁⲃⲏⲧⲁ ⲙ̄ⲡⲡⲁⲧⲣⲓⲁⲣⲭⲏⲥ ⲥⲉⲩⲏⲣⲟⲥ:-

1 ⲁⲡⲉⲕⲟⲩⲟⲉⲓⲛ ⲡⲱⲣ̄ϣ̄ ⲉ̄ⲃⲟⲗ·
   ⲁϥⲙⲉϩⲡ̄ϩⲟ ⲛ̄ϯⲕⲟⲩⲙⲉⲛⲏ ⲧⲏⲣⲥ̄·
   ⲱ̄ ⲥⲉⲩⲏⲣⲟⲥ ⲡ̄ⲡⲁⲧⲣⲓⲁⲣⲭⲏⲥ·
   ⲡ̄ⲛⲟϭ ⲙ̄ⲫⲱⲥⲧⲏⲣ ⲉ̄ⲧⲣ̄ⲟⲩⲟ̄ⲉⲓⲛ⸗

2 ⲃⲓⲟⲥ ⲛⲓⲙ ⲛ̄ⲧⲉⲛⲉⲧⲟⲩⲁⲁⲃ·
   ⲙ̄ⲛ̄ⲛⲉⲥⲁϩ ⲛ̄ⲧⲉⲕⲗⲏⲥⲓⲁ̄·
   ⲁⲕⲉⲛⲧⲟⲩ ⲉⲧⲙⲏⲧⲉ ⲁⲕϣⲁϫⲉ ⲉ̄ⲣⲟⲟⲩ·
   ϣⲁⲛⲧⲉⲕⲧⲁϩⲉⲧ̄ⲡⲓⲥⲧⲓⲥ ⲉ̄ⲣⲁⲧⲥ̄⸗

3 ⲅⲉⲅⲁⲣ ⲁⲩⲙⲟⲩⲧⲉ ⲉ̄ⲣⲟⲕ·
   ϫⲉⲥ̄ϣ̄ⲣ̄ ⲙ̄ⲛ̄ⲥⲁⲡⲥ̄ϣ̄ⲣ̄·
   ⲁ̄ⲛⲟⲛ ⲛⲉⲭⲣⲏⲥⲧⲓⲁⲛⲟⲥ·
   ⲙⲁⲣⲉⲛϯⲉ̄ⲟⲟⲩ ⲉ̄ⲡⲉⲭ̄ⲥ̄⸗

4 ⲇⲓⲕⲁⲓⲟⲥ ⲛⲁⲙⲉ ⲁ̄ⲗⲏⲑⲱⲥ·
   ⲁⲕϣⲱⲡⲉ ⲛⲟⲩⲣⲉϥϣⲟⲣϣⲉⲣ·
   ⲉ̄ⲛⲉϩⲣⲉⲧⲓⲕⲟⲥ ⲉ̄ⲑⲟⲟⲩ·
   ϩⲓⲧⲛ̄ⲛⲉⲕⲇⲟⲅⲙⲁ ⲉⲧⲥⲟⲩⲧⲱⲛ⸗

66

◄ HYMN SIX ►

The alphabetic acrostic on the Patriarch Severus

1   Your light has spread forth;
    it has filled the face of the whole world,
    O Patriarch Severus,
    great, shining luminary.

2   All the lives of the saints
    and the teachers of the Church
    you have introduced, and you have spoken about them
    to establish the faith.

3   For you were called
    saviour after the Saviour.
    We are Christians,
    let us glorify Christ.

4   Justly, truly, verily,
    you became a destroyer
    of the wicked heretics
    through your orthodox doctrines.

5   ⲉⲛⲑⲉ ⲛⲟⲩⲃⲱ ⲛ̄ϫⲓⲧⲛⲟⲩⲧⲉⲙ·
     ϩⲁⲡⲉⲥⲟⲩⲧⲁϩ ϩⲙ̄ⲡⲏⲓ ⲙ̄ⲡⲛⲟⲩⲧⲉ·
     ⲧⲁⲓⲧⲉ ⲑⲉ ⲙ̄ⲡⲓⲛⲟϭ ⲥⲉⲩⲏⲣⲟⲥ·
     ⲉϥϩⲛ̄ⲧⲙⲏⲧⲉ ⲛ̄ⲧⲉⲕⲗⲏⲥⲓⲁ⳾

6   ⲍⲱⲣⲱⲃⲁⲃⲉⲗ ⲁϥⲕⲱⲥⲙⲓ ⲙ̄ⲡⲣⲡⲉ·
     ⲡⲉⲛⲧⲁϥⲕⲟⲧϥ ⲛ̄ϭⲓⲥⲟⲗⲟⲙⲱⲛ·
     ⲁϥⲕⲱⲥⲙⲓ ⲛ̄ⲧⲉⲕⲗⲏⲥⲓⲁ̄ ⲙ̄ⲡⲟ̅ⲥ̅·
     ⲧⲉⲛⲧⲁϥϯⲡⲉϥⲥ̄ⲛⲟϥ ϩⲁⲣⲟⲥ⳾

7   ⲏ̄ ⲧⲓⲱⲥ ⲁⲕϣⲱⲡⲉ ⲛⲟⲩⲣⲉϥϣⲟⲣϣⲉⲣ·
     ⲛ̄ⲛⲉϩⲣⲉⲧⲓⲕⲟⲥ ⲉⲑⲟⲟⲩ·
     ⲁⲕⲑⲃ̄ⲃⲓⲟⲟⲩ ϣⲁⲡⲉⲥⲏⲧ ⲉ̄ⲁⲙⲛⲧⲉ·
     ϩⲓⲧⲛ̄ⲛⲉⲕⲇⲟⲅⲙⲁ ⲉⲧⲥⲟⲩⲧⲱⲛ⳾

8   ⲑⲉⲱ̄ⲇⲱⲣⲁ ⲧⲉⲣⲱ ⲛⲉⲩⲥⲉⲃⲏⲥ·
     ⲁ̄ⲡⲉⲥⲥⲓⲟⲩⲣ̄ ⲛⲁⲩ ⲉⲡⲛⲟϭ ⲛ̄ⲧⲁⲓⲟ̄·
     ⲉⲥⲁⲙⲁϩⲧⲉ ⲛ̄ⲧϭⲓϫ ⲛ̄ⲥⲉⲩⲏⲣⲟⲥ·
     ⲁϥϩⲉ ⲉ̄ϫⲙ̄ⲡⲉϥϩⲟ ϩⲁⲑⲟⲧⲉ⳾

9   ⲓⲉ ⲧⲓ·[1] ⲉ̄ⲥⲉⲗⲉⲧⲓⲛ ⲙ̄ⲙⲟϥ·
     ϫⲉϯⲥⲟⲡⲥ̄ ⲙ̄ⲙⲟⲕ ⲡⲁϭ̅ⲥ̅ ⲛⲓⲱⲧ·
     ⲧⲁⲙⲁⲓ ϫⲉⲛⲧⲁϥⲛⲁⲩ ⲉ̄ⲟⲩ·
     ⲧⲁϯⲉ̄ⲟⲟⲩ ⲉ̄ⲡⲉⲭ̅ⲥ̅⳾

---

[1]   ⲓⲉ ⲧⲓ is difficult to interpret. ⲓⲉ may be assumed to be the Fayyumic form of the interrogative particle ⲉⲓⲉ. ⲧⲓ is probably the Greek interrogative pronoun τί, although this does not appear to be attested in Coptic. There is, however, attestation for the use of ⲉⲓⲉ followed by the Coptic interrogative pronoun ⲛⲓⲙ, e.g. ⲉⲓⲉ ⲛⲓⲙ in the Sahidic text of Mt. 19.25. The alternative of taking ⲓⲉ as the Greek exclamatory particle ἰέ = ἰή is less probable. The following ⲉⲥⲉⲗⲉⲧⲓⲛ is the Fayyumic equivalent of Sahidic ⲉⲥⲁⲓⲧⲉⲓ.

5   Like a good olive tree
    beneath its fruit in the house of God,[1]
    so is the great Severus
    in the midst of the Church.

6   Zerubbabel adorned the temple,[1]
    which Solomon had built.
    He (Severus) adorned the Church of the Lord,
    for which he (Jesus) had given his blood.

7   Meanwhile, you became a destroyer
    of the wicked heretics.
    You brought them low, down to hell,
    through your orthodox doctrines.

8   As for the pious Empress Theodora,
    her eunuch saw the great honour,
    when she grasped the hand of Severus.
    He (the eunuch) fell upon his face for fear.

9   Why?, she asked him,
    I pray you, my lord father,
    tell me what he (the eunuch) saw,
    that I may glorify Christ.

---

[1]   Cf. Zech. 4.

69

10 ⲕⲉⲅⲁⲣ ⲁϥⲛⲁⲩ ⲉⲡⲥⲱⲣ·
ⲉϥϩⲙⲟⲟⲥ ⲉϥϣⲁϫⲉ ⲛⲙⲙⲁϥ·
ϫⲉⲥⲉⲩⲏⲣⲟⲥ ⲙⲡⲣϭⲱ ⲙⲡⲉⲓⲙⲁ·
ϫⲉⲁⲧⲙⲛ̄ⲧⲁⲧⲛⲁϩⲧⲉ ϣⲱⲡⲉ ⲛ̄ϩⲏⲧϥ⳪

11 |ⲗⲟⲓⲡⲟⲛ[1] ⲁⲥϫⲱⲕ ⲉ̄ⲃⲟⲗ ⲉ̄ϫⲱⲕ·
ⲛ̄ϭⲓⲧⲉⲡⲣⲟⲫⲏⲧⲓⲁ̄ ⲛ̄ⲇⲁ̄ⲇ̄·
ϫⲉⲡⲣⲱⲙⲉ ⲛⲁϯⲡⲉϥⲟⲩⲟⲓ ϩ̄ⲛⲟⲩϩⲏⲧ ⲉϥϩⲏⲙ·[2]
ⲛ̄ϥ̄ϫⲓⲥⲉ ⲛ̄ϭⲓⲡ̄ⲛⲟⲩⲧⲉ⳪

12 ⲙⲁⲣⲟⲛ ⲉ̄ⲃⲟⲗ ϣⲁⲧⲁⲛⲧⲓⲟ̄ⲭⲓⲁ̄·
ⲧⲛ̄ⲛⲁⲩ ⲉⲡⲧⲁⲓⲟ̄ ⲛ̄ⲥⲉⲩⲏⲣⲟⲥ·
ⲡⲉⲓⲫⲱⲥⲧⲏⲣ ⲛⲁⲗⲏⲑⲓⲛⲟⲛ·
ⲛ̄ⲧⲁⲫ̄ϯ ⲧⲛ̄ⲛⲟⲟⲩϥ ⲛⲁⲛ⳪

13 ⲛⲉⲉ̄ⲡⲓⲥⲕⲟⲡⲟⲥ ⲛ̄ⲭⲁⲗⲭⲏⲇⲱⲛ·
ⲁⲩϫⲓϣⲓⲡⲉ ϩ̄ⲛⲟⲩⲃⲉⲡⲏ·
ϫⲉⲁⲡⲛⲟⲩⲧⲉ ⲧⲛ̄ⲛⲟⲟⲩ ⲛⲥⲉⲩⲏⲣⲟⲥ·
ⲁϥϣⲉⲣϣⲱⲣⲛⲉⲩⲉⲕⲕⲗⲏⲥⲓⲁ⳪

14 ϫⲉⲛⲱⲥ ⲛⲓⲙ ⲛ̄ⲧⲉⲛⲉⲡⲓⲥⲧⲟⲥ·
ⲕⲱ ⲛⲏⲧⲛ̄ ⲙⲡⲣ̄ⲡⲙⲉⲉⲩⲉ̄ ⲛ̄ⲥⲉⲩⲏⲣⲟⲥ·
ϫⲉϥⲛⲁϣϭⲙ̄ϭⲟⲙ ⲉ̄ⲣⲱⲧⲛ̄ ⲁⲛ·
ⲛ̄ϭⲓⲡ̄ϫⲁϫⲉ ⲛⲁⲡⲟⲥⲧⲁⲧⲏⲥ⳪

---

[1] Page ⲣ̄ⲝ̄ⲃ begins.
[2] The reading ⲉϥϩⲏⲙ makes perfectly good sense in the context, but note that the Sahidic Psalter, Ps. 63.6, E.A.W. Budge, *The Earliest Known Coptic Psalter* (London 1898), 65, reads ⲉϥϩⲏⲡ (cf. Bohairic Psalter, Ps. 63.7, O.H.E. Burmester and E. Dévaud, *Psalterii versio memphitica e recognitione Pauli de Lagarde* (Louvain 1925), 72: ⲉϥϣⲏⲕ), translating the Greek βαθεῖα. The reading here may be a conscious adaptation, or it may be due to a scribal error somewhere in the course of transmission, perhaps encouraged by the similarity of the two letters in some types of hand.

10 For he saw the Saviour,
    sitting and speaking with him (Severus),
    saying, Severus, do not stay in this place,
    for unbelief has entered herein.

11 Then was fulfilled in you
    the prophecy of David:
    The man shall go forth with an ardent heart
    and God shall be exalted.[1]

12 Let us go forth to Antioch
    and see the renown of Severus,
    this true luminary,
    whom God sent to us.

13 The bishops of Chalcedon
    were quickly put to shame,
    for God sent Severus;
    he destroyed their churches.

14 All you friends[2] of the faithful
    keep the memory of Severus,
    that he may have no power over you—
    the apostate enemy.

---

[1] Cf. Ps. 63.7-8 (see note to the Coptic text).
[2] Lit.: 'stranger', 'guest-friend'.

15 ογπετϣογειτπε πϣⲙϣε тнрϥ·
ⲛⲛееⲡⲓⲥⲕⲟⲡⲟⲥ ⲛⲭⲁⲗⲕⲏⲁⲱⲛ·
ⲭⲉⲁⲛⲉⲇⲱⲅⲙⲁ ⲛⲥⲉγⲏⲣⲟⲥ·
ϣⲉⲣϣⲱⲣⲟγ ⲍⲛⲟγϭⲉⲡⲏ⳥

16 ⲡⲡⲁⲣⲁⲇⲓⲥⲟⲥ ⲱϣ ⲉⲃⲟⲗ·
ⲙⲛⲛⲉⲣⲏⲧ тнⲣⲟγ ⲉⲧⲣⲏⲧ¹ ⲛⲍⲏⲧϥ·
ⲭⲉϣⲁⲧⲛⲁγ ⲛϥⲉⲓ ⲛϭⲓⲥⲉγⲏⲣⲟⲥ·
ⲛϥⲧⲃⲃⲟ ⲙⲡⲓⲙⲁ ⲛⲉⲗⲟⲟⲗⲉ⳥

17 ⲣⲙⲙⲁⲟ ⲛⲓⲙ ⲙⲛⲛⲉⲍⲏⲕⲉ·
ⲛⲓⲍⲗⲗⲟ ⲙⲛⲛⲓϣⲏⲣⲉ ϣⲏⲙ·
ⲕⲱ ⲛⲏⲧⲛ ⲙⲡⲉⲣⲡⲙⲉⲉγⲉ ⲛⲥⲉγⲏⲣⲟⲥ·
ⲉϥⲣⲟγⲟⲉⲓⲛ ⲉⲛⲉⲧⲛⲍⲏⲧ⳥

18 ⲥⲱⲧⲙ ⲉⲛⲉⲭⲣⲏⲥⲧⲓⲁⲛⲟⲥ·
ⲉⲧⲟγⲱϣ ⲉⲱⲛⲍ ⲍⲛⲟγⲙⲛⲧⲥⲁⲃⲉ·
ⲭⲉⲁⲥⲉγⲏⲣⲟⲥ ⲡⲓⲥⲟⲫⲟⲥ·
ⲇⲟⲅⲙⲁⲧⲓⲍⲉ ⲍⲛⲟγⲙⲛⲧⲭⲱⲱⲣⲉ⳥

19 ⲧⲙⲛⲧⲥⲉⲙⲛⲟⲥ ⲛⲁⲛⲟγⲥ ⲛⲁⲥⲛⲏγ·
ⲑγⲡⲟⲙⲟⲛⲏ ⲟγⲁⲧϣⲁⲭⲉ ⲉⲣⲟⲥⲧⲉ·
ϣⲁⲧⲉⲛⲟγ ⲛⲉⲇⲟⲅⲙⲁ ⲛⲥⲉγⲏⲣⲟⲥ·
ϣⲟⲣϣⲉⲣ ⲉⲛⲉⲍⲣⲉⲧⲓⲕⲟⲥ⳥

---

¹ ⲉⲧⲣⲏⲧ either stands for ⲉⲧⲉⲣⲏⲧ (note that ⲣⲏⲧ is attested
as an alternative form of ⲉⲣⲏⲧ), or must be considered to be the
qualitative form of ⲣⲱⲧ, 'to grow'. If the latter be accepted, the
preceding ⲙⲛⲛⲉⲣⲏⲧ may be interpreted as ⲙⲛ-ⲛⲉ-ⲣⲏⲧ, and it
would have to be assumed that ⲣⲏⲧ stands for ⲣⲱⲧ, pl. ⲣⲁⲧⲉ,
'growth', 'vegetation'.

15   Vain is all the worship
      of the bishops of Chalcedon,
      for the doctrines of Severus
      destroyed them quickly.

16   Paradise cries out
      and all the promises promised therein:[1]
      When will Severus come
      and purify this vineyard?

17   All rich and poor,
      old men and youths,
      keep the memory of Severus
      who illumines your hearts.

18   Listen to the Christians
      who wish to live wisely:
      The wise Severus
      taught doctrine powerfully.

19   Piety is good, my brethren,
      steadfastness is ineffable.
      Even now the doctrines of Severus
      destroy the heretics.

---

[1] Or: 'and all the plants grown in it' (see note to the Coptic
text).

20 ΥΠΟΜΟΝΗ ΝΙΜ ΑΥϢΩΠΕ ΝΑΚ·
ⲱ̄ ⲤΕΥⲎΡΟⲤ ΠΙΠΑΤΡΙΑΡΧΗⲤ·
ΕΚΜΟΟϢΕ ϨⲘΜΑ ΝΙΜ·
ϢΑΝΤΕΚ†ΠΛΩΒϢ ⲈΤΕΚⲔⲖⲎⲤΙⲀ⸗

21 ΦΩΒ ⲚΤΑΚΑΑϤ ϨⲘΠΙΜΟΝΑⲤΤΗΡΙΟΝ·
ⲠϢΟΡΠ ⲘΜΑ ⲚΤΑΚΟΥΩϨ ⲚϨⲎΤϤ·
ΕΚ† ΟΥⲂⲈΝΕϨΡΕΤΙΚΟⲤ·
ΕΚϢΟΡϢⲢ ⲘΜΟΟΥ ϨⲚΟΥϬΕΠΗ⸗

22 ΧΕΡΕ ⲤΕΥⲎΡΟⲤ ΠΙΠΑΤΡΙΑΡΧΗⲤ·
ΠΑΓΩΝΩΘΕΤΗⲤ ⲚΡΕϤΧΡΟ·
ΑΚΜΙϢΕ ΚΑΛΩⲤ ϨⲘΠΑΓΩΝ·
ϢΑΝΤΕΚΤΟΥΧΟΝ ⲈΝΕΠΑϢ ⲈΘΟΟΥ⸗

23 ΨΑΟΥⲚ ⲘⲠΝΟΥΤΕ | ϨΟⲖⳆ¹ ⲈΜΑΤΕ·
ΕϤΚΑΛΙⲰⲠΙΖΕ ϨⲚⲤΕΥⲎΡΟⲤ·
ΧΕΑΝΕϤⲆΟΓΜΑ ΕΤⲤΟΥΤΩΝ·
ϢΟΡϢⲢ ⲈΝΕϨΡΕ†ΚΟⲤ⸗

24 ⲱ̄ ⲤΕΥⲎΡΟⲤ ΠΑΠΡΑΝ ΕΤϨΟⲖϬ·
ΠΙⲤΩΤΗΡ ⲘⲚⲚⲤΑⲠⲤⲰⲢ·
ⲤΟΠⲤ ⲈⲠϬⲤ ΕϨΡΑΙ ΕΧΩΝ·
ⲚϤΚΑΝΕΝΝΟΒΕ <ΝΑΝ ΕΒΟⲖ>:-²

---

¹ Page ⲣ̅ⲝ̅ⲅ̅ begins.
² The scribe has omitted ΝΑΝ ΕΒΟⲖ, or possibly merely
ΕΒΟⲖ.

74

20   All steadfastness has become yours,
     O Patriarch Severus,
     as you journey everywhere
     to set the crown on the Church.

21   The work which you did in the monastery,
     the first place in which you dwelt,
     was your fighting against the heretics
     and your destroying them quickly.

22   Hail, Patriarch Severus,
     victorious judge.
     You have fought well in the fight
     to save us from the evil snares.

23   The knowledge of God is very sweet,
     making a fine display in Severus,
     for his orthodox doctrines
     have destroyed the heretics.

24   O Severus of the sweet name,
     saviour after the Saviour,
     pray to the Lord for us,
     that he may forgive our sins.[1]

---

[1]   Or: 'that he may forgive us our sins' (see note to the Coptic text).

(pp. P̄ϧΓ, line 5 – P̄ϧΔ)

ζ ⲡⲁⲗⲫⲁⲃⲏⲧⲁ ⲛ̄ⲧⲁⲛⲁⲥⲧⲁⲥⲓⲥ: ⲙⲉⲧⲁⲛⲁⲗⲩⲙⲯⲓⲥ:-

1 ⲁⲡ⳪ⲥ ⲧⲱⲟⲩⲛ̄ ⲛ̄ⲑⲉ ⲙ̄ⲡⲉⲧⲟⲃϣ̄·
   ⲛ̄ⲑⲉ ⲛⲟⲩⲭⲱ⳥ⲣⲉ ⲉϥⲧⲁϩⲉ ⲙ̄ⲡⲏⲣⲡ̄·
   ⲁϥⲡⲁⲧⲁⲥⲥⲉ ⲛ̄ⲛⲉϥϫⲁϫⲉ ⲉⲡⲁϩⲟⲩ·
   ⲁϥⲧⲁⲁⲩ ⲉⲩⲛⲟⳓⲛⲉⳓ ⲛ̄ϣⲁⲉⲛⲉϩ⸗

2 ⲃⲓ ⲛ̄ⲛⲉⲧⲛ̄ⲃⲁⲗ ⲉϩⲣⲁⲓ ⲉⲧⲡⲉ·
   ϣⲁⲡⲉⲛⲧⲁϥⲧⲱⲟⲩⲛ̄ ϩⲉⲛⲉⲧⲙⲟⲟⲩⲧ̄·
   ⲱϣ ⲉ̄ⲃⲟⲗ ⲙⲛ̄ⲛⲉⲁⲅⲅⲉⲗⲟⲥ·
   ϫⲉⲁ̄ⲛⲉⲡⲏⲩⲉ̄ ⲟⲩⲛⲟϥ ⲁⲡⲕⲁϩ ⲧⲉⲗⲏⲗ⸗

3 ⲅⲉⲅⲁⲣ ⲛⲉⲅⲣⲁⲫⲏ ⲉ̄ⲧⲟⲩⲁⲁ̄ⲃ·
   ⲧ̄ⲡⲁⲗⲉⲁ̄ ⲙⲛ̄ⲧⲕⲩⲛⲏ·
   ⲉⲣⲙⲛ̄ⲧⲣⲉ ϩⲁⲧⲁⲛⲁⲥⲧⲁⲥⲓⲥ·
   ⲙⲛ̄ⲧⲁⲛⲁⲗⲩⲙⲯⲓⲥ ⲉⲡ⳪ⲥ⸗

4 ⲁⲗ̄ⲗ̄ ⲡⲉⲣⲟ ⲱϣ ⲉ̄ⲃⲟⲗ·
   ϩⲉⲡⲉⲯⲁⲗⲧⲏⲣⲓⲟⲛ ⲉϥϫⲱ ⲙ̄ⲙⲟⲥ·
   ϫⲉⲧⲱⲇⲏ ⲛ̄ⲧⲁⲛⲁⲥⲧⲁⲥⲓⲥ·
   ⲡ̄ⲕⲁϩ ⲧⲏⲣϥ̄ ϯⲗⲟⲩⲗⲁⲓ ⲉ̄ϥ̄ϯ⸗

The alphabetic acrostic on
the Resurrection and Ascension

1   The Lord has arisen as one out of sleep,
    as a mighty man drunk with wine.
    He smote his enemies backward;
    he put them to perpetual reproach.[1]

2   Lift up your eyes to heaven
    to him who has risen from the dead.
    Proclaim with the angels:
    The heavens rejoiced and the earth was glad.[2]

3   For the holy scriptures,
    the Old and the New (Testament),
    bear witness to the resurrection
    and the ascension of the Lord.

4   King David proclaims
    in the psalter, saying:
    The song of the resurrection.
    Shout unto God, all the earth.[3]

---

[1]   Ps. 77.65–6.
[2]   Cf. Ps. 95.11.
[3]   Cf. Ps. 65, title and verse 1 (cf. Ps. 97.4).

5 ⲉϥⲣⲙⲛ̄ⲧⲣⲉ ⲟⲛ ⲉϥϫⲱ ⲙ̄ⲙⲟⲥ·
ⲛ̄ϭⲓⲡⲓⲡ̄ⲣⲟⲫⲏⲧⲏⲥ ⲛⲟⲩⲱⲧ·
ϫⲉⲁ̄ⲛⲉⲕⲣⲱⲟⲩ ⲧⲏⲣⲟⲩ ⲙ̄ⲡⲕⲁϩ·
ⲛⲁⲩ ⲉ̄ⲡⲟⲩϫⲁⲓ ⲉ̄ⲡⲉⲛⲛⲟⲩⲧⲉ⸗

6 ϩⲩⲙⲁⲛⲉ ⲛⲁⲛ ⲉ̄ⲛⲉϣⲡⲏⲣⲉ·
ⲡⲁⲅⲅⲉⲗⲟⲥ ⲉⲧϩⲓϫⲙ̄ⲡⲱⲛⲉ·
ⲉϥⲣⲙⲛ̄ⲧⲣⲉ ϩⲁⲧⲁⲛⲁⲥⲧⲁⲥⲓⲥ·
ϫⲉⲁ̄ⲡϭ̄ⲥ ⲧⲱⲟⲩⲛ̄ ϩⲛ̄ⲛⲉⲧⲙⲟⲟⲩⲧ̄⸗

7 ⲏ̄ⲥⲁⲓⲁⲥ ⲡⲉⲡⲣⲟⲫⲏⲧⲏⲥ·
ⲣ̄ⲙⲛ̄ⲧⲣⲉ ϩⲁⲧⲁⲛⲁⲥⲧⲁⲥⲓⲥ·
ϫⲉϯⲛⲁⲧⲱⲟⲩⲛ ⲡⲉϫⲉⲡϭ̄ⲥ·
ⲧⲁϫⲓⲥⲉ ⲧⲁϫⲓⲉ̄ⲟⲟⲩ⸗

8 ⲑⲱⲙⲁⲥ ϩⲱⲱϥ ⲡⲁⲡⲟⲥⲧⲟⲗⲟⲥ·
ϫⲱ ⲙ̄ⲡⲧⲁⲓⲟ̄ ⲛⲧⲁⲛⲁⲥⲧⲁⲥⲓⲥ·
ⲛ̄ⲧⲉⲣⲉⲡϭ̄ⲥ ⲟⲩⲟⲛϩ̄ϥ ⲉ̄ⲣⲟϥ·
ϫⲉⲡⲁϭ̄ⲥ ⲁⲩⲱ̄ ⲡⲁⲛⲟⲩⲧⲉ·
ϯⲡⲓⲥⲧⲉⲩⲉ̄ ⲉ̄ⲧⲉⲕⲁⲛⲁⲥⲧⲁⲥⲓⲥ⸗[1]

9 ⲓⲱϩⲁⲛⲛⲏⲥ ⲡⲉⲩⲁⲅⲅⲉⲗⲓⲥⲧⲏⲥ·
ϫⲉⲛⲧⲉⲣⲉϥⲧⲱⲟⲩⲛ̄ ⲉ̄ⲃⲟⲗ ϩⲛ̄ⲛⲉⲧⲙⲟⲟⲩⲧ̄·
ⲁϥⲟⲩⲟⲛϩ̄ϥ ⲉ̄ⲛⲉϥⲙⲁⲑⲏⲧⲏⲥ·
ϩⲓϫⲉⲛⲑⲁⲗⲁⲥⲥⲁ ⲛ̄ⲧⲓⲃⲉⲣⲓⲁⲥ⸗

---

[1] The arrangement of this stanza in five verses is almost certainly correct (see p. 10, n. 2).

5   He also testifies, saying
    —this same prophet—:
    All the ends of the earth
    have seen the salvation of our God.[1]

6   Declare the wonders to us.
    The angel who is upon the stone
    bears witness to the resurrection:
    The Lord has risen from the dead.[2]

7   The prophet Isaiah
    bears witness to the resurrection:
    I will arise, said the Lord,
    and will be exalted and glorified.[3]

8   The apostle Thomas also
    tells of the glory of the resurrection,
    when the Lord appeared to him:
    My Lord and my God,
    I believe in your resurrection.[4]

9   John, the evangelist, says:
    When he had risen from the dead,
    he appeared to his disciples
    at the sea of Tiberias.[5]

---

[1]   Ps. 97.3.
[2]   Cf. Mt. 28.2–6.
[3]   Cf. Is. 33.10.
[4]   Cf. John 20.28.
[5]   Cf. John 21.1.

10 ΚΛΕѠΠΑ Μ̄Π̄ΕϤΚΕϢΒΗΡ·
ΕΥΡ̄Μ̄Ν̄Τ̄ΡΕ ϨΑΤΑΝΑСΤΑСΙС·
ϪΕΑΠϬ̄С̄ ΤѠΟΥΝ̄·
ΑΥѠ ΑϤΟΥΟΝϨϤ̄ Ε̄СΙΜѠΝ⸗

11 ΛΟΥΚΑС ΑΝ ΚΑΤΑΤΕΙϨΕ·
ϪΕΤΕΤΝ̄ϢΙΝΕ Ν̄САΝΙΜ Ε̄ΠΕΙΜΑ·
|Ν̄САΠΕΤΟΝϨ[1] Μ̄Ν̄ΝΕΤΜΟΟΥΤ̄·
ΑϤΤѠΟΥΝ̄ Ν̄ϤΜ̄ΠΕΙΜΑ ΑΝ⸗

12 ΜΑΡΚΟС ΟΝ ϪΕΠϬ̄С̄ ῙС̄·
Ν̄ΤΕΡΕϤΟΥѠ ΕϤϢΑϪΕ ΝΜ̄ΜΑΥ·
ΑΥϪΙΤϤ̄ ΕϨΡΑΙ Ε̄ΝΜ̄ΠΗΥΕ̄·
ΑϤϨΜΟΟС Ν̄САΟΥΝΑΜ Μ̄ΠΕϤΕΙѠΤ⸗

13 ΝΕΠΡΑϪΙС ΟΝ ΕΡΜ̄Ν̄Τ̄ΡΕ·
ϨΑΝΕΑΠΟСΤΟΛΟС Ε̄ΤΟΥΑΑΒ·
ΕΥᾹϨΕΡΑΤΟΥ ΕΥϬѠϢΤ̄ Ν̄СѠϤ·
ΕϤΝΑΒѠΚ ΕϨΡΑΙ ΕΤΠΕ⸗

14 ϪΑΟΥΝΑΜ[2] ΕΠΕΚΙѠΤ ϨΕΝΕΤϪΟСΕ·
Ѡ ΠϬ̄С̄ Ν̄ΤΠΕ ΜΝ̄Π̄ΚΑϨ·
ΕΚСѠΚ ϢΑΡΟΚ ΝΟΥΟΝ ΝΙΜ·
ϨΙΤΝ̄ΤΕΚΑΝΑСΤΑСΙС Ε̄ΤΟΥΑΑΒ⸗

---

[1] Page Ρ̄Ξ̄Δ̄ begins.
[2] For Κ(Ν)СΑ-.

10　Cleopas and his companion also
　　bear witness to the resurrection:
　　The Lord has risen
　　and has appeared to Simon.[1]

11　Again, Luke says thus:
　　Whom do you seek here,
　　the living among the dead?
　　He has risen, he is not here.[2]

12　Again, Mark says: The Lord Jesus,
　　when he had finished speaking with them,
　　was taken up into heaven,
　　and sat down at the right hand of his Father.[3]

13　The Acts also bear witness
　　to the holy apostles,
　　standing and looking after him,
　　as he is about to go up into heaven.[4]

14　You are at the right hand of your Father in the highest,
　　O Lord of heaven and earth,
　　drawing everyone to you
　　through your holy resurrection.

---

[1]　Luke 24.34.
[2]　Cf. Luke 24.5–6.
[3]　Cf. Mark 16.19.
[4]　Cf. Acts 1.11.

15 ογϣπηρε αληθωςτε·
τϭιΝερρωμε μπενсⲱⲣ·
ογϩογⲉϣπηρετε τεϥⲁ̄ναϲταϲιϲ·
ⲙ̄ⲛⲧⲉϥⲁ̄ⲛⲁⲗⲩⲙⲯⲓⲥ ⲉ̄ⲧⲟⲩⲁ̄ⲁⲃ⳾

16 ⲡⲉⲧⲣⲟⲥ ⲣ̄ⲙⲛ̄ⲧⲣⲉ ⲉϥⲭⲱ ⲙ̄ⲙⲟⲥ·
ⲭⲉⲁϥⲃⲱⲕ ⲉ̄ϩⲣⲁⲓ ⲉⲧⲡⲉ·
ⲁ̄ⲛⲁⲅⲅⲉⲗⲟⲥ ϩⲩⲡⲟⲧⲁⲥⲥⲉ ⲛⲁϥ·
ⲙ̄ⲛ̄ⲛⲉϩⲟⲩⲥⲓⲁ̄ ⲙ̄ⲛ̄ⲛϭⲟⲙ⳾

17 ⲣⲱⲙⲉ ⲛⲓⲙ ⲉⲧⲡⲓⲥⲧⲉⲩⲉ ⲉ̄ⲡϭ̄ⲥ̄·
ϥⲥⲱⲧⲙ̄ ⲉ̄ⲡⲁⲩⲗⲟⲥ ⲉϥⲭⲱ ⲙ̄ⲙⲟⲥ·
ⲭⲉⲁⲩⲧⲁⲛϩⲟⲩⲧϥ̄ ϩⲙ̄ⲡⲕⲟⲥⲙⲟⲥ·
ⲁⲩϥⲓⲧϥ̄ ⲉ̄ϩⲣⲁⲓ ϩⲛ̄ⲟⲩⲉ̄ⲟⲟⲩ⳾

18 ⲥⲱⲧⲙ̄ ⲛⲓϩⲉⲑⲛⲟⲥ ⲧⲏⲣⲟⲩ·
ⲉ̄ⲛⲓⲙⲛ̄ⲧⲙⲛ̄ⲧⲣⲉ ⲉ̄ⲧⲟ ⲛϩⲟⲧ·
ⲛ̄ⲧⲉϯⲁ̄ⲛⲁⲥⲧⲁⲥⲓⲥ ⲉ̄ⲧⲟⲩⲁ̄ⲁⲃ·
ⲙ̄ⲛ̄ⲧⲁⲛⲁⲗⲩⲙⲯⲓⲥ ⲉ̄ⲡϭ̄ⲥ̄⳾

19 ⲧⲟⲧⲉ ⲁ̄ⲧⲉⲛⲧⲁⲡⲣⲟ ⲙⲟⲩϩ ⲛ̄ⲣⲁϣⲉ·
ⲁⲩⲱ̄ ⲁ̄ⲡⲉⲛⲗⲁⲥ ⲧⲉⲗⲏⲗ·
ⲭⲉⲁϥⲧⲟⲩⲛⲉⲥⲧⲉⲛⲁ̄ⲡⲁⲣⲭⲏ·
ⲁϥⲭⲓⲧϥ̄ ⲛⲙ̄ⲙⲁϥ ⲉ̄ϩⲣⲁⲓ ⲉⲧⲡⲉ⳾

15 The incarnation of our Saviour
is truly a wonder;
a greater wonder is his resurrection
and his holy ascension.

16 Peter bears witness, saying:
He went up into heaven
and the angels were subject to him
with the authorities and powers.[1]

17 Every man who believes in the Lord
listens to Paul, saying:
He was believed in the world,
and he was received up in glory.[2]

18 Listen all you nations
to the trustworthy testimonies
of the holy resurrection
and the ascension of the Lord.

19 Then our mouth was filled with joy
and our tongue was glad,
for he raised our first-fruits[3]
and took it with him up into heaven.

---

[1] I Peter 3.22.
[2] I Tim. 3.16.
[3] Cf. I Cor. 15.20.

20 ϨΜΝΕⲨⲈ̄ Ⲉ̄ⲢⲞϤ ϨⲚ̄ⲞⲨⲤⲘⲞⲨ·
ⲘⲚ̄ϨⲈⲚⲰⲆⲎ Ⲙ̄ⲠⲚ̄Ⲓ̄ⲕ̄Ⲟ̄Ⲛ̄·
ϪⲈⲀϤϨⲘⲞⲞⲤ Ⲛ̄ⲤⲀⲞⲨⲚⲀⲘ Ⲉ̄ⲠⲈϤⲒⲰⲦ·
Ⲛ̄ⲦⲞϤ ⲈⲦⲤⲘ̄ⲘⲈ Ⲉ̄ϨⲢⲀⲒ ϨⲀⲢⲞⲚ⳥

21 ⲪⲰⲢⲒ ⲚⲎⲦⲚ̄ ⲚⲞⲨϬⲞⲘ·
Ⲱ̄ ⲚⲈⲀ̄ⲠⲞⲤⲦⲞⲖⲞⲤ Ⲉ̄ⲦⲞⲨⲀⲀⲂ·
ϬⲰϢ̄Ⲧ̄ ϨⲎⲦϤ̄ Ⲙ̄ⲠⲠⲀⲢⲀⲕⲖⲎⲦⲞⲤ·
ϢⲀⲚⲦⲈϤⲈⲒ Ⲉ̄ϨⲢⲀⲒ Ⲉ̄ϪⲰⲦⲚ̄⳥

22 ϪⲰⲢⲈⲨⲈ̄ Ⲛ̄ⲦⲈⲦⲚ̄ⲦⲈⲖⲎⲖ·
ⲘⲚ̄ⲞⲨⲞⲚ ⲚⲒⲘ ⲈⲦⲤⲞⲞⲨϨ̄ Ⲉ̄ⲢⲀⲦⲈⲚ·
ϪⲈϨⲘ̄Ⲡ̄ϪⲰⲕ Ⲛ̄Ⲧ̄ⲠⲈⲚⲦⲎⲕⲞⲤⲦⲎ·
ⲠⲈⲠⲚ̄Ⲁ̄ ⲚⲎⲨ Ⲉ̄ϨⲢⲀⲒ Ⲉ̄ϪⲰⲦⲚ̄⳥

23 ⲮⲀⲖⲒ Ⲉ̄ⲦⲈⲦⲢⲒⲀⲤ Ⲉ̄ⲦⲞⲨⲀⲀⲂ·
ⲈⲤϨⲚ̄ⲞⲨⲘⲚ̄ⲦⲞⲨⲀ̄ ⲚⲀⲦⲠⲰⲢϪ̄·
ⲈⲦⲈⲠⲀⲒⲠⲈ ⲠⲒⲰⲦ·
ⲘⲚ̄Ⲡ̄ϢⲎⲢⲈ ⲘⲚ̄ⲠⲈⲠⲚ̄Ⲁ̄ Ⲉ̄ⲦⲞⲨⲀⲀⲂ⳥

24 Ⲱ̄ ⲚⲈⲖⲀⲞⲤ ⲦⲎⲢⲞⲨ Ⲙ̄ⲠⲕⲞⲤⲘⲞⲤ·
Ⲁ̄ⲘⲎⲒⲦⲚ̄ ⲦⲚ̄ⲠⲀϨⲦⲚ̄ ⲚⲀϤ·
ⲦⲀⲢⲈϤϢⲚ̄ϨⲦⲎϤ ϨⲀⲢⲞⲚ·
Ⲛ̄ϤⲕⲀⲚⲈⲚⲚⲞⲂⲈ ⲚⲀⲚ Ⲉ̄ⲂⲞⲖ:-

20 Sing to him with a hymn
and spiritual songs,[1]
for he sat down at the right hand of his Father,
he who makes intercession for us.

21 Take possession of power,
O holy apostles;
look forward to the Paraclete
until he comes upon you.

22 Dance and be joyful
with everyone who is gathered unto us,
for at the end of the Fifty Days[2]
the Spirit will come upon you.[3]

23 Sing to the holy Trinity
that is in indivisible unity,
which is the Father
and the Son and the Holy Spirit.

24 O all peoples of the world,
come and let us prostrate ourselves before him,
that he may have mercy upon us
and forgive us our sins.

---

[1] Cf. Eph. 5.19; Col. 3.16.
[2] Pentecost.
[3] Cf. Acts 1.5 (Sahidic).

(pp. P̄ᴣ̄Є-P̄ᴣ̄Ϛ, line 32)

Ꮆ̄   ΠΑΛΦΑΒΗΤΑ Ṃ̄ΠΑΡΧΑΓΓΕΛΟϹ ΜΙΧΑΗΛ:-

1   ΑΛΗΘΩϹ Ᾱ̄ΠΕΚϢΑ Ē̄ΤΟΥΑΑΒ·
    ΕΥΦΡΑΝΕ Ṃ̄ΜΟΝ Ω̄ ΜΙΧΑΗΛ·
    Ē̄ΡΕΝΕΠΡΟΦΗΤΗϹ ΤΗΡΟΥ·
    ϢΑΧΕ ΕΠΤΑΙΟ̄ Ν̄ΝΕΚΜΝ̄ⲦΧΩΩΡΕ⸗

2   ΒΩϢ Ē̄ΒΟΛ Ν̄ϬΙΜΩΥϹΗϹ·
    ΧΕϤΝΑΤΝ̄ΝΟΟΥ Ṃ̄ΠΕϤΑΓΓΕΛΟϹ·
    Ν̄ϤΝΟΥΧ Ē̄ΒΟΛ ϨΙΘΗ Ṃ̄ΜΟΚ·
    Ē̄ΝΕϨΕΘΝΟϹ ΕΤϯ Ν̄Ṃ̄ΜΑΚ⸗

3   ΓΕΓΑΡ ΝΕΝΙΟΤΕ ΝΑΠΟϹΤΟΛΟϹ·
    ΜΝ̄ΝΕϹΑϨ Ν̄ΤΕΚΛΗϹΙΑ·
    ΜΝ̄ΝΕΤΑΓΜΑ Ν̄ΝΕΜΑΡΤΥΡΟϹ·
    ΜΙΧΑΗΛ ΠΕΤΟ ΝΝΑϢΤΕ ΝΑΥ⸗

4   ΔΑΝΙΗΛ ΠΕΠΡΟΦΗΤΗϹ·
    ϢΑΧΕ ΕΠΤΑΙΟ̄ Ṃ̄ΜΙΧΑΗΛ·
    ΧΕΜΠΕΛΑΑΥ Ᾱ̄ϨΕΡΑΤϤ Ν̄Ṃ̄ΜΑΙ·
    Ν̄ϹΑΜΙΧΑΗΛ ΠΕΤΟ ΝΑΡΧΩΝ⸗[1]

---

[1]   The abbreviation ⲁⲣ̄ⳉ could stand for either ⲁⲣⲭⲱⲛ or
ⲁⲣⲭⲁⲅⲅⲉⲗⲟⲥ. The former has been chosen in conformity with the
reading of Dan. 10.21.

◄ HYMN EIGHT ►

The alphabetic acrostic on the Archangel Michael

1 Truly, your holy feast
   has gladdened us, O Michael,
   and all the prophets
   speak of the renown of your feats.

2 Moses proclaims:
   He shall send his angel
   that he may cast out before you
   the nations that fight against you.[1]

3 For our fathers, the apostles,
   and the teachers of the Church
   and the ranks of the martyrs
   have Michael for their protector.

4 The prophet Daniel
   speaks of Michael's renown:
   No one stood by me
   except Michael who is the prince.[2]

---

[1] Cf. perhaps Ex. 33.2.
[2] Cf. Dan. 10.21.

5 ⲁϥϣ̅ⲧⲁⲙ ⲉⲧⲧⲁⲡⲣⲟ ⲛ̄ⲛⲉⲙⲟⲩⲓ·
ⲁϥϯ ⲛⲁϥ ⲉ̄ⲡⲁⲣⲓⲥⲧⲟⲛ·
ⲡⲉϫⲁϥ ϫⲉⲁ̄ⲕⲉⲣⲡⲁⲙⲉⲉⲩⲉ̄ ⲡϭ̅ⲥ̅·
ⲙ̄ⲡⲉⲕⲕⲱ ⲛ̄ⲥⲱⲕ ⲛ̄ⲛⲉⲧⲙⲉ ⲙ̄ⲙⲟⲕ⸗[1]

6 ⲉⲣⲉⲓⲏⲥⲟⲩ ⲡ̄ϣⲏⲣⲉ ⲛ̄ⲛⲁⲩⲏ̄·
ϩⲛ̄ⲣⲱⲥ ⲛ̄ϩⲓⲉ̄ⲣⲓⲭⲱ·
ⲁϥϥⲓ ⲛ̄ⲛⲉϥⲃⲁⲗ ⲉϩⲣⲁⲓ ⲉⲧⲡⲉ·
ⲁϥⲛⲁⲩ ⲉ̄ⲙⲓⲭⲁⲏⲗ ⲉϥⲙⲓϣⲉ ⲉ̄ϫⲱϥ⸗

7 ⲍⲁⲭⲁⲣⲓⲁⲥ ⲡⲉⲡⲣⲟⲫⲏⲧⲏⲥ·
ϫⲉⲁⲓⲛⲁⲩ ⲉ̄ⲡⲁⲅⲅⲉⲗⲟⲥ·
ϩⲓϫⲙ̄ⲡⲉⲑⲩⲥⲓⲁⲥⲧⲏⲣⲓⲟⲛ·
ⲉϥⲁ̄ϩⲉⲣⲁⲧϥ̄ ⲙⲛ̄ⲓⲏⲥⲟⲩ⸗

8 ⲏ̄ⲥⲁⲓⲁⲥ ⲡⲉⲡⲣⲟⲫⲏⲧⲏⲥ·
ϫⲉⲉⲓⲥϩⲏⲏ̄ⲧⲉ ⲁ̄ⲛⲟⲕ·
ϯⲛⲁϫⲁⲩ ⲙ̄ⲡⲁⲁⲅⲅⲉⲗⲟⲥ ϩⲁⲧⲉⲕϩⲏ·
ⲉⲧⲣⲉϥⲥⲟⲃⲧⲉ ⲛ̄ⲛⲉⲕϩⲓⲟⲟⲩⲉ⸗

9 ⲑⲉⲱ̄ⲣⲓ ⲟⲛ ⲉ̄ⲙⲓⲭⲁⲏⲗ·
ⲛ̄ⲧⲁϥⲁ̄ⲙⲁϩⲧⲉ ⲛ̄ⲧⲁⲡⲉ ⲛⲁⲃⲁⲕⲟⲩⲙ·
ⲁϥϫⲓ ⲙ̄ⲙⲟϥ ⲙⲉⲡⲁⲣⲓⲥⲧⲟⲛ·
ⲉⲡϣⲏⲓ <ⲛ>ⲛⲉⲙⲟⲩⲓ ϣⲁⲇⲁⲛⲓⲏⲗ⸗

---

[1] Note that, contrary to the usual practice, two stanzas are devoted to ⲇ (ⲇⲁⲛⲓⲏⲗ), and that therefore this hymn has 25 stanzas. The alphabetic arrangement is taken up again in stanza 6.

5   He shut the mouth of the lions.[1]
    He gave him the dinner.
    He (Daniel) said: You have remembered me, Lord.
    You have not forsaken those who love you.[2]

6   While Joshua, the son of Nun,
    was in the gate of Jericho,
    he lifted his eyes up to heaven
    and saw Michael fighting for him.[3]

7   The prophet Zechariah says:
    I saw the angel
    by the altar,
    standing with Joshua.[4]

8   The prophet Isaiah says:
    Behold, I
    shall send my angel before you
    to prepare your ways.[5]

9   Look again at Michael
    who took hold of Habakkuk's head
    and took him with the dinner
    to the lions' den to Daniel.[6]

---

[1]   Cf. Dan. 6.18.
[2]   Cf. Bel and the Dragon 34–8.
[3]   Cf. Josh. 5.13.
[4]   Cf. Zech. 3.1.
[5]   Cf. Mk. 1.2 (Mal. 3.1).
[6]   Cf. Bel and the Dragon 34–6.

10 ιωсΗφ π̅ϩλλο ⲛ̅ϩⲁⲙϣⲏ·
   ⲁⲡⲁⲅⲅⲉⲗⲟⲥ ϣⲁϫⲉ ⲛⲙⲙⲁϥ·
   ϫⲉⲙⲡⲣ̅ⲣ̅ϩⲟⲧⲉ ⲉⲕϫⲓ ⲙ̅ⲙⲁⲣⲓⲁ·
   ⲧⲉⲕⲥ̅ϩⲓⲙⲉ ⲉ̅ϩⲟⲩⲛ̅ ⲉ̅ⲡⲉⲕⲏⲓ⳥

11 ⲕⲁⲗⲱⲥ ⲁϥϫⲟⲟⲥ ⲛ̅ϭⲓⲇⲁ̅ⲇ̅·
   ϩⲙ̅ⲡⲉⲯⲁⲗⲧⲏⲣⲓⲟⲛ ⲉⲧⲧⲁⲓⲏⲩ·
   ϫⲉϣⲁⲣⲉⲡⲁⲅⲅⲉⲗⲟⲥ ⲙ̅ⲡϭ̅ⲥ̅·
   ⲕⲱⲧⲉ ⲉ̅ⲛⲉⲧⲣ̅ϩⲟⲧⲉ ϩⲏⲧϥ̅⳥

12 ⲗⲁⲟⲥ ⲛⲓⲙ ⲉⲧϩⲓϫⲙ̅ⲡⲕⲁϩ·
   ⲙⲛ̅ⲛⲉⲧⲁⲅⲙⲁ ⲛⲁⲅⲅⲉⲗⲓⲕⲟⲛ·
   ⲥⲉⲣⲁϣⲉ ϩⲙ̅ⲡ̅ϣⲁ ⲙ̅ⲙⲓⲭⲁⲏⲗ·
   ⲡⲁⲅⲅⲉⲗⲟⲥ ⲛ̅ϣⲁⲛϩⲧⲏϥ⳥

13 ⲙⲓⲭⲁⲏⲗ ⲡⲁⲣⲭⲁⲅⲅⲉⲗⲟⲥ·
   ⲁϥⲉⲓ ⲉ̅ⲡⲉⲥⲏⲧ ⲉ̅ⲃⲟⲗ ϩⲛ̅ⲧⲡⲉ·
   ⲁϥⲃⲱⲕ ⲉⲧⲃⲁⲃⲩⲗⲱⲛ ⲁϥⲛⲟⲩϩⲙ̅ ⲉⲡⲅ̅ ⲛ̅ϩⲁⲅⲓⲟⲥ·
   ⲙ̅ⲡⲉⲗⲁⲁⲩ ⲙ̅ⲡⲉⲑⲟⲟⲩ ⲧⲁϩⲟⲟⲩ⳥

14 |ⲛⲉϩⲓⲟ̅ⲙⲉ[1] ⲛ̅ⲧⲁⲩⲡⲱⲧ ⲉⲡⲧⲁⲫⲟⲥ·
   ⲁ̅ⲡⲁⲅⲅⲉⲗⲟⲥ ϣⲁϫⲉ ⲛⲉⲙⲁⲩ·
   ϫⲉⲁ̅ⲧⲉⲧⲛ̅ϣⲓⲛⲉ ⲛ̅ⲥⲁⲓ̅ⲥ̅·
   ⲁϥⲧⲱⲟⲩⲛ̅ ⲛ̅ϥⲉⲙⲡⲉⲓⲙⲁ ⲁⲛ⳥

---

[1] Page ⲣ̅ⲗ̅ⲋ begins.

10   As for Joseph, the aged carpenter,
the angel spoke with him:
Do not be afraid to take Mary
your wife into your house.[1]

11   David spoke well
in the precious psalter:
The angel of the Lord
surrounds those who fear him.[2]

12   All peoples upon earth
and the angelic ranks
rejoice on the feast of Michael,
the merciful angel.

13   The archangel Michael
came down from heaven.
He went to Babylon and delivered the three holy men.
No evil befell them.[3]

14   The women who went to the tomb,
the angel spoke with them:
You seek Jesus;
he has risen, he is not here.[4]

---

[1] Cf. Mt. 1.20.
[2] Ps. 33.8.
[3] Cf. Dan. 3.91–4 (24–7).
[4] Cf. Mt. 28.5–6; Mk. 16.5–6; Lk. 24.5–6.

15 ϫⲱⲕ ⲙ̄ⲙⲟⲛ ⲉ̄†ⲑⲉⲱⲣⲓⲁ·
ⲱ̅ ⲗⲟⲩⲕⲁⲥ ⲉⲧⲃⲉⲡⲁⲅⲅⲉⲗⲟⲥ·
ⲡⲉⲛⲧⲁϥⲟⲩⲟⲛ𝄐ϥ̄ ⲉ̄ⲛⲉⲱⲟⲟⲥ·
ϫⲉⲁⲩϫⲡⲟ ⲛⲏⲧⲛ̄ ⲙ̄ⲡⲥⲱ̅ⲣ̅⳼

16 ⲟⲩϣⲁⲛ𝄐ⲧⲏϥⲡⲉ ⲡⲉⲭ̅ⲥ̅·
ⲟⲩⲡ̅ⲣⲉⲥⲃⲉⲩⲧⲏⲥ ⲉ̄ⲧⲟ ⲛ𝄐ⲟⲧ·[1]
ⲧⲉ[2] ⲡⲓⲁⲣⲭⲏⲁⲅⲅⲉⲗⲟⲥ·
ⲉϥⲥⲟⲡ̅ⲥ̅ ⲉ̄ϫⲙ̄ⲡⲅⲉⲛⲟⲥ ⲛⲁⲇⲁⲙ⳼

17 ⲡⲉⲧⲣⲟⲥ ⲡ̄ⲛⲟϭ ⲛⲁⲡⲟⲥⲧⲟⲗⲟⲥ·
ⲣⲁϣⲉ ⲙ̄ⲡⲟⲟⲩ ⲁⲩⲱ̅ ϥ̄ⲧⲉⲗⲏⲗ·
ϫⲉⲁ̄ⲙⲓⲭⲁⲏⲗ ⲡⲱⲧ ϣⲁⲣⲟϥ·
ⲁϥⲉⲛⲧϥ̄ ⲉ̄ⲃⲟⲗ 𝄐ⲉⲡⲉϣⲧⲉⲕⲟ⳼

18 ⲣⲁϣⲉ ⲛⲁⲕ ⲱ̅ ⲡⲁⲩⲗⲟⲥ·
ϫⲉⲁ̄ⲙⲓⲭⲁⲏⲗ ⲉⲓ ϣⲁⲣⲟⲕ·
𝄐ⲙ̄ⲡⲉⲥϭⲏⲣ ⲛ̄ⲑⲁⲗⲁⲥⲥⲁ·
ⲁϥⲧⲟⲩϫⲟⲕ ⲙⲛ̄ⲛⲉⲧⲛⲉⲙⲁⲕ⳼

19 ⲥⲱⲧⲙ̄ ⲉ̄ⲡⲉⲩⲁⲅⲅⲉⲗⲓⲥⲧⲏⲥ·
ⲡⲉⲭⲁϥ ϫⲉⲁⲅⲅⲉⲗⲟⲥ ⲉⲓ ⲉ̄ⲃⲟⲗ 𝄐ⲛ̄ⲧⲡⲉ·
ⲁϥⲥⲕⲉⲣⲕⲱⲣⲡⲱⲛⲉ ⲁϥ𝄐ⲙⲟⲟⲥ 𝄐ⲓϫⲱϥ·
𝄐ⲓⲣⲙ̄ⲡ̄ⲣⲟ ⲛ̄ⲧⲁⲛⲁⲥⲧⲁⲥⲓⲥ⳼

---

[1] Note the unusual division before the copula, as also in IX,15/
2, XI,21/2, and XII,15/2.
[2] For ⲡⲉ. Note the same irregular use in III,5/3, 7/4, 24/3.

15   You draw us to the contemplation,
O Luke, of the angel
who appeared to the shepherds,
saying: The Saviour has been born to you.[1]

16   Christ is merciful.
A faithful ambassador
is the archangel,
praying for the race of Adam.

17   The great apostle Peter
rejoices today and is glad,
for Michael went to him
and brought him out of prison.[2]

18   Rejoice, O Paul,
for Michael came to you
on the sea voyage,
and saved you and those with you.[3]

19   Listen to the evangelist.
He said: An angel came out of heaven.
He rolled away the stone and sat upon it[4]
at the door of the resurrection.

---

[1] Cf. Lk. 2.11.
[2] Cf. Acts 5.19.
[3] Cf. Acts 27.23–4.
[4] Cf. Mt. 28.2.

20 ΤΟΤΕ ΠΕΧΕΠΑΓΓΕΛΟϹ·
ⲈⲚⲈϨⲒⲞⲘⲈ ⲚⲦⲀⲨⲠⲰⲦ ⲈⲠⲦⲀⲪⲞϹ·
ⲬⲈⲀ̄ⲦⲈⲦⲚ̄ϢⲒⲚⲒ ⲚϹⲀⲒ̄Ϲ̄·
ⲀϥⲦⲰⲞⲨⲚ̄ ⲚϥⲈⲘⲠⲈⲒⲘⲀ ⲀⲚ⸗

21 ⲨⲘⲚⲈⲨⲈ̄ Ⲛ̄ⲦⲈⲦⲚ̄ⲦⲈⲖⲎⲖ·
ⲞⲨⲞⲚ ⲚⲒⲘ ⲈⲦϢⲞⲞⲠ ϨⲈⲠⲬⲀⲒⲈ̄·
ⲬⲈⲀ̄ⲠⲀⲄⲄⲈⲖⲞϹ ⲆⲒⲀ̄ⲔⲰⲚⲒ ⲈⲢⲰⲦⲚ̄·
ϢⲀⲚⲦⲈⲦⲚ̄ϪⲀⲔⲠⲈⲦⲈⲚⲀⲄⲰⲚ Ⲉ̄ⲂⲞⲖ⸗

22 ⲪⲒⲖⲒⲠⲠⲞϹ ⲠⲀⲠⲞϹⲦⲞⲖⲞϹ·
ⲀⲠⲀⲄⲄⲈⲖⲞϹ ϢⲀϪⲈ ⲚⲘ̄ⲘⲀϥ·
ⲬⲈⲦⲠⲈⲔⲞⲨⲞⲒ ⲦⲞⲂ̄Ⲕ̄ Ⲉ̄ⲠⲒϨⲀⲢⲘⲀ·
ⲦⲀⲢⲈⲔⲂⲀⲠⲦⲒⲌⲈ Ⲙ̄ⲠⲈϹⲒⲞⲨⲢ̄⸗

23 ⲬⲀⲢⲒϹⲘⲀ ⲚⲒⲘ Ⲛ̄ⲦⲀⲖϬⲞ·
ⲆⲰⲢⲈⲀ̄ ⲚⲒⲘ Ⲛ̄ⲔⲈⲚⲞⲂⲈ Ⲉ̄ⲂⲞⲖ·
ⲀⲨⲚⲎⲨ ⲚⲀⲚ Ⲉ̄ⲂⲞⲖ ϨⲚ̄Ⲧ̄ⲠⲈ·
ϨⲒⲦⲚ̄ⲚⲈϹⲞⲠⲤ̄ ⲈⲘⲒⲬⲀⲎⲖ⸗

24 ⲮⲀⲖⲖⲒ ⲈⲠⲈⲚⲚⲞⲨⲦⲈ ⲮⲀⲖⲖⲈⲒ·
ⲔⲀⲦⲀⲠ̄ϢⲀϪⲈ Ⲙ̄ⲠⲈⲠ̄ⲢⲞⲪⲎⲦⲎϹ·
ⲬⲈⲀⲨⲰ̄ ⲦⲚⲀⲮⲀⲖⲒ ⲈⲢⲞⲔ·
Ⲙ̄ⲠⲘ̄ⲦⲞ Ⲉ̄ⲂⲞⲖ ⲚⲚⲀⲄⲄⲈⲖⲞϹ⸗

25 Ⲱ̄ ⲚⲈⲖⲀⲞϹ ⲦⲎⲢⲞⲨ Ⲙ̄Ⲡ̄ⲔⲞϹⲘⲞϹ·
ⲘⲀⲢⲈⲚϹⲞⲠⲤ̄ Ⲉ̄ⲘⲒⲬⲀⲎⲖ·
Ⲛ̄ϥⲠⲀⲢⲀⲔⲀⲖⲒ Ⲙ̄Ⲡ̄ⲚⲞⲨⲦⲈ ϨⲀⲢⲞⲚ·
Ⲛ̄ϥⲔⲈⲚⲈⲚⲚⲞⲂⲈ ⲚⲀⲚ Ⲉ̄ⲂⲞⲖ:-

20 Then the angel said
to the women who went to the tomb:
You seek Jesus;
he has risen, he is not here.[1]

21 Sing and rejoice,
everyone who is in the wilderness,
for the angel ministered unto you
until you finished your contest.[2]

22 Philip the apostle,
the angel spoke with him:
Advance, join yourself to this chariot
that you may baptize the eunuch.[3]

23 All gifts of healing
and all gifts of forgiveness of sin
come to us from heaven
through the prayers of Michael.

24 Sing to our God, sing,[4]
according to the word of the prophet:
And I shall sing to you
before the angels.[5]

25 O all the peoples of the world,
let us pray to Michael
that he may beseech God for us
to forgive us our sins.

---

[1] Cf. Mt. 28.5–6; Mk. 16.5–6; Lk. 24.5–6.
[2] Cf. perhaps Mt. 4.11; Mk. 1.13.
[3] Cf. Acts 8.29–40.
[4] Ps. 46.7.
[5] Ps. 137.1.

(pp. p̄ⲗ̄ⲋ̄, line 33 – p̄ⲍ̄ⲏ)

ⲑ̄   ⲡⲁⲗⲫⲁⲃⲏⲧⲁ ⲛⲛⲉⲛⲓⲟⲧⲉ ⲛⲁⲡⲟⲥⲧⲟⲗⲟⲥ:-

1   ⲁⲗⲏⲑⲱⲥ ⲟⲩⲛⲟϭⲡⲉ ⲡⲉⲟ̄ⲟⲩ ⲙⲛ̄ⲡ̄ⲧⲁⲓⲟ̄·
    ⲙ̄ⲡⲓ·ⲓ̄ⲃ̄· | ⲛⲁⲡⲟⲥⲧⲟⲗⲟⲥ·[1]
    ⲛⲁⲓ ⲛ̄ⲧⲁⲡⲥⲱ̄ⲣ ⲥⲱⲧⲡ̄ ⲙ̄ⲙⲁⲩ·
    ⲁϥϫⲁⲩⲥⲟⲩ ⲉ̄ⲃⲟⲗ ⲉⲡⲧⲁϣⲉⲟⲉⲓϣⲝ

2   ⲃⲉⲣⲙ̄ⲛ̄ⲧ̄ⲣⲉ ⲛ̄ϭⲓⲡ̄ⲥⲱ̄ⲣ·
    ϩ̄ⲛ̄ⲛⲉⲩⲁⲅⲅⲉⲗⲓⲟⲛ ⲉⲧⲧⲁⲓⲏⲩ·
    ϫⲉⲙⲡⲓⲥⲱⲧⲡ̄ ⲛⲟⲩⲣⲙ̄ⲙⲁⲟ̄·
    ⲁⲗⲗⲁ ϩ̄ⲛ̄ϩⲏⲕⲉ ⲛⲉⲛⲧⲁⲓⲥⲱⲧⲡ̄ ⲙ̄ⲙⲟⲟⲩⲝ

3   ⲅⲉⲅⲁⲣ ⲡⲉϫⲉⲡϭ̄ⲥ̄ ⲛⲁⲩ·
    ϫⲉⲛ̄ϯⲛⲁⲙⲟⲩⲧⲉ ⲉ̄ⲣⲱⲧⲛ̄ ⲁⲛ ϫⲉⲛⲁϩⲙ̄ϩⲁⲗ·
    ϫⲉⲙⲡ̄ϩ̄ⲙ̄ϩⲁⲗ ⲥⲟⲟⲩⲛ̄ ⲁⲛ·
    ⲉ̄ⲡⲉⲧⲉⲣⲉⲡⲉϥϫⲟⲉⲓⲥ ⲉⲓⲣⲉ ⲙ̄ⲙⲟϥⲝ

4   ⲗⲁⲓⲧⲉ ⲑⲉ ⲛ̄ⲧⲁⲓⲙⲟⲩⲧⲉ ⲉ̄ⲣⲱⲧⲛ̄·
    ϫⲉⲛⲁⲥⲛⲏⲩ ⲁⲩⲱ̄ ⲛⲁϣ̄ⲃⲏⲣ·
    ϫⲉⲛⲉⲛⲧⲁⲓⲥⲟⲧⲙⲟⲩ ϩⲓⲧⲙ̄ⲡⲁⲓⲱⲧ·
    ⲛⲁⲓ ⲁ̄ⲛⲟⲕ ⲛⲉⲛⲧⲁⲓϫⲟⲟⲩ ⲛⲏⲧⲛ̄ⲝ

---

[1]   Page p̄ⲗ̄ⲍ begins.

◄ HYMN NINE ►

The alphabetic acrostic on our fathers, the apostles

1   Truly, great is the glory and the honour
    of the twelve apostles,
    whom the Saviour chose.
    He sent them forth to preach.[1]

2   The Saviour bears witness
    in the precious gospels:
    I did not choose a rich man,
    but I chose poor men.[2]

3   For the Lord said to them:
    I shall not call you my servants,
    for the servant does not know
    what his lord does.[3]

4   So I have called you
    my brethren and my friends,
    for the things that I heard from my Father,
    these I have told you.[4]

---

[1]   Cf. Mk. 3.14.
[2]   Cf. Lk. 6.20–4; James 2.5.
[3]   Jn. 15.15.
[4]   Cf. Jn. 15.15.

5 ⲉⲓⲥϩⲏⲏⲧⲉ ϯⲭⲁⲩ ⲙ̄ⲙⲁⲧ̄ⲛ ⲉ̄ⲃⲟⲗ·
ⲛ̄ⲑⲉ ⲛ̄ϩ̄ⲛⲉ̄ⲥⲟⲟⲩ ϩⲛ̄ⲧ̄ⲙⲏⲧⲉ ⲛ̄ϩ̄ⲛⲟⲩⲱⲛϣ̄·
ϣⲱⲡⲉ ⲛ̄ⲥⲁⲃⲏ ⲛ̄ⲑⲏ ⲛ̄ⲛⲓϩⲟϥ·
ⲁⲩⲱ̄ ⲛⲁⲕⲉⲣⲉⲟⲥ ⲛⲟⲑⲉ ⲛ̄ⲛⲓϭⲣⲟⲙⲡⲉ⸗

6 ϩⲱⲧⲉⲙ ⲉⲡⲉⲧⲣⲟⲥ·
ⲉϥϣⲁϫⲉ ⲙⲛ̄ⲡ̄ⲥⲱ̄ⲣ·
ϫⲉⲙⲁⲧⲁⲙⲟⲛ ⲡϭ̄ⲥ ⲉⲡⲉⲛⲃⲉⲕⲉ·
ⲡⲉⲭ̄ⲥ̄ ⲛ̄ⲧⲁⲛⲟⲩⲁ̄ϩⲛ̄ ⲛ̄ⲥⲱⲕ⸗

7 ⲏ̄ⲧⲁ ⲙ̄ⲡⲉⲭⲉⲡϭ̄ⲥ̄ ⲛⲁⲩ·
ϫⲉⲛⲧⲱⲧⲛ̄ⲡⲉ ⲛⲁϣⲃⲏⲣ·
ⲛⲉⲛⲧⲁⲡⲁⲓⲱⲧ ⲥⲱⲧⲡ̄ ⲙ̄ⲙⲁⲩ·
ⲧⲁⲉⲓⲣⲏⲛⲏ ϯⲛⲁϯ ⲙ̄ⲙⲟⲥ ⲛⲏⲧⲛ̄⸗

8 ⲑⲉⲱⲣⲓ ⲛ̄ⲛⲓⲣⲉⲙⲥⲁⲣⲝ̄·
ⲉ̄ⲣⲉⲡⲛⲟⲩⲧⲉ ϣⲁϫⲉ ⲛⲙ̄ⲙⲁⲩ·
ϫⲉϩⲣⲁⲓ ϩ̄ⲙⲡⲉϫⲡⲟ ⲛ̄ⲕⲉⲥⲟⲡ·
ϯⲛⲁⲥⲟⲃⲧⲉ ⲛ̄ϩ̄ⲛⲑⲣⲟⲛⲟⲥ ⲛⲏⲧⲛ̄⸗

9 ⲓ̄ⲥ̄ ⲇⲉ ⲡⲉϫⲁϥ ⲛⲁⲩ·
ϫⲉϯⲛⲁⲥⲱⲟⲩϩ̄ ⲉⲡⲕⲟⲥⲙⲟⲥ ⲧⲏⲣϥ̄·
ⲧⲁⲉⲛⲧ̄ϥ ⲉ̄ⲡⲓ̄ⲁ̄ ⲛⲓⲱⲥⲁⲫⲁⲧ·
ϫⲉⲉ̄ⲣⲉⲡ̄ⲃⲉⲕⲉ ϩ̄ⲙ̄ⲡⲙⲁ ⲉ̄ⲧⲙ̄ⲙⲁⲩ⸗

5 Behold, I send you forth
as sheep in the midst of wolves.
Be wise as the serpents
and harmless as the doves.[1]

6 Listen to Peter
speaking with the Saviour:
Tell us, Lord, our reward,
O Christ, whom we have followed.[2]

7 Then the Lord said to them:
You are my friends,[3]
whom my Father has chosen.
My peace I shall give to you.[4]

8 Look at these men of flesh
with whom God speaks:
In the regeneration
I shall prepare thrones for you.[5]

9 And Jesus said to them:
I shall gather all the world,
and shall bring it to the valley of Jehoshaphat,[6]
for the reward is in that place.

---

[1] Mt. 10.16.
[2] Cf. Mt. 19.27.
[3] Cf. Jn. 15.14.
[4] Cf. Jn. 14.27.
[5] Cf. Mt. 19.28.
[6] Cf. Joel 3.2.

10 ⲕⲁⲗⲱⲥ ⲁϥϫⲟⲟⲥ ⲛ̄ϭⲓⲁ̄ⲇ̄·
ϩⲙ̄ⲡⲉⲯⲁⲗⲧⲏⲣⲓⲟⲛ ⲉⲧⲧⲁⲓⲏⲩ·
ϫⲉⲁⲡⲉⲩϩ̄ⲣⲟⲟⲩ ⲉⲓ ⲉ̄ⲃⲟⲗ ⲉ̄ϫⲙ̄ⲡⲕⲁϩ ⲧⲏⲣϥ̄·
ⲁⲩⲱ̄ ⲛⲉⲩϣⲁϫⲉ ϣⲁ†ⲕⲟⲩⲙⲉⲛⲏ⸗

11 ⲗⲁⲟⲥ ⲛⲓⲙ ⲉⲧϩⲓϫⲙ̄ⲡⲕⲁϩ·
ⲙⲛ̄ⲛⲉⲫⲩⲗⲏ· ⲙ̄ⲛ̄ⲛⲓⲉ̄ⲑⲉⲛⲟⲥ·[1]
ⲥⲉⲁ̄ϩⲉⲣⲁⲧⲟⲩ ⲉⲡⲙⲁ ⲛ†ϩⲁⲡ·
ⲉ̄ⲣⲉⲡⲓ·ⲓ̄ⲃ̄· ⲛ̄ⲣⲱⲙⲉ ϩⲙⲟⲟⲥ⸗

12 ⲙⲁⲣⲉⲛⲥⲱⲧⲙ̄ ⲉⲡⲁⲩⲗⲟⲥ·
ⲉϥⲣ̄ⲙⲛ̄ⲧⲣⲉ ⲛⲁⲛ ⲉϥϫⲱ ⲙ̄ⲙⲟⲥ·
ϫⲉⲧⲛ̄ⲛⲁ†ϩⲁⲡ ⲉ̄ϩⲛ̄ⲁⲅⲅⲉⲗⲟⲥ·
ⲙ̄ⲡⲁⲧⲉⲛⲡⲱϩ ⲣⲱ ⲉ̄ⲛⲁⲡⲕⲟⲥⲙⲟⲥ⸗

13 ⲛⲁⲓⲛⲉ ⲛⲉⲣⲁⲛ ⲙ̄ⲡⲓ·ⲓ̄ⲃ̄·
ⲛⲁⲡⲟⲥⲧⲟⲗⲟⲥ ⲉⲧⲧⲁⲓⲏⲩ·
ⲛⲉⲛⲧⲁⲡⲥⲱ̄ⲣ̄ |ⲥⲱⲧⲡ̄[2] ⲙ̄ⲙⲟⲟⲩ·
ⲁϥϫⲁⲩⲥⲟⲩ ⲉ̄ⲃⲟⲗ ⲉⲡⲧⲁϣⲉⲟⲉⲓϣ⸗

14 ϫⲱⲧⲡ̄[3] ⲉ̄ⲡⲉⲧⲣⲟⲥ ⲉ̄ⲕⲉⲓⲣⲉ ⲙ̄ⲙⲟϥ·
ⲛⲓⲱⲧ ⲛ̄ⲛⲁⲡⲟⲥⲧⲟⲗⲟⲥ·
ⲁϥⲁⲣⲛⲁ ⲙ̄ⲙⲟⲕ ⲛ̄·ⲅ̄·ⲛ̄ⲥⲟⲡ·
ⲁⲩⲱ ⲁⲕⲕⲱ ⲛⲁϥ ⲉ̄ⲃⲟⲗ⸗

---

[1] Scribal error for ⲉⲑⲛⲟⲥ.
[2] Page ⲣ̄ⲝ̄ⲏ̄ begins.
[3] The use of the Present Tense, instead of the expected Perfect I, is probably due to the alphabetic arrangement of the hymn.

10   David spoke well
     in the precious psalter:
     Their voice has gone forth over the whole earth
     and their words to the world.[1]

11   All peoples upon the earth,
     and the tribes and the nations
     stand at the place of judgement,
     where these twelve men are seated.[2]

12   Let us listen to Paul,
     who bears witness to us, saying:
     We shall judge angels,
     though we have not yet even got as far
          as judging worldly things.[3]

13   These are the names of the twelve
     honoured apostles
     whom the Saviour chose.
     He sent them forth to preach.[4]

14   You chose[5] Peter, making him
     father of the apostles.
     He denied you three times[6]
     and you forgave him.

---

[1]   Cf. Ps. 18.5.
[2]   Cf. Mt. 19.28.
[3]   Cf. I Cor. 6.3.
[4]   Cf. Mk. 3.14.
[5]   Lit. 'You choose …'.
[6]   Cf. Mt. 26.75; Mk. 14.72; Lk. 22.61.

15 ΟΥΡѠΜΕ ̄ΝΡΕϤϢѠΤ ĒΒΟΛ·[1]
ΠΕ ΑΝΔΡΕΑC Π̄CΟΝ Μ̄ΠΕΤΡΟC·
ΑΠϬ̄C CѠΤⲠ̄ Μ̄ΜΟϤ·
ΑϤΧΟΟΥϤ ĒΤΕΧѠΡΑ Ν̄ΝΕΟΥΑΜΡѠΜΕ⸗

16 ΠΙΚΕΟΥΑ ΟΝ ΧΕΙΑΚѠΒΟC·
Ν̄ΤΟϤΠΕ ΠϢΗΡΕ Μ̄ΠΕϨΡΟΥΒΑΙ·
ΑϤΝΑΥ ĒΠΕΟΟΥ Μ̄Π̄ΝΟΥΤΕ·
ϨΙΧΜ̄Π̄ΤΟΟΥ ΝΝΕΧΟΕΙΤ⸗

17 ΡΑϢΕ ΝΑΚ Ѡ ΙѠϨΑΝΝΗC·
ΧΕΕΙC ΤΑΜΑΑΥ ΑΙΤΑΝϨΟΥΤΚ ĒΡΟC·
†ΝΑϨΑΡΕϨ ĒΡΟΚ ĒΚΟΝϨ·
ϢΑΝΤΕΚΝΑΥ ĒΡΟΙ ΕΙ͞Ο ΝΕΡΟ⸗

18 CѠΤⲘ̄ ĒΦΙΛΙΠΠΟC·
ΕϤϢΑΧΕ ΜΕΠΕΝC͞Ѡ͞Ρ·
ΧΕΜΑΤΑΜΟΙ ĒΠΕΟΟΥ Μ̄ΠΙѠΤ·
Μ̄ΠΑΤΕΝΠѠΤ ΕΠΤΑϢΕΟ͞ΕΙϢ⸗

19 ΤΟΤΕ ΒΑΡΘΟΛΟΜΕΟC ϨѠѠϤ·
ΑϤΚΡΕΜΡΕΜ ΕϤΧѠ Μ̄ΜΟC·
ΧΕΑΝΟΚ ΑΙΝΑΥ ĒΠΕΝC͞Ѡ͞Ρ·
ΕϤϢΑΧΕ Μ̄ΝΟΥCΑΜΑΡΙΤΗC⸗

---

[1] Note the unusual division before the copula, as also in
VIII,16/3, XI,21/2, and XII,15/2.

15 A man of determination[1]
    was Andrew, the brother of Peter.
    The Lord chose him
    and sent him to the land of the man-eaters.[2]

16 Yet another one, James,
    is the son of thunder.[3]
    He saw the glory of God
    on the mount of Olives.[4]

17 Rejoice, O John,
    for behold, I have entrusted you to my mother.[5]
    I shall keep you alive
    until you see me being king.[6]

18 Listen to Philip,
    speaking with the Saviour:
    Show me the glory of the Father[7]
    before we go to preach.

19 Then Bartholomew, for his part,
    murmured, saying:
    I saw our Saviour,
    speaking with a Samaritan.[8]

---

[1] Possibly a reference to the meaning of the Greek name
Ἀνδρέας ('manly').
[2] Cf. the Acts of Andrew and Matthias (for editions and translations, see p. 6, n. 1).
[3] Cf. Mk. 3.17.
[4] Cf. Mk. 13.3. See also Mt. 17.1–2; Mk. 9.2–3; Lk. 9.28–9.
[5] Cf. Jn. 19.26–7.
[6] Cf. Jn. 21.21–3.
[7] Cf. Jn. 14.8–9.
[8] Cf. perhaps Jn. 4.7–30.

20 ϥⲓ¹ ⲙⲁⲑⲉⲟⲥ ⲡⲓⲧⲉⲗⲱⲛⲏⲥ·
   ⲁϥϫⲓ² ⲙ̄ⲡⲧⲉⲗⲱⲛⲏⲥ ⲉ̄ⲡⲉⲛⲥⲱⲣ·
   ϩⲱⲥ ⲣⲱⲙⲉ ⲉ̄ⲡⲉϥⲙⲁ ⲛⲧⲉⲗⲱⲛⲏⲥ·
   ⲁⲩⲱ ⲁⲩⲕⲱ ⲛⲁϥ ⲉ̄ⲃⲟⲗ⳹

21 ⲫⲱⲣⲓ ⲛⲁⲕ ⲉ̄ⲛⲟⲩⲡⲓⲥⲧⲓⲥ·³
   ⲱ̄ ⲑⲱⲙⲁⲥ ⲡⲁⲡⲟⲥⲧⲟⲗⲟⲥ·
   ⲉⲣⲉⲡⲉⲛⲥⲱⲣ ⲧⲁⲙⲟ ⲙ̄ⲙⲟⲕ·
   ⲉ̄ⲛⲉϣⲥⲛ̄ⲉⲓⲃⲧ̄ ⲉⲧϩⲛ̄ⲛⲉϥϭⲓⲝ⳹

22 ⲭⲉⲣⲉ ⲓⲁⲕⲱⲃⲟⲥ·
   ⲙⲛ̄ⲑⲁⲇⲉⲟⲥ ⲡⲉϥⲥⲟⲛ·
   ⲡϣⲏⲣⲉ ·ⲃ̄· ⲛⲓⲱⲥⲏⲫ·
   ⲛⲉⲛⲧⲁⲩϣⲱⲡⲉ ⲛ̄ⲥⲟⲛ ⲉ̄ⲡϭⲥ̄⳹

23 ⲯⲁⲗⲗⲉⲓ ⲉ̄ⲡⲉⲛⲛⲟⲩⲧⲉ ⲯⲁⲗⲗⲉⲓ·
   ⲯⲁⲗⲗⲓ ⲉ̄ⲡⲉⲛⲉⲣⲟ ⲯⲁⲗⲓ·
   ⲱ̄ ⲡ̄ⲗⲁⲥ ⲉ̄ⲡⲉⲥϯⲛⲟⲩⲃⲉ·
   ⲡⲁⲩⲗⲟⲥ ⲡⲁⲡⲟⲥⲧⲟⲗⲟⲥ⳹

24 ⲱϣ ⲉ̄ⲃⲟⲗ ϩⲛ̄ⲟⲩⲡⲓⲥⲧⲓⲥ·
   ⲱ̄ ⲥⲓⲙⲱⲛ ⲡ̄ⲕⲩⲣⲓⲛⲛⲉⲟⲥ·
   ⲙⲛ̄ⲗⲟⲩⲕⲁⲥ ⲡⲁⲡⲟⲥⲧⲟⲗⲟⲥ·
   ⲙⲛ̄ⲙⲁⲣⲕⲟⲥ ⲡⲉⲩⲁⲅⲅⲉⲗⲓⲥⲧⲏⲥ:-
   ⲥⲟⲡⲥ̄ ⲉ̄ⲡϭⲥ̄⁴

---

¹ Perhaps ϥⲓ, which also occurs in III,20/1 and IV,5/1, stands for ⲟⲩⲏⲓ.
² Possibly for ⲁⲩϫⲓ, as one expects the Passive; but see L. Stern, *Koptische Grammatik* (Leipzig 1880), §479 end.
³ For ⲛⲟⲩⲡⲓⲥⲧⲓⲥ.
⁴ The last verse is clearly not part of the hymn, but a later scribal addition (see p. 9).

20 Truly, as for the tax-collector Matthew,
the tax-collector was taken to our Saviour,[1]
as a man is taken to his tax office,
and he was forgiven.

21 Take possession of faith,
O Thomas, the apostle,
when our Saviour shows you
the wounds of the nails which are in his hands.[2]

22 Hail James
and Thaddaeus, his brother,[3]
the two sons of Joseph
who became brothers of the Lord.[4]

23 Sing to our God, sing,
sing to our king, sing,[5]
O perfumed tongue,
Paul, the apostle.

24 Proclaim in faith,
O Simon of Cyrene,[6]
and Luke, the apostle,
and Mark, the evangelist.
Pray to the Lord.[7]

---

[1] Cf. perhaps Mt. 9.9.
[2] Cf. Jn. 20.25.
[3] Cf. Mt. 10.3; Mk. 3.18.
[4] Perhaps a confused reference to Mt. 13.55; Mk. 6.3.
[5] Ps. 46.7.
[6] Cf. Mt. 27.32; Mk. 15.21; Lk. 23.26.
[7] The last verse is clearly not part of the hymn, but a later scribal addition (see p. 9).

◄ HYMN TEN ►

(pp. р̄з̄ө-р̄о̄, line 29)

ī ετвεπ̄вапτιсма:-

1 апкосмос τηρϥ̄ моγз̄ ῑ̄раϣε μ̄πооγ·
   ετвετ̄бιнει μ̄πενс̄ω̄р̄·
   εζραι ε̄χμ̄пιορααннс·
   ε̄χιχωκμ̄ з̄ν̄νεμооγ⸗

2 вωϣ ε̄вол ν̄бιιωзаннс·
   εϥχω μ̄мосназр̄ν̄εμннϣε·
   χεπαιπε πεзιειв επноγτε·
   ν̄ταϥει αϥϥιπ̄ν̄овε μ̄π̄космос⸗

3 гεгар νενειоτε μ̄π̄рофнтнс·
   раϣε μ̄πооγ αγω̄ сετεληλ·
   χεᾱπενс̄ω̄р̄ νагаθос·
   ει αϥχεκνεγϣαχε ε̄вол⸗

4 ααγεια ωϣ ε̄вол εϥχω μ̄мос·
   χετεсмн μ̄π̄с̄ зιχν̄νεμαγ·
   апноγτε μ̄πεō̄оγ ωϣ ε̄вол·
   π̄с̄ зιχν̄зενμооγ ε̄ναϣωоγ⸗

106

━◄ HYMN TEN ►━

On Baptism

1   The whole world has been filled with rejoicing today
    because of the coming of our Saviour
    to the Jordan
    to be baptized in the waters.[1]

2   John proclaims,
    saying before the multitudes:
    This is the Lamb of God,
    which has come and has taken away the sin
            of the world.[2]

3   For our fathers, the prophets,
    rejoice today and are glad,
    for our good Saviour
    has come and has fulfilled their words.

4   David proclaims, saying:
    The voice of the Lord is upon the waters.
    The God of glory has cried out,
    the Lord is upon many waters.[3]

---

[1]   Cf. Mt. 3.13; Mk. 1.9.
[2]   Cf. Jn. 1.29.
[3]   Ps. 28.3.

5   εις πε϶ιειβ επνογτε ετον϶·
πενταϥει αϥϫιπνοβε μ̄πκοσμος·
εϥναϫακμεν τηρεν·
϶ν̄ογπ̄ν̄ᾱ εϥογᾱαβ μ̄νογμοογ⸗

6   ζωγραφι ναν επϫωκ επραϣε·
ω̄ πεπροφητης εκϫω μ̄μος·
ϫε϶ιτ̄νογκω϶τ̄ μ̄νογμοογ·
ακεντεν ε̄βολ εγμα νεμτον⸗

7   н̄σαιας πεπροφητης·
ϫετεσμη μ̄πετωϣ ε̄βολ ϶ῑπϫαιε·
ϫεс̄βτετε϶ιн̄ μ̄π̄ς̄·
ν̄τετ̄νσοογτ̄ν̄ ν̄νεϥ϶ιᾱοογε̄⸗

8   θεω̄ρι ον νнσαιας·
ϫεμαρεн̄ϫαιε̄ μ̄πιορλανнς·
ωϣ εβολ ϶ν̄ογτελнλ·
ϫεαγϯ ναγ ε̄πεᾱογ μ̄π̄λιβανος⸗

9   ιω϶αннης· ον· πεπροдромος·
παρακαλι μ̄πενсω̄р·
ϫεᾱνοκ ε̄τр̄х̄ριᾱ π̄ς̄·
ε̄ϫιϫωκ̄μ ϶ενεκбιϫ⸗

5   Behold, the Lamb of the living God,
    which has come and has taken away the sin
            of the world[1]
    will baptize us all
    with the Holy Spirit and water.[2]

6   Describe to us the fullness of joy,
    O prophet, by saying:
    Through fire and water
    you brought us into a place of rest.[3]

7   The prophet Isaiah says:
    The voice of him who cries in the wilderness,
    Prepare the way of the Lord
    and make straight his ways.[4]

8   Consider Isaiah again:
    Let the desert places of Jordan
    cry out in gladness,
    for the glory of Lebanon has been given to them.[5]

9   John, the forerunner, also
    beseeches our Saviour:
    I have need, Lord,
    to be baptized by your hands.[6]

---

[1]   Cf. Jn. 1.29.
[2]   Cf. Jn. 1.33.
[3]   Ps. 65.12.
[4]   Cf. Is. 40.3.
[5]   Cf. Is. 35.2.
[6]   Cf. Mt. 3.14.

10 ΚΑΛΩC ΑϥΧΟΟC Ñ6ΙΔΑᾹ·
ϨΜ̅ΠΕΨΑΛΤΗΡΙΟΝ ΕΤΤΑΙΗΥ·
ΧΕΘΑΛΑCCΑ ΝΑΥ ΑCΠΩΤ·
Ᾱ̅ΠΙΟΡΔΑΝΗC ΚΟΤϥ Ē̅ΠΑϨΟΥ≠

11 ΛΑΟC ΝΙΜ ΕΤϨΙΧΜ̅ΠΚΑϨ·
Ᾱ̅ΜΗΙΤΝ̅ Ē̅ΧΜ̅ΠΙΟΡΔΑΝΗC·
ΘΕΩ̅ΡΙ Μ̅ΠΕϨΙΕΙΒ ΕΠΝΟΥΤΕ·
ΕΡΕΙΩϨΑΝΝΗC ΒΑΠΤΙΖΕ Μ̅ΜΟϥ≠

12 ΜΑΡΕΝΑΜΠΗΥĒ ΟΥΝΟϥ·
Ν̅ΤΕΝΑΠΚΑϨ ΤΗΡϤ ΤΕΛΗΛ·
ϨΑΧΩϥ Ē̅ΝΜ̅ΜΑΝΟΥΗΛ·[1]
ΧΕΑϥΕΙ ΑϥΤΒΒΟ Ν̅ΝΕΜΟΟΥ≠

13 ΝΕΝΤΑΥΒΑΠΤΙΖΕ Ē̅ΠΕΧ̅C̅·
ΑΥϮΠΕΧ̅C̅ ϨΙΩ̅ΟΥ·
ΚΑΤΑΠΩϣΑΧΕ Μ̅ΠΑΥΛΟC·
ΦΙĒ̅ΡΟC ΝΑΠΟCΤΟΛΟΝ≠[2]

14 |ϨΥΜΑΝΕ[3] ΝΑΝ Ω̅ ΙΩϨΑΝΝΗC·
ΧΕΝΤΕΡΕΚΒΑΠΤΙΖΕ Μ̅ΠCΩ̅Ρ̅·
Ᾱ̅ΝΜ̅ΠΗΥĒ ΟΥΩΝ Ν̅ΤΕΥΝΟΥ·
ΑΠΕΠΝ̅Ᾱ̅ Ē̅ΤΟΥΑΑΒ ΕΙ Ē̅ΧΩϥ≠

---

¹ For ΝΕΜΜΑΝΟΥΗΛ.
² The reading ΝΑΠΟCΤΟΛΟΝ, rather than the expected
ΝΑΠΟCΤΟΛΟC, seems inescapable; see p. 152, n. ad loc.
³ Page ρ̅ο̅ begins.

10 David spoke well
    in the precious psalter:
    The sea saw, it fled;
    Jordan was turned back.[1]

11 All peoples on earth,
    come to the Jordan.
    Look at the Lamb of God
    as John baptizes him.[2]

12 Let those of heaven rejoice
    and those of the whole earth be glad[3]
    before Immanuel,
    for he has come and purified the waters.

13 Those who were baptized in Christ
    put on Christ,[4]
    according to the word of Paul,
    the apostolic priest.

14 You tell us, O John,
    that, when you had baptized the Saviour,
    at once the heavens opened
    and the Holy Spirit came upon him.[5]

---

[1] Ps. 113.3.
[2] Cf. Jn. 1.29–36.
[3] Cf. Ps. 95.11.
[4] Cf. Gal. 3.27.
[5] Cf. Mt. 3.16; Mk. 1.10; Lk. 3.21–2.

15 ογνοϭ ⲙ̄ⲙⲩⲥⲧⲏⲣⲓⲟⲛⲡⲉ·
ⲡⲉⲓϩⲱⲃ ⲉ̄ⲧⲟ ⲛ̄ϣⲡⲏⲣⲉ·
ϫⲉⲁⲩϩⲙ̄ϩⲁⲗ ⲙ̄ⲡ̄ϣⲁ·
ⲁϥⲃⲁⲡⲧⲓⵂⲉ ⲙ̄ⲡⲉϥϫⲟⲉⲓⲥ⳺

16 ⲡⲁⲓ ⲡⲉⲛⲧⲁⲧⲉⲥⲙⲏ ⲙ̄ⲡⲉϥⲉⲓⲱⲧ·
ⲉⲓ ⲉ̄ϫⲱϥ ϩⲓϫⲙ̄ⲡⲓⲟⲣⲇⲁⲁⲛⲏⲥ·
ϫⲉⲡⲁⲓⲡⲉ ⲡⲁϣⲏⲣⲉ ⲙ̄ⲙⲉⲣⲓⲧ·
ⲡⲉⲛⲧⲁⲡⲁⲟⲩⲱϣ ϣⲱⲡⲉ ϩⲓϫⲱϥ⳺

17 ⲣⲱⲙⲉ ⲛⲓⲙ ⲉⲧϩⲓϫⲙ̄ⲡⲕⲁϩ·
ⲉⲩⲡⲓⲥⲧⲉⲩⲉ ⲉⲡⲉⲭ̄ⲥ̄·
ⲛ̄ⲥⲉϫⲓⲡ̄ⲃⲁⲡⲧⲓⲥⲙⲁ ⲙ̄ⲡⲉϥⲣⲁⲛ·
ϣⲁⲓⲕⲁⲛⲉϥⲛⲟⲃⲉ ⲛⲁϥ ⲉⲃⲟⲗ⳺

18 ⲥⲱⲧⲙ̄ ⲉ̄ⲡⲁⲩⲗⲟⲥ ϫⲉⲁϥⲧⲟⲩϫⲟⲛ·
ϩⲓⲧⲙ̄ⲡ̄ϫⲱⲕⲙ̄ ⲙ̄ⲡⲉϫⲡⲟ ⲛ̄ⲕⲉⲥⲟⲡ·
ⲙⲛ̄ⲧⲙⲛⲧⲃ̄ⲣⲣⲉ ⲙ̄ⲡⲉⲡⲛ̄ⲁ̄·
ⲡⲁⲓ ⲛ̄ⲧⲁϥⲡⲁϩⲧϥ̄ ⲉϩⲣⲁⲓ ⲉϫⲱⲛ⳺

19 ϯⲛⲁⲉⲣⲡⲉⲕⲙⲉⲉⲩⲉ̄ ⲡϭ̄ⲥ̄·
ⲉⲓϩⲙ̄ⲡ̄ⲕⲁϩ ⲙ̄ⲡⲓⲟⲣⲇⲁⲁⲛⲏⲥ·
ⲕ̄ⲛⲁϫⲟⲕⲙⲉⲧ ⲉ̄ⲃⲟⲗ ⲛ̄ϩⲏⲧϥ·
ϯⲛⲁⲟⲩⲃⲁϣ ⲉ̄ϩⲟⲩⲉ̄ⲟⲩⲭⲓⲱⲛ⳺

15   It is a great mystery,
        this marvellous thing,
        that a servant was worthy
        to baptize his lord.

16   This is he to whom the voice of his Father
        came by the Jordan:
        This is my beloved Son,
        on whom my good pleasure has come.[1]

17   All men upon earth,
        who believe in Christ
        and are baptized in his name,
        to them I shall forgive their sins.

18   Listen to Paul: He saved us
        through the baptism of rebirth
        and the renewing of the Spirit,
        which he poured upon us.[2]

19   I shall remember you, Lord,
        while I am in the land of the Jordan.[3]
        You will wash me therewith,
        I shall be whiter than snow.[4]

---

[1] Mt. 3.17.
[2] Titus 3.5–6.
[3] Ps. 41.7.
[4] Ps. 50.9.

20 ϩγΜΝΕγΕ ΕΤΠΗ ΜΝΝΕΤΝϩΗΤϹ·
ΜΑΡΕΠΚΑϩ ΤΗΡϥ ΟγΝΟϥ·
ΜΑΡΕΠΙΟΡΔΑΝΗϹ ΤΕΛΗΛ ΕΜΑϥ·[1]
ϪΕΑΠϢΗΡΕ ΜΠΝΟγΤΕ ϪΩΚΜ ΝϩΗΤϥ⸗

21 ΦΙΛΙΠΠΟϹ ΠΑΠΟϹΤΟΛΟϹ·
ΡΑϢΕ ΜΠΟΟγ ΑγΩ ϥΤΕΛΗΛ·
ϪΕΑϥΒΑΠΤΙΖΕ ΜΠΕϹΙΟγΡ·
ϩΜΠΡΑΝ ΝΤΕΤΡΙΑϹ ΕΤΟγΑΑΒ⸗

22 ΧΑΙΡΕ ΠΙΟΡΔΑΝΗϹ·
ΠΙΕΡΟ ΕΤϩΑΤΕ ΝΟγΟΕΙΝ·
ϩΝϩΕΝΚΡΙΝΟΝ ΝϹϯΝΟγΒΕ·
ΝΤΑΠΕΝϹΩΡ ϪΙϪΩΚΕΜ ΝϩΗΤΟγ⸗

23 ΨΩΤΗΡ ΩϢ ΕΒΟΛ ΕΟγΟΝ ΝΙΜ·
ϪΕΠΕΤΝΑΠΙϹΤΕγΕ ΕΡΟΙ·
ΝϥϪΙΠΒΑΠΤΙϹΜΑ ΜΠΟγϪΑΙ·
ϯΝΑΚΕΝΕγΝΟΒΕ ΝΑγ ΕΒΟΛ⸗

24 Ω ΝΛΑΟϹ ΤΗΡΟγ ΜΠΚΟϹΜΟϹ·
ΜΑΡΕΝϯΕΟΟγ ΕΠΝΟγΤΕ·
ϪΕΑϥΚΑΤΕΝ ΕΤΕΝΑΡΧΗ·
ϩΙΤΜΠϪΩΚΜ ΜΠΕϪΠΟ ΝΚΕϹΟΠ:-

---

[1] For ΜΜΟϥ.

20 Sing to the heaven and those therein.
    Let the whole earth rejoice.
    Let the Jordan be glad,
    for the Son of God was baptized in it.

21 The apostle Philip
    rejoices today and is glad,
    for he baptized the eunuch[1]
    in the name of the Holy Trinity.

22 Hail Jordan,
    the river that flows with light,
    with scented lilies
    among which our Saviour was baptized.

23 The Saviour proclaims to everyone:
    He who shall believe in me
    and shall receive the baptism of salvation,
    to him I shall forgive his sins.[2]

24 O all the peoples of the world,
    let us glorify God,
    for he turned us to our beginning
    through the baptism of rebirth.[3]

---

[1] Cf. Acts 8.38.
[2] Cf. Mk. 16.16.
[3] Cf. Titus 3.5.

◄ HYMN ELEVEN ►

(pp. ρō, line 30 – ρōв, line 24)

ιᾱ   ετвεππατριαρχηс сεγηρος:-

1   απб̄с ω̄ρ̄κ̄ ν̄ϥναρ̄ϩτηϥ αν·
χεντοκπε πογ̄ηηв ν̄ϣαενεϩ·
καταττα϶ιс μμελχιсελεκ·
ω̄ π̄πατριαρχηс сεγηρος⸗

2   вωϣ ε̄вολ ν̄б̄ιπсω̄ρ̄·
εϥχω μμος ε̄πενιωτ πετρος·
χεαι† ν̄τε϶ογсιᾱ νακ·
εμογρ εвωλ ϩιχμ̄π̄καϩ⸗

3   γεκαρ †ε϶ογсια νογωτ·
απνογτε χαρι϶ε |μμος[1] νακ·
ω̄ π̄πατριαρχηс сεγηρος·
μ̄νογον νιμ ε̄τινε μμοκ⸗

4   αλ̄λ̄ π̄ρρο ωϣ εвολ·
χεαιχιсε νογсωτπ̄ ϩμ̄παλλος·
αιбινε ναλ̄λ̄ παϩμ̄ϩαλ·
αιτωϩб̄ <μμοϥ> μπανεϩ ε̄τογλ̄λ̄в⸗

---

[1]   Page ρōλ begins.

116

◄ HYMN ELEVEN ►

On the Patriarch Severus

1   The Lord has sworn and will not repent:
You are a priest for ever
after the order of Melchizedek,[1]
O Patriarch Severus.

2   The Saviour proclaims,
saying to our father Peter:
I have given you authority
to bind and to loose upon earth.[2]

3   For this same authority
God granted to you,
O Patriarch Severus,
and to everyone who is like you.

4   King David proclaims:
I have exalted one chosen out of my people.
I have found David, my servant.
I have anointed him with my holy oil.[3]

---

[1]   Ps. 109.4.
[2]   Cf. Mt. 18.18.
[3]   Ps. 88.20–1.

5 ⲉϥⲉⲣⲙⲛ̄ⲧⲣⲉ ⲟⲛ ⲉϥϫⲱ ⲙ̄ⲙⲟⲥ·
   ϫⲉⲧⲁϭⲓϫ ⲧⲉⲧⲛⲁϯ ⲛ̄ⲧⲟⲟⲧϥ·
   ⲁⲩⲱ ⲡⲁⲃⲟⲓ ⲛⲁϯϭⲟⲙ ⲛⲁϥ·
   ⲙ̄ⲡ̄ϫⲁϫⲉ ⲛⲁϭⲉⲛ2ⲏⲩ ⲛ̄2ⲏⲧϥ̄ ⲁⲛ⳾

6 ⲍⲱⲅⲣⲁⲫⲓ ⲛⲁⲛ ⲉ̄ⲡⲉⲕⲃⲓⲟⲥ ⲉ̄ⲧⲟⲩⲁⲁⲃ·
   ⲱ̄ ⲡ̄ⲛⲟϭ ⲛ̄ⲇⲓⲇⲁⲥⲕⲁⲗⲱⲥ·
   ⲧⲁⲣⲉⲛⲙⲉⲗⲉⲧⲁ 2ⲛ̄ⲟⲩⲥⲟⲟⲩⲧⲛ̄·
   2ⲛ̄ⲛⲉⲕⲗⲟⲅⲟⲥ ⲉⲧⲧⲁⲓⲏⲩ⳾

7 ⲏ̄ⲗⲓⲁⲥ ⲡⲓⲣⲉϥⲕⲱ2 ⲉⲡⲛⲟⲩⲧⲉ·
   ⲁⲕϣⲱⲡⲉ ⲉⲕⲧⲛ̄ⲧⲱⲛ ⲉ̄ⲣⲟϥ·
   2ⲛ̄ⲛⲉⲕⲇⲟⲅⲙⲁ ⲉⲧⲥⲟⲩⲧⲱⲛ·
   ⲉⲕϣⲟⲣϣⲣ̄ ⲉ̄ⲛⲉ2ⲣⲉϯⲕⲟⲥ⳾

8 ⲑⲟⲙⲟⲗⲟⲅⲓⲁ̄ ⲙ̄ⲡⲉⲭ̄ⲥ̄·
   ⲙ̄ⲛⲧⲉϥⲡⲓⲥⲧⲓⲥ ⲉⲧⲥⲟⲩⲧⲱⲛ·
   ⲁⲕⲧ̄ⲥⲁⲃⲉⲟⲩⲟⲛ ⲛⲓⲙ ⲉ̄ⲣⲟⲟⲩ·
   2ⲓⲧⲛ̄ⲛⲉⲕⲗⲟⲅⲟⲥ ⲉⲕⲧⲁⲩⲟ̄ ⲙ̄ⲙⲟⲟⲩ⳾

9 ⲓ̄ⲥ̄ ⲡⲉⲛⲧⲁϥⲥⲱⲧⲡ̄ ⲙ̄ⲙⲟⲕ·
   ⲱ̄ ⲡ̄ⲡⲁⲧⲣⲓⲁⲣⲭⲏⲥ ⲥⲉⲩⲏⲣⲟⲥ·
   ⲛⲟⲩϣⲱⲥ 2ⲓϫⲙ̄ⲡⲉⲕⲗⲁⲟⲥ·
   ⲉⲧⲣⲉⲕⲙⲟⲟ̄ⲛⲉ ⲛ̄ⲛⲉϥⲉ̄ⲥⲟⲟⲩ⳾

5   Again he testifies, saying:
My hand shall help him,
and my arm shall strengthen him.
The enemy shall not have advantage over him.[1]

6   Describe to us your holy life,
O great teacher,
that we may meditate rightly
on your precious words.

7   Elijah, the zealot of God—
you were like him
in your right beliefs,
overturning the heretics.[2]

8   The confession of Christ
and his right faith
you taught to everyone
by your words which you preached.

9   Jesus chose you,
O Patriarch Severus,
a shepherd over your people,
to feed his sheep.

---

[1]   Ps. 88.22–3.
[2]   Cf. e.g. III Kg. 18.

10 ⲕⲁⲓⲅⲁⲣ ⲁⲡϬⲥ ϫⲟⲟⲥ ⲉ̄ⲡⲉⲧⲣⲟⲥ·
ϫⲉⲕⲙⲉ ⲙ̄ⲙⲟⲓ ⲡⲉϫⲁϥ ϫⲉⲥⲉ·
ⲡⲉϫⲉⲡϬⲥ ⲛⲁϥ ϩⲛ̄ⲟⲩⲣⲁϣⲉ·
ϫⲉⲙⲟⲟⲛⲉ ⲛ̄ⲛⲁϩⲓⲉⲓⲃ ⲙⲛ̄ⲛⲁⲉ̄ⲥⲟⲟⲩ⸗

11 ⲗⲟⲅⲟⲥ ⲛⲓⲙ ⲉⲕⲧⲁⲟⲩⲟ̄ ⲙ̄ⲙⲟⲟⲩ·
ⲱ̄ ⲡⲥⲁϩ ⲉⲧⲙⲉⲧⲉⲩⲥⲉⲃⲏⲥ·
ⲕ̄ϣⲁϫⲉ ⲛ̄ϩⲏⲧⲟⲩ ⲉⲧⲃⲉⲡϩⲏⲩ·
ⲁⲩⲱ̄ ⲡ̄ⲧⲱⲃⲉⲥ ⲛ̄ⲛⲉⲙⲯⲩⲭⲏ⸗

12 ⲙⲱⲩⲥⲏⲥ ⲡ̄ⲛⲟϬ ⲙ̄ⲡ̄ⲣⲟⲫⲏⲧⲏⲥ·
ⲁⲕϣⲱⲡⲉ ⲉⲕⲧⲛ̄ⲧⲱⲛ ⲉ̄ⲣⲟϥ·
ϫⲉⲁⲕⲥ̄ⲙⲉⲛⲛⲟⲙⲟⲥ ⲉ̄ⲡⲉⲕⲗⲁⲟⲥ·
ⲉⲧⲇⲓⲕⲁⲓⲟ̄ⲥⲩⲛⲏ· ⲙⲉϯⲣⲏⲛⲏ⸗

13 ⲛⲉⲥⲁϩ ⲧⲏⲣⲟⲩ ⲛ̄ⲧⲉⲕⲕⲗⲏⲥⲓⲁ̄·
ⲥⲉⲣ̄ϣ̄ⲡⲏⲣⲉ ⲙ̄ⲡ̄ⲥⲁ ⲛ̄ⲛⲉⲕⲗⲉϫⲓⲥ·
ⲉⲕⲧⲁⲩⲟ̄ ⲙ̄ⲙⲟⲟⲩ ϩⲓⲧⲙ̄ⲡⲉⲡⲛ̄ⲁ̄·
ⲉⲧϣⲁϫⲉ ϩⲛ̄ⲧⲉⲕⲧⲁⲡⲣⲟ⸗

14 ϫⲱⲕ ϣⲁⲣⲟⲕ ⲛⲟⲩⲟⲛ ⲛⲓⲙ·
ⲱ̄ ⲡⲡⲁⲧⲣⲓⲁⲣⲭⲏⲥ ⲥⲉⲩⲏⲣⲟⲥ·
ϩⲓⲧⲙ̄ⲡⲉϩⲗⲟϬ ⲉⲛⲉⲕϣⲁϫⲉ ⲉ̄ⲧⲟⲩⲁⲁⲃ·
ⲁⲩⲱ ⲛⲉⲕⲥ̄ⲃⲟⲟⲩⲉ̄ ⲛⲱⲛϩ⸗

10 For the Lord said to Peter:
    Do you love me? He said: Yes.
    The Lord said to him joyfully:
    Feed my lambs and my sheep.[1]

11 All the words which you preach,
    O teacher of godliness,
    you speak therewith for the benefit
    and the admonition of our souls.

12 Moses, the great prophet—
    you were like him,
    for you laid down laws for your people
    for righteousness and peace.

13 All the teachers of the Church
    marvel at the beauty of your language
    which you utter through the Spirit
    which speaks with your mouth.

14 You draw everyone to you,
    O Patriarch Severus,
    by the sweetness of your holy words
    and your teachings of life.

---

[1] Cf. Jn. 21.15–17.

15 ογνοбπε πταιō μπεισαϩ·
ογνοбπε πταιō μπειϣως·
ογνοбπε πταιō μπειρωμε·
ετφορει μπνογτε ϩνογμε⸗

16 |πεισαϩ¹ ναποστολικος·
πεισαϩ ⲛⲇογματικος·
πειφωстηρ ναληθινον·
ēⲧρογōⲉⲓⲛ ētоικογμενη⸗

17 ρωμε ⲛⲓⲙ ετϩιⲭⲙⲡκαϩ·
εγϣανμελετα ϩνογсоογⲧⲛ·
ϩⲛⲛεⲕⲗогос εⲕταγō μμоογ·
ϣαγογⲭⲁⲓ ēⲃоⲗ ϩⲓⲧооⲧⲕ⸗

18 соογⲛ ⲛⲓⲙ ⲛⲧετεгραφη·
ⲁ̄ⲡⲉⲭ̄ⲥ̄ ⲉⲣογōⲉⲓⲛ ēⲣоⲕ·
ⲁⲕⲉⲓⲙⲉ ēⲛⲉγϩⲉⲣⲙⲏⲛⲓⲁ·
ⲁⲕⲭⲱ ēⲣоог ēⲡⲉγⲃⲱⲗ⸗

19 ⲧотⲉ ⲡⲉⲭⲁϥ ⲛ̄бⲓⲡⲉⲡⲣоφⲏⲧⲏⲥ·
ⲭⲉⲛⲧоⲕ ⲡⲉⲛⲧⲁⲕ̄ⲡⲗⲁⲥⲥⲉ ⲙ̄ⲙоⲓ·
ⲁⲕⲕⲁⲧⲉⲕбⲓⲭ ⲉϩⲣⲁⲓ ē̄ⲭⲱⲓ·
ⲁγⲉⲣϣ̄ⲡⲏⲣⲉ ⲙ̄ⲡⲉⲕⲥоогⲛ̄ ē̄ϩⲏⲧ⸗

---

¹ Page ⲣ̄ⲟ̄ⲃ̄ begins.

15 Great is the honour of this teacher,
    great is the honour of this shepherd,
    great is the honour of this man
    who truly bears God.

16 This apostolic teacher,
    this teacher of doctrine,
    this true luminary
    who gives light to the world.

17 All people upon earth,
    if they meditate rightly
    on your words, which you preach,
    shall be saved by you.

18 All knowledge of the scriptures
    Christ has illumined for you.
    You have known their interpretations,
    you have told them their exposition.

19 Then the prophet said:
    You formed me,
    you laid your hand upon me,
    they marvelled at the knowledge of you in me.[1]

---

[1] Cf. Ps. 138.5–6.

20 ⲨⲖⲎⲔⲒⲀ̄ ⲚⲒⲘ Ⲛ̄ⲢⲰⲘⲈ·
Ⲛ̄ⲒⲀ̄ⲖⲞ ⲘⲚ̄Ⲛ̄ϢⲎⲢⲈ ϢⲎⲘ·
Ⲕ̄ⲦⲤ̄ⲂⲰ ⲚⲀⲨ Ⲏ̄Ⲛ̄ⲚⲈⲄⲢⲀⲪⲎ·
ⲘⲚ̄Ⲡ̄ⲦⲀϢⲈⲞ̄ⲈⲒϢ Ⲛ̄ⲚⲈⲨⲀⲄⲄⲈⲖⲒⲞⲚ⳾

21 ⲪⲎ Ⲃ̄Ⲥ̄ Ⲉ̄Ⲧ̄ⲢⲞⲨⲞⲈⲒⲚ·[1]
ⲠⲈ Ⲡ̄ⲠⲀⲦⲢⲒⲀⲢⲬⲎⲤ ⲤⲈⲨⲎ̄ⲢⲞⲤ·
ⲔⲀⲦⲀⲦⲈⲪⲰⲚⲎ Ⲙ̄Ⲡ̄Ⲥ̄Ⲱ̄Ⲣ̄·
ϪⲈⲚⲦⲰⲦⲚ̄ⲠⲈ ⲠⲞⲨⲞ̄ⲈⲒⲚ Ⲙ̄Ⲡ̄ⲔⲞⲤⲘⲞⲤ⳾

22 ⲬⲀⲒⲢⲈ ⲤⲈⲨⲎ̄ⲢⲞⲤ Ⲡ̄ⲠⲀⲦⲢⲒⲀⲢⲬⲎⲤ·
ⲬⲈⲢⲈ Ⲡ̄ⲚⲞϬ ⲚⲤⲞⲪⲞⲤ·
ⲬⲈⲢⲈ Ⲡ̄ⲢⲈϤⲘⲒϢⲈ Ⲉ̄ϪⲚ̄Ⲧ̄ⲠⲒⲤⲦⲒⲤ·
Ⲛ̄ⲦⲈⲦⲢⲒⲀⲤ ⲈⲦϪⲎⲔ Ⲉ̄ⲂⲞⲖ⳾

23 ⲮⲰⲦⲎⲢ ⲰϢ Ⲉ̄ⲂⲞⲖ Ⲉ̄ⲢⲞⲔ·
ⲘⲚ̄ⲞⲨⲞⲚ ⲚⲒⲘ Ⲉ̄ⲦⲒⲚⲈ Ⲙ̄ⲘⲞⲔ·
ϪⲈⲔⲀⲖⲰⲤ Ⲡ̄Ⲏ̄ⲘϨⲀⲖ ⲈⲦⲚⲀⲚⲞⲨϤ Ⲙ̄ⲠⲒⲤⲦⲞⲤ·
ⲂⲰⲔ Ⲉ̄ϨⲞⲨⲚ̄ ⲈⲠⲢⲀϢⲈ Ⲙ̄ⲠⲈⲔϬ̄Ⲥ̄⳾

24 Ⲱ Ⲡ̄ⲠⲀⲦⲢⲒⲀⲢⲬⲎⲤ ⲤⲈⲨⲎ̄ⲢⲞⲤ·
Ⲡ̄ϢⲞⲨϢⲞⲨ Ⲛ̄ⲚⲞⲢⲐⲞⲆⲞⲜⲞⲤ ⲦⲎⲢⲞⲨ·
ⲠⲀⲢⲀⲔⲀⲖⲒ Ⲙ̄Ⲡ̄Ϭ̄Ⲥ̄ ⲈϨⲢⲀⲒ ⲈϪⲰⲚ·
Ⲛ̄ϤⲔⲀⲚⲈⲚⲚⲞⲂⲈ ⲚⲀⲚ ⲈⲂⲞⲖ:-

---

[1] Note the unusual division before the copula, as also in VIII,16/3, IX,15/2, and XII,15/2.

20   All ages of man,
     old men and small children,
     you teach in the scriptures
     and the preaching of the gospels.

21   The lamp that shines
     is the Patriarch Severus
     according to the voice of the Saviour:
     You are the light of the world.[1]

22   Hail, Patriarch Severus,
     hail, great wise man,
     hail, fighter for the faith
     of the perfect Trinity.

23   The Saviour proclaims to you
     and to everyone who is like you:
     Well done, good and faithful servant,
     enter into the joy of your lord.[2]

24   O Patriarch Severus,
     the pride of all the orthodox,
     beseech the Lord for us
     to forgive us our sins.

---

[1]   Mt. 5.14.
[2]   Cf. Mt. 25.21, 23.

◄ HYMN TWELVE ►

(pp. P̄O̅B̅, line 25 – P̄O̅Δ̅, line 19)

I̅B̅   ετвεαπα αντωνιος:-

1   απεϲϯноγвε ñнεκᾱρετн·
     ϯоγрот εнεнψγхн·
     ω̄ πεнιωτ αντωνιοс·
     ноε μπεϲτοι μπϣнн μπωнζ⸗

2   вωϣ ε̄вол ñбιπϲω̄ρ·
     χεπετоγεϣερμαθнтнϲ ναι·
     μαρεϥαрна μμоϥ μμιн μμоϥ·
     ñϥϥι μπεϥϲ̄ϯо̄ϲ ñϥоγαζϥ ñϲωι⸗

3   гεκαρ πεнιωτ αντωνιос·
     αϥταλο μπεϥϲ̄ϯο̄ϲ ζιχωϥ·
     μñоγоν нιμ ε̄τιнε μμоϥ·
     αγоγᾱζоγ ñϲαπχоειϲ ῑϲ̄⸗

4 |αᾱᾱ¹ ωϣ ε̄вол εϥχω μμоϲ·
     χεᾱκαμαζτε ñταбιх нoγнαμ·
     ακχιмоειτ ζнт ζμπεκϣαχε·²
     ακϣοπⲧ̄ ε̄ρоκ ζñоγε̄ооγ⸗

---

¹   Page P̄O̅Γ̅ begins.
²   The Sahidic version of Psalm 72.24 reads ζμπεκϣоχнε,
following the Septuagint. It is impossible to say whether the reading in this hymn is due to a scribal error or is a conscious
adaptation.

◄ HYMN TWELVE ►

On Apa Antony

1   The perfume of your virtues
     has gladdened our souls,
     O our father Antony,
     as the scent of the tree of life.

2   The Saviour proclaims:
     He who wishes to be my disciple,
     let him deny himself
     and take up his cross and follow me.[1]

3   For our father Antony
     laid his cross upon himself,
     and so did everyone who is like him,
     and they followed the Lord Jesus.

4   David proclaims, saying:
     You have grasped my right hand.
     You have guided me by your word.[2]
     You have received me in glory.[3]

---

[1]   Cf. Mt. 16.24; Mk. 8.34; Lk. 9.23.
[2]   The Sahidic version of Ps. 72.24, following the Septuagint, reads 'counsel', rather than 'word'.
[3]   Cf. Ps. 72.23-4.

5 ⲉϥⲣ̅ⲙⲛ̅ⲧⲣⲉ ⲟⲛ ⲉϥϫⲱ ⲙ̅ⲙⲟⲥ·
    ϫⲉⲡⲉⲕⲟⲩⲟⲉⲓⲛ ⲙⲛ̅ⲧⲉⲕⲙⲉ·
    ⲛ̅ⲧⲟⲟⲩ ⲛⲉⲛⲧⲁⲩϫⲓⲙⲟⲉⲓⲧ ϩⲏⲧ·
    ⲁⲅⲉⲛⲧ̅ ⲉ̄ϫⲉⲙⲡⲉⲕⲧⲟⲟⲩ ⲉ̄ⲧⲟⲩⲁ̄ⲁⲃ⸗

6 ⲍⲩⲛⲏⲇⲏⲥⲓⲥ ⲛⲓⲙ ⲉⲧⲛⲁⲛⲟⲩⲟⲩ·
    ⲁⲕϣⲱⲡⲉ ⲛ̅ϩⲏⲧⲟⲩ ϩ̄ⲛⲟⲩⲧⲃ̄ⲃⲟ·
    ⲉⲕⲧⲱϩ̄ⲙ ⲉ̄ⲟⲩⲟⲛ ⲛⲓⲙ·
    ⲉ̄ϩⲟⲩⲛ̄ ⲉⲡⲃⲓⲟⲥ ⲛ̅ⲧⲙⲛ̅ⲧ̄ⲙⲟⲛⲁⲭⲟⲥ⸗

7 ⲏ̅ⲥⲁⲓⲁⲥ ⲡⲉⲡⲣⲟⲫⲏⲧⲏⲥ·
    ϫⲉⲛⲉⲧϩⲩⲡⲟⲙⲓⲛⲉ ⲉ̄ⲡϭ̅ⲥ̅·
    ⲥⲉⲛⲁϣⲓⲃⲉ ϩ̄ⲛ̅ⲧⲉⲩϭⲟⲙ·
    ⲥⲉⲛⲁⲣⲉⲧⲧⲏⲛⲁϩ ⲛ̄ⲑⲉ ⲛ̄ⲛⲓⲁ̄ϩⲱⲙ⸗

8 ⲑⲟⲧⲉ ⲛⲉⲛⲇⲉⲙⲱⲛⲓⲟⲛ·[1]
    ⲙⲛ̅ⲛⲉⲩⲫⲁⲛⲧⲁⲥⲓⲁ̄ ⲉ̄ⲧⲟϣ·
    ⲉⲩⲙⲓϣⲉ ⲛⲟⲩⲟ̄ⲉⲓϣ ⲛⲓⲙ·
    ⲙⲛ̅ⲛⲉⲛⲓⲟ̄ⲧⲉ ϩⲓⲡ̅ϫⲁⲓⲉ̄⸗

9 ⲓ̅ⲥ̅ ⲕⲁⲧⲁⲣⲅⲓ ⲙ̅ⲙⲟⲟⲩ·
    ⲉϥϯϭⲟⲙ ⲉ̄ⲛⲉϥⲡⲉⲧⲟⲩⲁⲁⲃ·
    ϩⲓⲧⲙ̅ⲡ̄ϥⲓ ⲉϩⲣⲁⲓ ⲛ̄ⲛⲉⲩϭⲓϫ·
    ⲉⲩⲥⲟⲡⲥ̅ ⲉ̄ⲧⲉϥⲙⲛⲧⲁⲅⲁⲑⲟⲥ⸗

---

[1] For ⲛⲛⲁⲉⲙⲱⲛⲓⲟⲛ.

5   Again he testifies, saying:
    Your light and your truth,
    they have guided me.
    They brought me upon your holy mountain.[1]

6   With clear conscience
    you have dwelt in purity,
    summoning everyone
    to the monastic life.

7   The prophet Isaiah says:
    They who wait upon the Lord
    shall renew their strength;
    they shall grow wings like eagles.[2]

8   The fearsomeness of demons
    and their many delusions
    always war
    with our fathers in the desert.

9   Jesus brings them to naught,
    giving strength to his saints,
    through the lifting up of their hands,
    as they pray to his goodness.

---

[1]   Cf. Ps. 42.3.
[2]   Is. 40.31.

10   ⲕⲁⲧⲁⲡϣⲁϫⲉ ⲙ̄ⲡⲉⲛⲥⲱ̄ⲣ·
     ϫⲉⲁⲓ† ⲛ̄ⲧⲉϫⲟⲩⲥⲓⲁ̄ ⲛⲏⲧⲛ̄·
     ⲉ̄ϩⲱⲙ ⲉ̄ϫⲛ̄ⲛ̄ϩⲟϥ ⲙⲛ̄ⲛⲟⲩⲟⲟϩⲉ·
     ⲁⲩⲱ̄ ⲉ̄ϫⲛ̄ⲧϭⲟⲙ ⲧⲏⲣⲥ̄ ⲉⲡϫⲁϫⲉ⳾

11   ⲗⲟⲓⲡⲟⲛ ⲁ̄ⲡⲉⲧⲥⲏϩ ϫⲱⲕ ⲉ̄ⲃⲟⲗ ⲉ̄ϫⲱⲟⲩ·
     ϫⲉⲛⲉⲧ<ⲧ>ⲑⲗⲓⲃⲉ ⲙ̄ⲙⲟⲓ ⲙⲛ̄ⲛⲁϫⲁϫⲉ·
     ⲛ̄ⲧⲟⲟⲩ ⲁⲩϭⲃⲃⲉ ⲁⲩⲱ̄ ⲁⲩϩⲉ·
     ⲁ̄ⲛⲟⲛ ⲁⲛⲧⲱⲟⲩⲛ ⲁⲩⲱ ⲁⲛⲥⲟⲟⲩⲧⲛ̄⳾[1]

12   ⲙⲁⲣⲉⲛⲧⲁϫⲣⲉⲡⲉⲛϩⲏⲧ ϩⲛ̄ⲧ̄ⲡⲓⲥⲧⲓⲥ·
     ⲉⲧⲥⲟⲩⲧⲱⲛ ⲛ̄ⲧⲉⲛⲉⲛⲉⲓⲟ̄ⲧⲉ·
     ⲁ̄ⲛⲟⲛ ⲛⲉϣⲏⲣⲉ ⲛ̄ⲛⲉⲡⲓⲥⲧⲟⲥ·
     ϫⲉⲕⲁⲥ ⲉⲛⲛⲁⲙⲁⲧⲉ ⲙ̄ⲡⲉⲩⲕⲗⲏⲣⲟⲥ⳾

13   ⲛⲉⲛⲉⲓⲟⲧⲉ ⲙ̄ⲡⲛ̄ⲁ̄ⲧⲟⲫⲟⲣⲟⲥ·
     ⲁⲩϣⲱⲡⲉ ⲛⲁⲛ ⲛ̄ϫⲁⲩⲙⲟⲉⲓⲧ·
     ⲉ̄ⲁⲩⲕⲱϩ ⲛⲁⲛ ⲉ̄ⲧⲉϩⲓⲏ·
     ⲉⲧⲣⲉⲛⲃⲱⲕ ϣⲁⲡ̄ⲛⲟⲩⲧⲉ ⲛ̄ϩⲏⲧⲥ̄⳾

14   ϫⲱⲕ ϣⲁⲣⲟⲕ ⲉ̄ⲟⲩⲟⲛ ⲛⲓⲙ·
     ⲱ ⲡⲉⲛⲓⲱⲧ ⲁⲛⲧⲱⲛⲓⲟⲥ·
     ϩⲓⲧⲙ̄ⲡⲉⲕⲃⲓⲟⲥ ⲉⲧⲥⲟⲧⲡ̄·
     ⲙⲛ̄ⲛⲉⲕⲁ̄ⲣⲉⲧⲏ ⲉⲧⲧⲁⲓⲏⲩ⳾

---

[1] Note that the last three verses of the stanza contain a conflated quotation from Ps. 26.2 and Ps. 19.9. This may have arisen because the quotation from Ps. 26.2 ends in ⲁⲩⲱ ⲁⲩϩⲉ, and the line preceding the quotation from Ps. 19.9 has the same ending.

10   According to the word of our Saviour:
I have given you authority
to tread upon serpents and scorpions,
and over all the power of the enemy.[1]

11   Then that which is written was fulfilled upon them:
My oppressors and my enemies
grew feeble and fell,[2]
but we have risen and have stood upright.[3]

12   Let us strengthen our hearts
in the right faith of our fathers.
We are the children of the faithful
that we may obtain their lot.

13   Our spirit-bearing fathers
became our guides,
and smoothed the way for us
that we should walk in it to God.

14   You draw everyone to you,
O our father Antony,
by your choice life
and your precious virtues.

---

[1] Lk. 10.19.
[2] Ps. 26.2.
[3] Ps. 19.9.

15 ογΝΟ6 ΜΜΑΤΕ ᾱΛΗΘΩΣ·[1]
    ΠΕ ΠΤΑΙō ΝΝΕΙΡΩΜΕ ĒΤΟΥᾱᾱΒ·
    ΝΤΑΥΚΩ ΝΣΩΟΥ ΜΠΕΙΚΟΣΜΟΣ·
    ΑΥΟΥᾱ2ΟΥ ΝΣΑΠ6̄Σ ῙΣ̄⸗

16 ΠΕΝΕΙΩΤ ĒΤΟΥΑᾱΒ ΑΝΤΩΝΙΟΣ·
    ĒΡΕΠΕϥΟΥΩϣ ϢΟΟΠ 2Α2ΤΜΠΝΟΥΤΕ·
    ΑΥΩ ΕϥΜΕΕΥĒ ĒΝΑΤΠΕ·
    ΠΜΑ ĒΡΕΠΕΧ̄Σ̄ Ν2ΗΤϥ⸗

17 Ι ΡΩΜΕ[2] ΝΙΜ ΕΤ2ΙΧΜΠΚΑ2·
    ΕΥϢΑΝΣΩΤΜ ΕΠΒΙΟΣ ĒΝΕΝΕΙΟΤΕ·
    ϢΑΥΡϢΠΗΡΕ ΝΝΕΥᾱΡΕΤΗ·
    ΜΝΝΕΥΠΟΛΗΤΙᾱ ΕΤΧΟΣΕ⸗

18 ΣΩΤΜ ΕΠ2ΙĒΡΟΣ ΝΑΠΟΣΤΟΛΟΣ·
    ΕϥϢΑΧΕ ΕΠΒΙΟΣ ĒΝΕΝΕΙōΤΕ·
    ΕΥΣΟΡΜ 2ΜΠΧΑΙĒ ΜΝΝΙᾱ·
    ΜΝΝΕϢΚΑΛ ΕΠΚΑ2⸗

19 ΤΟΤΕ ΠΕΧΑϥ Ν6Ιᾱᾱᾱ·
    ΧΕΕΙΣ2ΗΗΤΕ ΑΙΟΥĒ ΕΙΠΗΤ·
    ΑΥῶ ΑΙϢΩΠΕ 2ΜΠΧΑΙΕ·
    ΕΙ6ΩϣΤ̄ ĒΒΟΛ 2ΗΤϥ̄ ĒΠΕΤΝΟΥ2Μ ΜΜΟΙ⸗

---

[1] Note the unusual division before the copula, as also in VIII,16/3, IX,15/2, and XI,21/2.

[2] Page Ρ̄Οᾱ, the last page of quire Ῑᾱ, begins.

15 Truly, very great
  is the honour of these holy men,
  who forsook this world
  and followed the Lord Jesus.

16 Our holy father Antony's
  desire is with God,
  and he thinks of the things of heaven,
  the place where Christ is.

17 All men upon earth,
  when they hear of the life of our fathers,
  marvel at their virtues
  and their exalted way of life.

18 Listen to the apostolic priest
  speaking of the life of our fathers,
  wandering in the desert and in ravines
  and the holes of the earth.[1]

19 Then David said:
  Behold, I have fled afar off,
  and have dwelt in the wilderness,
  waiting for him who delivers me.[2]

---

[1] Cf. Hebr. 11.38.
[2] Ps. 54.8-9.

20 ⲎⲖⲓⲁⲥ ⲙⲛⲉ̄ⲗⲓⲥⲥⲁⲓⲟⲥ·
ⲙⲉⲛⲓⲱ2ⲁⲛⲛⲏⲥ ⲡ̄ⲃⲁⲡⲧⲓⲥⲧⲏⲥ·
ⲁⲩⲱⲱⲡⲉ ⲛ̄ⲱⲟⲣⲡ̄ 2ⲓⲡϫⲁⲓⲉ·
ⲱⲁⲛⲧⲉⲛⲉⲛⲉⲓⲟⲧⲉ ⲟⲩⲁ2ⲟⲩ ⲛ̄ⲥⲱⲟⲩ⸗

21 ⲫⲏⲧ ⲉ̄ⲛⲉⲛⲉⲓⲟ̄ⲧⲉ ⲙⲉ2 ⲉ̄ⲣⲁⲱⲉ·
ⲛⲟⲩⲟⲉⲓⲱ ⲛⲓⲙ 2ⲙ̄ⲡ̄ϫⲁⲓⲉ·
ⲉⲩⲱⲟⲟⲡ 2ⲛ̄ⲟⲩⲉⲥⲩⲭⲓⲁ·
ⲉⲩⲧ̇ ⲛ̄ⲛⲉⲩⲱⲗⲏⲗ ⲉⲡⲡⲉⲧϫⲟⲥⲉ⸗

22 ⲭⲁⲣⲓⲥⲙⲁ ⲛⲓⲙ ⲛ̄ⲧⲁⲗϭⲟ·
ⲁⲡⲛⲟⲩⲧⲉ ⲭⲁⲣⲓ2ⲉ ⲙ̄ⲙⲟⲟⲩ ⲛⲁⲕ·
ⲱ ⲡⲉⲛⲓⲱⲧ ⲁⲛⲧⲱⲛⲓⲟⲥ·
ⲙⲛ̄ⲟⲩⲟⲛ ⲛⲓⲙ ⲉ̄ⲧⲓⲛⲉ ⲙ̄ⲙⲟⲕ⸗

23 ⲯⲩⲭⲏ ⲛⲓⲙ ⲛ̄ⲇⲓⲕⲁⲓⲱⲥ·
ⲡⲥⲱ̄ⲣ ⲱⲱ ⲉ̄ⲃⲟⲗ ⲉ̄ⲣⲟⲟⲩ·
ϫⲉⲁ̄ⲙⲏⲓⲧⲛ̄ ⲱⲁⲣⲟⲓ·
ⲛⲉⲧⲥⲙⲁⲙⲁⲁⲧ ⲛⲧⲉⲡⲁⲓⲱⲧ⸗

24 ⲱ̄ ⲡⲉⲛⲓⲱⲧ ⲁⲛⲧⲱⲛⲓⲟⲥ·
ⲥⲟⲡⲥ̄ ⲉ̄ⲡϭ̄ⲥ̄ ⲉ2ⲣⲁⲓ ⲉ̄ϫⲱⲛ·
ⲛ̄ϥⲱⲛ̄2ⲧⲏϥ 2ⲁⲣⲟⲛ·
ⲛ̄ϥⲕⲁⲛⲉⲛⲛⲟⲃⲉ ⲛⲁⲛ ⲉ̄ⲃⲟⲗ:-

20 Elijah and Elisha
    and John the Baptist
    made their abode first in the desert,
    until our fathers followed them.

21 The heart of our fathers is filled with joy
    at all times in the wilderness,
    for they are in solitude,
    offering their prayers to the exalted one.

22 Every gift of healing
    God granted to you,
    O our father Antony,
    and to everyone who is like you.

23 To all righteous souls
    the Saviour proclaims:
    Come to me,
    you blessed of my Father.[1]

24 O our father Antony,
    pray to the Lord for us
    that he may have mercy on us
    and forgive us our sins.

---

[1] Cf. Mt. 25.34.

(pp. ‾ρ‾ο‾δ, line 20 – ‾ρ‾ο‾ϛ, line 13)

ι‾γ   ⲉⲧⲃⲉⲡⲉⲡⲣⲟⲫⲏⲧⲏⲥ ⲁⲡⲁ ϣⲉⲛⲟⲩⲧⲉ:-

1   ⲁⲡⲛⲟⲩⲧⲉ ϣⲁϫⲉ ⲛ̅ϫⲓⲛⲉϣⲟⲣⲡ·
ϩⲛ̅ⲧ̅ⲧⲁⲡⲣⲟ ⲛ̅ⲛⲉϥⲡ̅ⲣⲟⲫⲏⲧⲏⲥ·
ϫⲓⲛⲙⲱⲩⲥⲏⲥ ⲡⲉⲡⲣⲟⲫⲏⲧⲏⲥ·
ϣⲁⲡⲉⲛⲉⲓⲱⲧ ⲁⲡⲁ ϣⲉⲛⲟⲩⲧⲉ⳿

2   ⲃⲁⲃⲁⲓ ⲡⲓϩⲱⲃ ⲉϥⲟ ⲛϣⲡⲏⲣⲉ·
ϫⲉⲁⲡⲛⲟⲩⲧⲉ ϣⲁϫⲉ ⲙⲛ̅ⲙⲱⲩⲥⲏⲥ·
ⲛ̅ⲧⲟⲩ ⲛϣⲉ ⲋϥⲉ ⲛ̅ⲥⲟⲡ·
ⲟⲩⲥⲟⲡ ⲛⲟⲩⲱⲧ ⲁϥⲛⲁⲩ ⲉ̅ⲣⲟϥ⳿

3   ⲅⲁⲓⲅⲁⲣ ⲡⲉⲛⲉⲓⲱⲧ ⲁⲡⲁ ϣⲉⲛⲟⲩⲧⲉ·
ⲡⲁⲣⲭⲏⲙⲁ<ⲛ>ⲇⲣⲓⲧⲏⲥ ⲉⲧⲧⲁⲓⲏⲩ·
ⲁϥϣⲁϫⲉ ⲛ̅ⲧⲟϥ ⲙⲉⲡⲉⲛⲥⲱ̅ⲣ·
ⲛ̅ϩⲁϩ ⲛ̅ⲥⲟⲡ ⲛⲑⲉ ⲛⲟⲩⲣⲱⲙⲉ⳿

4   ⲇⲁ̅ⲇ̅ ⲡⲣ̅ⲣⲟ ⲱϣ ⲉ̅ⲃⲟⲗ·
ϩⲉⲡⲉⲯⲁⲗⲧⲏⲣⲓⲟⲛ ⲉⲧⲧⲁⲓⲏⲩ·
ϫⲉⲛⲉⲕⲟⲩⲏⲏⲃ ⲡ̅ⲛⲟⲩⲧⲉ·
ⲛⲁⲧ ϩⲓⲱ̅ⲟⲩ ⲛⲟⲩⲇⲓⲕⲁⲓⲟⲥⲩⲛⲏ⳿

◄ HYMN THIRTEEN ►

On the prophet Apa Shenoute

1 God spoke of old
by the mouth of his prophets,
from Moses, the prophet,
to our father Apa Shenoute.

2 O this marvel
that God spoke with Moses
five hundred and seventy times;
but only once he saw him.[1]

3 For our father Apa Shenoute,
the renowned archimandrite,
spoke with our Saviour
many times as with a man.

4 King David proclaims
in the precious psalter:
Your priests, God,
shall clothe themselves with righteousness.[2]

---

[1] Cf. Ex. 33.20–3.
[2] Ps. 131.9.

5 εκϣανϣινε ϩⲛ̄ⲡ̄ⲡⲁⲗⲉⲁ·
ϣⲁⲛϭⲉⲛⲙⲱⲩⲥⲏⲥ ⲡⲉⲡⲣⲟⲫⲏⲧⲏⲥ·
εκϣανϣινε ϩⲛ̄ⲧ̄ⲕⲩⲛⲏ·
ϣⲁⲛϭⲉⲛⲡⲉⲛⲉⲓⲱⲧ ⲁ̄ⲡⲁ ϣⲉⲛⲟⲩⲧⲉ⳥

6 ⲍⲱⲅⲣⲁⲫⲓ ⲛⲁⲛ ⲉ̄ⲡⲉⲕⲃⲓⲟⲥ ⲉⲧⲟⲩⲁⲁⲃ·
ⲱ ⲡⲉⲛⲓⲱⲧ ⲁⲡⲁ ϣⲉⲛⲟⲩⲧⲉ·
ⲛ̄ⲭⲓⲛⲉⲕⲉⲛϩⲏⲧⲥ̄ ⲉ̄ⲧⲉⲕⲙⲁⲁⲩ·
ⲁⲩⲙⲟⲩⲧⲉ ⲉ̄ⲣⲟⲕ ⳼ⲉⲡⲉⲡⲣⲟⲫⲏⲧⲏⲥ⳥

7 ⲛ̄ⲧⲁ ⲙⲱⲩⲥⲏⲥ |ϩⲓⲭⲙ̄ⲡ̄ⲧⲟⲟⲩ·[1]
ⲁ̄ⲧⲉⲥⲙⲏ ⲙ̄ⲡϭ̄ⲥ ϣⲱⲡⲉ ϣⲁⲣⲟϥ·
ϫⲉⲙⲡ̄ⲣϩⲱⲛ ⲉ̄ϩⲟⲩⲛ̄ ⲉ̄ⲡⲓⲙⲁ·
ϫⲉⲟⲩⲕⲁϩ ⲉϥⲟⲩⲁⲁⲃ ⲡⲉⲧⲉⲕϩⲓϫⲱϥ⳥

8 ⲑⲉⲱ̄ⲣⲓ ⲟⲛ ⲙ̄ⲡⲉⲡⲣⲟⲫⲏⲧⲏⲥ·
ⲡⲉⲛⲓⲱⲧ ⲉ̄ⲧⲟⲩⲁ̄ⲁⲃ ⲁ̄ⲡⲁ ϣⲉⲛⲟⲩⲧⲉ·
ⲉϥϣⲁϫⲉ ⲛ̄ⲧⲟϥ ⲙⲉⲡⲉⲛⲥⲱ̄ⲣ·
ⲛ̄ϩⲁϩ ⲛⲥⲟⲡ ⲛ̄ⲑⲉ ⲛ̄ⲣⲱⲙⲉ ⲥ̄ⲛⲁⲩ⳥

9 ⲓ̄ⲥ̄ ⲁϥϣⲁϫⲉ ⲙ̄ⲛⲙⲱⲩⲥⲏⲥ·
ϫⲉϫⲓ ⲛⲡ̄ⲗⲁⲟⲥ ⲉϩⲣⲁⲓ ⲉ̄ⲕⲏⲙⲉ·
ϫⲓⲟ̄ⲟⲣ ⲙ̄ⲙⲟⲟⲩ ϩⲛ̄ⲑⲁⲗⲁⲥⲥⲁ·
ⲧⲁⲥⲁⲛⲟⲩϣⲟⲩ ϩ̄ⲛⲧⲉⲣⲏⲙⲟⲥ⳥

---

[1] Page ⲣ̄ⲟ̄ⲉ̄, the first page of quire ⲓ̄ⲃ̄, begins.

5   If you seek in the old (dispensation),
    we find the prophet Moses.
    If you seek in the new,
    we find our father Apa Shenoute.

6   Describe to us your holy life,
    O our father Apa Shenoute.
    While you were yet in your mother's womb,
    you were called prophet.

7   Then Moses was upon the mountain.
    The voice of the Lord came to him:
    Do not approach this place,
    for where you are is holy ground.[1]

8   Consider again the prophet,
    our holy father Apa Shenoute,
    who spoke with our Saviour
    many times as two men speak.

9   Jesus spoke with Moses:
    Take the people down to Egypt.[2]
    Make them cross the sea
    and I shall feed them in the wilderness.

---

[1]   Cf. Ex. 3.5.
[2]   One would expect 'out of Egypt'; cf. Ex. 3.10.

10   ΚΑΙΓΑΡ ΠΕΝΕΙΩΤ ΑΠΑ ϢΕΝΟΥΤΕ·
       ΑϤϢΩΠΕ ΝΙΩΤ Ε̄ϨΝ̄ΜΗΗϢΕ·
       ΑϤΤ̄ΡΕΠΕΥΒΙΟC ϢΩΠΕ·
       Ν̄ΘΕ Μ̄ΠΑΝΕΑΓΓΕΛΟC Ε̄ΤΟΥᾹΑΒ⳽

11   ΛΙΠΟΝ ΜΩΥCΗC ΠΕΠΡΟΦΗΤΗC·
       Ν̄ΤΕΡΕΠ̄ΛΑΟC ΕΡΝΟΒΕ·
       ΑϤϢΛΗΛ ΑΠΚΑϨ Ω̄ΜΚ̄·
       Ν̄ΤΑΘΑΝ Μ̄Ν̄ΑΒΙΡΩΝ⳽

12   ΜΑΡΕΠΕΝΒΙΟC ϢΩΠΕ Ν̄ΘΕ ΜΠΑΠΕΝΙΩΤ ΑΠΑ
        ϢΕΝΟΥΤΕ·
       Ν̄ΤΕΡΕΠΑΝΟΥΗΡϢΕ Ρ̄ΝΟΒΕ·
       ΑϤϢΛΗΛ ΑΠΚΑϨ ΟΥΩΝ Ν̄ΡΩϤ·
       ΑϤΩΜΚ̄ Μ̄ΜΟϤ⳽[1]

13   ΝΕΑΠΝΟΥΤΕ ϢΑΧΕ ΜΝΜΩΥCΗC·
       ΧΕΤΑΜΙΟ̄ ΝΑΙ ΝΟΥC̄ΚΥΝΗ·
       ΑϤΤΑΜΙΟC ΑϤΧΟΚC̄ Ε̄ΒΟΛ·
       ΚΑΤΑΘΕ Ν̄ΤΑϤΧΟΟC ΝΑϤ⳽

14   ϨΑΟΥΝ̄ ΧΕΠΟΥΕϨCΑϨΝΕ Μ̄Π̄Ϭ̄C·
       ΠΕΝΤΑϤϢΩΠΕ Ν̄ΧΙΝΕϢΟΡΠ̄·
       ϢΑΝΤΕΜΩΥCΗC ΤΑΜΙΟ̄ Ν̄ΤΕCΚΥΝΗ·
       Ν̄ΤΕΠ̄ΛΑΟC ϢΛΗΛ Ν̄ϨΗΤC̄⳽

---

[1]   For two corrections in stanzas 11 and 12, see n. ad loc.,
Appendix p. 153 below.

10 For our father Apa Shenoute
   became a father of many.
   He caused their life to become
   like that of the holy angels.

11 Then the prophet Moses,
   when the people sinned,
   prayed and the earth swallowed
   Dathan and Abiram.[1]

12 Let our life be like that of our father Apa Shenoute.
   When the guard[2] sinned,
   he prayed. The earth opened its mouth
   and swallowed him.

13 God had told Moses:
   Make me a tabernacle.
   He made it and completed it,
   as he told him.[3]

14 You know that the command of the Lord
   was from the beginning,
   that Moses should make the tabernacle
   and the people pray therein.

---

[1] Cf. Num. 16.20–35.

[2] I.e. jailer. For the story alluded to, see the Arabic Life of Shenoute: E.Amélineau, *Monuments pour servir à l'histoire de l'Égypte chrétienne aux IVᵉ et Vᵉ siècles* (Mémoires publiés par les membres de la Mission archéologique française au Caire 4,i, Paris 1888), 382-4, and also the Ethiopic version: G. Colin, *La version éthiopenne de la vie de Schenoudi* (CSCO 444–5/Aeth. 75–6, Louvain 1982), translation (445/76), 29–30.

[3] Cf. Ex. 25.7–8.

15 ογνοбπε πταιō μπεⲡⲣοφΗτΗⲥ·
ⲡⲉⲛⲓⲱⲧ ⲁ̄ⲡⲁ ϣⲉⲛⲟⲩⲧⲉ·
ⲛ̄ⲧⲉⲣⲉϥⲥⲱⲣ ⲉⲃⲟⲗ·
ⲉⲡⲙⲟⲛⲁⲥⲧΗⲣⲓⲟⲛ⸗

16 ⲡⲱⲛⲉ ⲛ̄ⲧⲁⲛⲉⲧⲕⲱⲧ ⲥ̄ⲧⲟϥ ⲉ̄ⲃⲟⲗ·
ⲁ̄ⲡⲉⲛⲥⲱⲣ̄ ⲁ̄ⲙⲁϩⲧⲉ ⲙ̄ⲙⲟϥ·
ⲙ̄ⲛ̄ⲡⲉⲛⲓⲱⲧ ⲁ̄ⲡⲁ ϣⲉⲛⲟⲩⲧⲉ·
ⲁϥϯⲟⲩϣⲓⲙⲉ ⲉ̄ⲧⲉⲕⲗΗⲥⲓⲁ̄⸗

17 ⲣⲱⲙⲉ ⲛⲓⲙ ⲉⲧϩⲓⲭⲙ̄ⲡⲕⲁϩ·
ⲉⲩϣⲁⲛⲉⲓ ⲉⲡⲉⲕⲙⲟⲛⲁⲥⲧΗⲣⲓⲟⲛ·
ϣⲁⲩⲣ̄ϣ̄ⲡΗⲣⲉ ⲙ̄ⲡⲱⲛⲉ ⲉⲧⲙ̄ⲙⲁⲩ·
ⲭⲉⲙ̄ⲛ̄ⲗⲁⲁⲩ ⲙ̄ⲡⲱⲗϩ ⲛ̄ϩΗⲧⲟ̄ϥ⸗

18 ⲥⲱⲧⲙ̄ ⲉⲡⲛⲟⲩⲧⲉ ⲡϣⲁⲛⲁϩⲧΗϥ·
ⲉϥϣⲁⲭⲉ ⲙ̄ⲛ̄ⲙⲱⲩⲥΗⲥ·
ⲭⲉⲁ̄ⲙⲟⲩ ⲛⲁⲓ ϩⲓⲭⲙ̄ⲡ̄ⲧⲟⲟⲩ·
ⲧⲁϯ ⲛⲁⲕ ⲙ̄ⲡ̄ⲛⲟⲙⲟⲥ⸗

19 ⲧⲟⲧⲉ ⲁ̄ⲙⲱⲩ̄ⲥΗⲥ ⲡⲱⲧ ⲉ̄ⲭⲙ̄ⲡ̄ⲧⲟⲟⲩ·
ⲁϥⲁ̄ϩⲉⲣⲁⲧϥ̄ ⲁϥϣⲗΗⲗ·
ⲁ̄ⲧⲉⲕⲗⲟⲟ̄ⲗⲉ ϩⲱⲃⲉ̄ ⲙ̄ⲙⲟϥ·
ϣⲁⲛⲧⲉⲡⲛⲟⲩⲧⲉ ϯⲡ̄ⲛⲟⲙⲟⲥ ⲛⲁϥ⸗

15   Great is the honour of the prophet,
     our father Apa Shenoute,
     when he founded
     the monastery.

16   The stone which the builders rejected[1]
     was taken up by our Saviour
     with our father Apa Shenoute,
     and he laid the foundation of the church.[2]

17   All men upon earth,
     when they come to your monastery,
     marvel at that stone,
     for there is no mark on it.

18   Listen to the merciful God,
     speaking with Moses:
     Come to me upon the mountain,
     and I shall give you the law.[3]

19   Then Moses went upon the mountain.
     He stood and prayed.
     The cloud covered him
     until God gave him the law.[4]

---

[1]   Ps. 117.22 etc.
[2]   Cf. the Arabic Life of Shenoute (Amélineau, *Monuments*, 354).
[3]   Cf. Ex. 24.12.
[4]   Cf. Ex. 24.15–18.

20 ⲅ¹ ⲡⲉⲛⲉⲓⲱⲧ ⲁⲡⲁ ϣⲉⲛⲟⲩⲧⲉ·
ⲛⲧⲉⲣⲉⲡⲣ̅ⲣⲟ ϫⲁⲩ ⲓ ⲛ̅ⲥⲱϥ·²
ⲁ̄ⲧⲉⲕⲗⲟ̄ⲟ̄ⲗⲉ ϩⲁⲣⲡⲁⲍⲉ ⲙ̅ⲙⲟϥ·
ⲁⲥϫⲓⲧ̄ϥ̄ ⲉⲡⲡⲁⲗⲗⲁⲧⲓⲟⲛ⳥

21 ⲫⲱⲥⲟⲛ³ ⲛⲧⲉⲣⲉⲡⲣⲣⲟ ⲛⲁⲩ ⲉ̄ⲣⲟϥ·
ⲁϥϣⲱⲡⲉ ϩⲛ̄ⲟⲩⲛⲟ̄ϭ ⲛⲥ̄ⲧⲱⲧ·
ⲁϥⲥⲉⲡⲥⲱⲡϥ ⲁϥⲥ̄ⲙⲟⲩ ⲉ̄ⲣⲟϥ·
ⲁϥⲕⲁⲁϥ ⲉ̄ⲃⲟⲗ ϩⲛⲟⲩⲉⲓⲣⲏⲛⲏ⳥

22 ⲭⲁⲣⲓⲍⲉ ⲛⲁⲛ ⲛⲟⲩⲛⲟ̄ϭ ⲛ̄ϩⲙⲟⲧ·
ⲱ̄ ⲡⲉⲛⲉⲓⲱⲧ ⲁⲡⲁ ϣⲉⲛⲟⲩⲧⲉ·
ⲉⲧⲃⲉⲛⲉϩⲏⲕⲉ ⲙ̄ⲡⲉⲕⲗⲁⲟⲥ·
ϫⲉⲕⲁⲥ ⲛ̄ⲛⲉⲩϫⲓⲧⲟⲩ ⲛ̄ϭⲟⲛⲥ̄⳥

23 ⲯⲩⲭⲏ ⲛⲓⲙ ⲉⲧϩⲓϫⲙ̄ⲡ̄ⲕⲁϩ·
ⲉⲩϣⲁⲛⲉⲓ ⲉ̄ⲡⲉⲕⲙⲟⲛⲁⲥⲧⲏⲣⲓⲟⲛ·
ϣⲁⲩϫⲓ ⲙⲡⲕⲱ ⲉ̄ⲃⲟⲗ ⲛ̄ⲛⲉⲩⲛⲟⲃⲉ·
ϩⲓⲧⲙ̄ⲡⲛⲟⲩⲧⲉ ⲡ̄ϣⲁⲛⲁ ϩⲧⲏϥ⳥

24 ⲱ ⲡⲉⲛⲉⲓⲱⲧ ⲁ̄ⲡⲁ ϣⲉⲛⲟⲩⲧⲉ·
ⲡⲁⲣⲭⲏⲙⲁⲛⲇⲣⲓⲧⲏⲥ ⲉⲧⲧⲁⲓⲏⲩ·
ⲡⲁⲣⲁⲕⲁⲗⲓ ⲙⲡ̄ϭ̄ⲥ̄ ⲉ̄ϫⲱⲛ·
ⲛ̄ϥ̄ⲕⲁⲛⲉⲛⲛⲟⲃⲉ ⲛⲁⲛ ⲉ̄ⲃⲟⲗ:-

---

¹ Presumably for ⲏ.
² Page ⲣ̅ⲟ̅ⲥ̅ begins.
³ For ἐφ’ ὅσον.

144

20   Now our father Apa Shenoute,
      when the emperor sent for him,
      was seized by a cloud[1]
      and taken to the palace.[2]

21   When the emperor saw him,
      he trembled greatly.
      He entreated him, he[3] blessed him
      and he dismissed him in peace.[4]

22   Grant us a great favour,
      O our father Apa Shenoute,
      concerning the poor of your people,
      that they shall not be ill-treated.

23   All souls upon earth,
      if they come to your monastery,
      shall obtain the forgiveness of their sins
      through the merciful God.

24   O our father Apa Shenoute,
      renowned archimandrite,
      beseech the Lord for us
      to forgive us our sins.

---

[1]   Lit.: 'by the cloud'.
[2]   Cf. the Bohairic Life of Shenoute: J. Leipoldt, *Sinuthii archi-mandritae vita et opera omnia* 1 (CSCO 41/Copt. 1=ii,2, Louvain 1906, repr. 1951) 31, §58.
[3]   Presumably Shenoute.
[4]   Cf. the Bohairic Life of Shenoute (Leipoldt, n. 2 above, 33, §62).

APPENDIX

This appendix includes various matters of orthography and palaeography which have been excluded from the notes to the Coptic text
and its translation, and which are not covered by the general
remarks in the Introduction (see pp. 7–9, 13–14). Certain common-
place features (wherever they seem to raise no problem of reading)
are not noted here: the standard forms of final -ℕ and -ⲧ as raised
symbols; the monogram for ⲟⲩ; various letters written larger or
smaller than normal; and the frequent ornamental extension of letters into the top, bottom, and side margins.

Hymn I

2/1   Expected punctuation-mark lacking at the end of the verse.

2/4   ⲙⲡϭⲓⲱ̅ (at the end of the manuscript line).

5/2   ⲡⲉⲓⲡⲣⲟ̅ϥ (at the end of the manuscript line).

6/1   Expected punctuation-mark probably lacking at the end of
the verse.

7/3   ⲧ̇ⲡⲁⲣ

8/1   Expected punctuation-mark probably lacking at the end of
the verse.

9/1   ⲛ̅ⲡⲁⲧⲣⲓⲁⲣ; expected punctuation-mark lacking at the end of
the verse.

11/4   ϣⲁⲧⲡⲁⲣ

12/1   Expected punctuation-mark lacking at the end of the verse.

16/3   Expected punctuation-mark lacking at the end of the verse.

16/4   ⲡⲁⲣ

17/4   ⲡⲁⲣ

22/2   ⲧ̇ⲡⲁⲣ

22/4 ⲉⲡⲛⲟⲩ⳱ (at the end of the manuscript line).

24/4 Although the reading cannot be in doubt, there are only slight traces of the ⲉ̄ of ⲉ̄ⲃⲟⲗ, and a short gap must have been left in front of it. A small hole in the parchment in this area is visible on the photograph of the verso (p. 152), and this fault may have been responsible for the gap.

Hymn II

1 The first stanza can only be analysed as comprising three verses. The scribe may have omitted a verse, possibly confused by the similar beginnings of the verses: ⲁⲡⲟⲩ-, ⲁⲡⲟⲩ-, ⲡⲟⲩ-.

2/2 ⲉⲧⲧⲁⲓⲏⲩ: ⲉ̂ⲣ̂ⲩ (at the end of the manuscript line).

4/1 expected punctuation-mark lacking at the end of the verse: ⲙⲉⲣⲕⲟⲩⲣⲓ̊⸌ (at the end of the manuscript line).

10/1 Expected punctuation-mark lacking at the end of the verse— unless the extended tail from the final letter (which stands at the end of the manuscript line) can be said to fulfil this function.

20/1 Expected punctuation-mark lacking at the end of the verse.

22/1 Expected punctuation-mark lacking at the end of the verse.

Hymn III
Heading: ⲡⲉⲥⲧⲣⲁⲧⲉⲗⲁ⳱

1/3 ⲛⲉⲙⲁ̂ⲣ̂ (at the end of the manuscript line).

20/3 Expected punctuation-mark probably lacking at the end of the verse.

Hymn IV
Heading: ⲡⲉⲥ̄ⲧⲣⲁⲧⲉⲗⲁ⳱

6/1 Expected punctuation-mark lacking at the end of the verse.

9/1 Expected punctuation-mark lacking at the end of the verse.

17/1 ⲙ̄ⲛ̂ⲓ̄ⲱ̄ ⸱

18/3   Expected punctuation-mark probably lacking at the end of the verse.

20/3   ⲉϩⲱⲧⲃ̄ (at the end of the manuscript line).

Hymn V

Heading: ⲑⲉⲱⲁ̇ⲣⲡⲉⲥⲧⲣⲁⲧⲉⲗⲁ

1/4   ⲑⲉⲱⲁⲱ̂ⲣⲟⲥ in full, as also at 3/2. In both cases, the name stands at the end of a verse, and, as a result of being written out in full, exactly fills a manuscript line.

5/1   ⲉ̇ⲛ̈ⲉⲕ: the apparent supralinear mark over the ⲛ is probably an accidental mark.

8/2   ⲑⲉⲱⲁ̄ⲣ̄ ⸱

9/1   Expected punctuation-mark lacking at the end of the verse.

13/4   ⲑⲉⲱⲁ̄ⲣ̄ (at the end of the manuscript line).

14/2   ⲉⲧ⸴ⲧ⸴ ⸱

14/3   Expected punctuation-mark lacking at the end of the verse.

15/2   ⲑⲉⲱⲁ̄ⲣ̄ ⸜

16/3   ⲉⲧ⸴⸱

16/4   ⲑⲉⲱⲁ̄ⲣ̄ (at the end of the manuscript line).

18/3   ⲉⲧ⸴⸱

18/4   ⲑⲉⲱⲁ̄ⲣ̄ (at the end of the manuscript line).

20/2   ⲑⲉⲱⲁ̄ⲣ̄ ⸱

21/4   ⲉⲧ⸴ⲧ⸴ ⫻

23/3   ⲉⲛⲉⲣ̄⸱

24   The arrangement of this stanza in six verses is almost certainly correct, although the punctuation at the end of verse 5, which in the manuscript coincides with the end of a manuscript line, is missing (see p. 10, n. 3).

24/1   ⲙⲁⲣⲧⲩⲣⲟⲥ in full.

Hymn VI

Heading: ⲡⲁⲧⲣⲓⲁⲣ

3/3   Expected punctuation-mark probably lacking at the end of the verse.

4/2   Expected punctuation-mark probably added above the line.

13/4   ⲛⲉⲩⲉⲕⲕⲥ (at the end of the manuscript line).

15/2   ⲛⲛⲉⲉⲡⲓⲥⲕ (at the end of the manuscript line).

23/3   Expected punctuation-mark lacking at the end of the verse.

24/2   ⲥⲱⲣ: the word is also written in full in this verse, when referring to Severus; cf. the entry in the Index of Greek Loan-Words.

24/4   ⲛϥⲕⲁⲛⲉⲛⲛⲟⲃⲉ (at the end of the manuscript line).

Hymn VII

5/1   Expected punctuation-mark lacking at the end of the verse.

8/4   Expected punctuation-mark lacking at the end of the verse. Nevertheless, it seems inevitable that the stanza in its present form must be analysed as containing five verses.

9/1   ⲓⲱ

9/3   ⲉⲛⲉϥⲙⲁ ; expected punctuation-mark lacking at the end of the verse—unless the form of the abbreviation (which stands at the end of the manuscript line) can be said to fulfil this function.

14/3   Expected punctuation-mark lacking at the end of the verse.

15/1   Expected punctuation-mark lacking at the end of the verse.

20/1   Expected punctuation-mark lacking at the end of the verse.

21/3   Expected punctuation-mark lacking at the end of the verse.

23/3   ⲡⲓⲱ : the abbreviation stands at the end of the manuscript line; expected punctuation-mark lacking at the end of the verse (and the form of the abbreviation hardly fulfils this function).

24/2   Expected punctuation-mark lacking at the end of the verse.

24/3   Expected punctuation-mark lacking at the end of the verse.

Hymn VIII

1/3   Expected punctuation-mark lacking at the end of the verse.

2/2   Expected punctuation-mark lacking at the end of the verse.

3/3   NNEⲘ̄ .

4/4   ⲡⲉⲧⲟⲛⲁⲣ⳥   (at the end of the manuscript line). See p. 86, n. 1).

5/1   This stanza is not furnished with an enlarged letter in the left-hand margin (see p. 9).

6/4   ⲉ̄ⲙⲓⲭⲁⲏ̄

7/1   Expected punctuation-mark lacking at the end of the verse.

7/2   Expected punctuation-mark lacking at the end of the verse. However, a space was left in the manuscript line at this point. Some gap was required here to avoid the descending tail of a ⲍ from the line above, but the space extends substantially further than was necessary for this purpose.

8/1   Expected punctuation-mark lacking at the end of the verse.

11/3-4 The expected punctuation-mark at the end of the third verse may well be a later addition, and a clear space now stands between ⲕⲱⲧⲉ and ⲉ̄ⲛⲉⲧⲡ̄ϩⲟⲧⲉ. Probably the position of the punctuation-mark was altered.

20/1   Expected punctuation-mark perhaps added later.

22/1   Expected punctuation-mark lacking at the end of the verse.

Hymn IX

1/3   Expected punctuation-mark lacking at the end of the verse.

2/2   ⲉⲧ ⲧ⳽   (at the end of the manuscript line). Expected punctuation-mark lacking at the end of the verse (and the form of the abbreviation hardly fulfils this function).

17/1   ⲱⲓⲱ̄ •

18/1   Expected punctuation-mark perhaps added later.

21/3   Expected punctuation-mark lacking at the end of the verse.

22/1   Expected punctuation-mark probably added above the line.

Hymn X

2/1   ⲓⲱ ⁚

4/1   Expected punctuation-mark lacking at the end of the verse.

6/2   ⲡⲉⲡⲣⲟⲫ̄   (at the end of the manuscript line).

9/1   ⲓⲱ⁚ⲟⲛ⸗

9/3   Expected punctuation-mark probably lacking at the end of the verse.

10/1   Expected punctuation-mark lacking at the end of the verse.

10/2   ⲉⲧ̑ⲧ̑ ⁚

11/4   ⲉⲣⲉⲓ̄ⲱ

13/4   ⲛⲁⲡⲟⲥⲧⲟⲗⲟⲛ̄ //   occurs at the end of the last line of page ⲣ̄ⲗ̄ⲑ, and the final -ⲛ seems clearly to be indicated by the long supralinear stroke, although the reading ⲛⲁⲡⲟⲥⲧⲟⲗⲟⲥ would be expected.

14/1   ⲱⲓⲱ̄ ▪

15/1   Expected punctuation-mark lacking at the end of the verse.

22/2   Expected punctuation-mark lacking at the end of the verse.

Hymn XI

1/2   ⲡⲟⲩⲏ̑ (at the end of the manuscript line): ⲡⲟⲩⲏ̑ | ⲏⲃ

3/3   ⲡⲡⲁⲧⲣⲓⲁⲣ̄

6/4   ⲉⲧ̑ⲧ̑ //

14/1   ⲍⲱⲕ̑ϣⲣⲟⲕ: the ϣ is written noticeably smaller than usual. Possibly ⲉⲣⲟⲕ has been corrected to ϣⲁⲣⲟⲕ.

15/3   Expected punctuation-mark lacking at the end of the verse.

22/1 ⲡ̄ⲡⲁⲧⲣⲓⲁⲣⳉ·

23/1 Expected punctuation-mark lacking at the end of the verse.

Hymn XII

2/1 Expected punctuation-mark lacking at the end of the verse.

10/1 Expected punctuation-mark probably lacking at the end of the verse.

20/2 ⲙⲉⲛⲓⲱ̄

Hymn XIII

5/4 ⲁ̇ⲡⲁⳉⲉⲛⲟⲩ̄ ⫻ (at the end of the manuscript line).

11/1 Expected punctuation-mark probably lacking at the end of the verse.

11–12 Two corrections in these stanzas are probably the result of confusion between similar phrases which occur in them. In stanza 11, an erasure follows ⲁⲡⲕⲁⲅ (11/3), extending to, but not including, the final punctuation mark of the stanza (11/4). The words ⲱ̄ⲙ̄ⲕ·ⲛ̄ⲧⲁⲑⲁ |ⲙ̄ⲛⲁ̇ⲃⲓⲣⲱⲛ were written in place of the erased matter. As there was insufficient room available, the correction encroaches upon the side margins of the column. In 12/4, a similar, but longer, erasure follows ⲁϥⲱⲙ̄ⲕ, again ending immediately before the final punctuation mark of the stanza. In place of this erasure was written ⲙ̄ⲙⲟϥ, which occupies considerably less room than the deleted matter. Thus blank space stands before and after ⲙ̄ⲙⲟϥ; as an incidental consequence, it is followed by a double set of punctuation marks, with about 2 cm of blank space between them.

11/4 ⲛ̇ⲧⲁⲑⲁ ; this stands at the end of the manuscript line, and protrudes into the margin, as it forms part of one of the corrections described in the preceding note.

23/1 Expected punctuation-mark lacking at the end of the verse.

24/1 Expected punctuation-mark lacking at the end of the verse.

153

INDEXES

I. Personal Names

155

ⲙⲉⲣⲕⲟⲩⲣⲓⲟⲥ II, title; 3/1; 4/1; 6/2; 12/2; 14/1; 16/2; 21/1; 23/2; 24/1
ⲙⲓⲭⲁⲏⲗ II,9/2. VIII, title; 1/2; 3/4; 4/2, /4; 6/4; 9/1; 12/3; 13/1; 17/3; 18/2; 23/4; 25/2
ⲙⲱⲩⲥⲏⲥ I,3/1. VIII,2/1. XI,12/1. XIII,1/3; 2/2; 5/2; 7/1; 9/1; 11/1; 13/1; 14/3; 18/2; 19/1

ⲛⲁⲩⲏ II,9/1. VIII,6/1

ⲟⲩⲁⲗⲗⲏⲣⲓⲁⲛⲟⲥ (Valerian) II,7/2

ⲡⲁⲛⲥⲉ III,20/1; 21/2; 22/2; 23/3
ⲡⲁⲩⲗⲟⲥ IV,4/1; 9/1. VII,17/2. VIII,18/1. IX,12/1; 23/4. X,13/3; 18/1
ⲡⲉⲧⲣⲟⲥ IV,17/1. VII,16/1. VIII,17/1. IX,6/1; 14/1; 15/2. XI,2/2; 10/1. — See also ⲥⲓⲙⲱⲛ

ⲥⲉⲩⲏⲣⲟⲥ VI, title; 1/3; 5/3; 8/3; 10/3; 12/2; 13/3; 14/2; 15/3; 16/3; 17/3; 18/3; 19/3; 20/2; 22/1; 23/2; 24/1. XI, title; 1/4; 3/3; 9/2; 14/2; 21/2; 22/1; 24/1

ⲥⲓⲙⲱⲛ (of Cyrene) IX,24/2
ⲥⲓⲙⲱⲛ (Peter) VII,10/4. — See also ⲡⲉⲧⲣⲟⲥ
ⲥⲟⲗⲟⲙⲱⲛ I,21/1. IV,10/3. VI,6/2

ⲧⲁⲑⲁⲛ (Δαθάν) XIII,11/4

ⲫⲓⲗⲓⲡⲡⲟⲥ VIII,22/1. IX,18/1. X,21/1
ⲫⲓⲗⲱⲡⲁⲧⲏⲣ II,6/4; 21/1

ⲭⲣⲏⲥⲧⲓⲁⲛⲟⲥ V,8/4. VI,3/3; 18/1
ⲭ(ⲣⲓⲥⲧⲟ)ⲥ I,16/3. II,15/4. V,10/2; 24/4. VI,3/4; 9/4. VIII,16/1. IX,6/4. X,13/1, /2; 17/2. XI,8/1; 18/2. XII,16/4. — See also ⲓ(ⲏⲥⲟⲩ)ⲥ and ⲭ(ⲣⲓⲥⲧⲟ)ⲥ ⲓ(ⲏⲥⲟⲩ)ⲥ
ⲭ(ⲣⲓⲥⲧⲟ)ⲥ ⲓ(ⲏⲥⲟⲩ)ⲥ II,5/3

ϣⲉⲛⲟⲩⲧⲉ XIII, title; 1/4; 3/1; 5/4; 6/2; 8/2; 10/1; 12/1; 15/2; 16/3; 20/1; 22/2; 24/1

ϩⲁⲣⲙⲉⲛⲓⲟⲥ IV,20/2
ϩⲣⲱⲙⲁⲛⲟⲥ III,1/4; 10/3; 14/1, 3; 19/4. IV,20/4

II. Geographical

ⲁⲛⲧⲓⲛⲱⲟⲩ III,12/2
ⲁⲛⲧⲓⲟⲭⲉⲩⲥ IV,8/1
ⲁⲛⲧⲓⲟⲭⲓⲁ IV,16/2. VI,12/1

ⲃⲁⲃⲩⲗⲱⲛ VIII,13/3

ⲉⲩⲭⲏⲧⲟⲥ (Euchaites) V,6/2; 7/1

ⲓⲟⲣⲇⲁⲛⲏⲥ X,1/3; 8/2; 10/4; 11/2; 16/2; 19/2; 20/3; 22/1
ⲓⲱⲥⲁⲫⲁⲧ IX,9/3

ⲕⲁⲡⲡⲁⲇⲟⲕⲓⲁ II,16/3
ⲕⲏⲙⲉ III,11/2. IV,16/3; 24/1. XIII,19/2
ⲕⲩⲣⲓⲛⲛⲉⲟⲥ (Κυρηναῖος) IX,24/2

ⲗⲓⲃⲁⲛⲟⲥ X,8/4

ⲡⲉⲣⲥⲓⲥ II,24/2
ⲡⲟⲩⲥⲓⲣⲉ (Abusir) III,20/1

ⲣⲁⲕⲟⲧⲉ (ⲣⲉⲙ-) IV,20/1

ⲥⲁⲙⲁⲣⲓⲧⲏⲥ IX,19/4
ⲥⲓⲱⲛ I,17/1

ⲧⲓⲃⲉⲣⲓⲁⲥ VII,9/4

ⲭⲁⲗⲕⲉⲇⲱⲛ VI,15/2. — ⲭⲁⲗⲭⲏⲇⲱⲛ VI,13/1

ϩⲓⲉⲣⲓⲭⲱ VIII,6/2

III. Greek Loan-Words

ἀγαθός ⲁⲅⲁⲑⲟⲥ IV,1/2. X,3/3. — (ⲙⲛⲧ)ⲁⲅⲁⲑⲟⲥ XII,9/4
ἀγάπη (ⲙⲁⲓ)ⲁⲅⲁⲡⲏ III,11/4
ἀγγελικόν ⲁⲅⲅⲉⲗⲓⲕⲟⲛ I,20/4. VIII,12/2
ἄγγελος ⲁⲅⲅⲉⲗⲟⲥ II,3/4. III,21/2; 22/2; 23/3. V,16/2. VII,2/3; 6/2; 16/3. VIII,2/2; 7/2; 8/3; 10/2; 11/3; 12/4; 14/2; 15/2; 19/2; 20/1; 21/3; 22/2; 24/4. IX,12/3. XIII,10/4

ἅγιος ϩⲁⲅⲓⲟⲥ II, title; 3/1; 6/2; 12/2; 23/2; 24/1. III, title; 4/2. V, title; 1/4; 3/2; 8/2; 15/2; 16/4; 18/4; 20/2. VIII,13/3
ἀγών ⲁⲅⲱⲛ VI,22/3. VIII,21/4
ἀγωνοθέτης ⲁⲅⲱⲛⲱⲑⲉⲧⲏⲥ VI,22/2
ἀετός ⲁⲉⲧⲟⲥ III,9/2
ἀθλητής ⲁⲑⲗⲏⲧⲏⲥ IV,3/2

156

αἱρετικός ϨΡΕΤΙΚΟΣ VI,4/3; 7/2; 19/4; 21/3. XI,7/4. — ϨΡΕϮΚΟΣ VI,23/4
αἰτεῖν (ΕΛ)ΕΤΙΝ VI,9/1
ἀκέραιος ΑΚΕΡΕΟΣ IX,5/4
ἀληθινόν ΑΛΗΘΙΝΟΝ VI,12/3. XI,16/3
ἀληθῶς ΑΛΗΘѠΣ III,1/1. IV,24/1. V,1/1. VI,4/1. VII,15/1. VIII,1/1. IX,1/1. XII,15/1
ἀλλά ΑΛΛΑ III,17/3; 22/4. IV,21/2, /4. V,13/3. IX,2/4
ἀλφάβητα ΑΛΦΑΒΗΤΑ I, title. II, title. III, title. IV, title. V, title. VI, title. VII, title. VIII, title. IX, title
ἀνάγκη ΑΝΑΓΚΗ V,17/2
ἀνάλημψις ΑΝΑΛΥΜΨΙΣ VII, title; 3/4; 15/4; 18/4
ἀνάστασις ΑΝΑΣΤΑΣΙΣ VII, title; 3/3; 4/3; 6/3; 7/2; 8/2, /5; 10/2; 14/4; 15/3; 18/3. VIII,19/4
ἄνομος ΑΝΟΜΟΣ II,24/3
ἀξίωμα ΑΞΙѠΜΑ IV,19/4
ἀπαρχή ΑΠΑΡΧΗ VII,19/3
ἀπολογία ΑΠΟΛΟΓΙΑ II,22/3
ἀποστάτης ΑΠΟΣΤΑΤΗΣ VI,14/4
ἀποστολικός ΑΠΟΣΤΟΛΙΚΟΣ XI,16/1
ἀπόστολος ΑΠΟΣΤΟΛΟΣ IV,4/1. V,24/2. VII,8/1; 13/2; 21/2. VIII,3/1; 17/1; 22/1. IX, title; 1/2; 13/2; 14/2; 21/2; 23/4; 24/3. X,21/1. XII,18/1. — ΑΠΟΣΤΟΛΟΝ X,13/4
ἀρετή ΑΡΕΤΗ XII,1/1; 14/4; 17/3
ἀριθμός ΑΡΙΘΜΟΣ II,13/4
ἄριστον ΑΡΙΣΤΟΝ VIII,5/2; 9/3
ἅρμα ϨΑΡΜΑ VIII,22/3
ἀρνεῖσθαι ΑΡΝΑ IX,14/3. XII,2/3
ἁρπάζειν ϨΑΡΠΑΖΕ XIII,20/3
ἀρχάγγελος ΑΡΧΑΓΓΕΛΟΣ I,11/3. II,8/2. VIII, title; 13/1. — ΑΡΧΗΑΓΓΕΛΟΣ VIII,16/3
ἀρχή ΑΡΧΗ X,24/3
ἀρχιμανδρίτης ΑΡΧΗΜΑΝΔΡΙΤΗΣ XIII,3/2; 24/2
ἄρχων ΑΡΧѠΝ I,14/3. III,24/2. VIII,4/4
ἀσπάζεσθαι ΑΣΠΑΖΕ I,18/4

βαβαί ΒΑΒΑΙ XIII,2/1
βαπτίζειν ΒΑΠΤΙΖΕ VIII,22/4. X,11/4; 13/1; 14/2; 15/4; 21/3
βάπτισμα ΒΑΠΤΙΣΜΑ X, title; 17/3; 23/3
βαπτιστής ΒΑΠΤΙΣΤΗΣ XII,20/2
βάρβαρος ΒΑΡΒΑΡΟΣ II,3/3; 4/3; 12/3
βασανίζειν ΒΑΣΑΝΙΖΕ IV,19/3
βάτος ΒΑΤΟΣ I,3/3

βίος ΒΙΟΣ II,6/1. III,2/1. VI,2/1. XI,6/1. XII,6/4; 14/3; 17/2; 18/2. XIII,6/1; 10/3; 12/1
βοηθεῖν (ρ)ΒΟΙΘΙ V,9/3. — (ρ)ΒΟΗΘΙ V,10/3. — (ΕΡ)ΒΟΗΘΙ V,17/5

γάρ ΓΑΡ IV,7/1; 19/1. — See also καὶ γάρ
γενεά ΓΕΝΕΑ I,5/4 bis
γένος ΓΕΝΟΣ VIII,16/4
γραφή ΓΡΑΦΗ IV,13/1. VII,3/1. XI,18/1; 20/3

δαιμόνιον ΔΕΜѠΝΙΟΝ V,3/3; 22/4. XII,8/1
δέ ΔΕ II,19/1. IV,6/4. IX,9/1
διακονεῖν ΔΙΑΚѠΝΙ VIII,21/3
διδάσκαλος ΔΙΔΑΣΚΑΛѠΣ XI,6/2
δίκαιος ΔΙΚΑΙΟΣ II,1/1; 2/3. — ΔΙΚΕΟΣ II,1/3. — ΔΙΚΑΙѠΣ XII,23/1
δικαιοσύνη ΔΙΚΑΙΟΣΥΝΗ IV,2/3. XI,12/4. XIII,4/4
δικαίως ΔΙΚΑΙΟΣ VI,4/1
δόγμα ΔΟΓΜΑ VI,4/4; 7/4; 19/3; 23/3. XI,7/3. — ΔѠΓΜΑ VI,15/3
δογματίζειν ΔΟΓΜΑΤΙΖΕ VI,18/4
δογματικός ΔΟΓΜΑΤΙΚΟΣ XI,16/2
δούξ (dux) ΔΟΥϤ IV,23/2
δράκων ΔΡΑΚѠΝ V,11/3
δυνατός ΔΥΝΑΤΟΣ II,10/4
δωρεά ΔѠΡΕΑ VIII,23/2
δῶρον ΔѠΡΟΝ V,15/4

ἔθνος ϨΕΘΝΟΣ I,13/3. VII,18/1. VIII,2/4. — ΕΘΕΝΟΣ IX,11/2
εἰρήνη ϨΙΡΗΝΗ V,8/1. — ΕΙΡΗΝΗ IX,7/4. XIII,21/4. — ΙΡΗΝΗ XI,12/4
εἶτα ΕΙΤΑ III,5/1. — ΗΤΑ III,7/1. V,7/1. IX,7/1. XIII,7/1
ἐκκλησία ΕΚΛΗΣΙΑ II,22/1. VI,2/2; 5/4; 6/3. VIII,3/2. XIII,16/4. — ΕΚΚΛΗΣΙΑ VI,13/4; 20/4. XI,13/1
ἐλευθεροῦν ΕΛΕΓΘΕΡΟΥ V,11/2
ἐξουσία ΕϤΟΥΣΙΑ V,3/1. VII,16/4. XI,2/3; 3/1. XII,10/2
ἐπιθυμεῖν ΕΠΙΘΥΜΙ IV,12/2
ἐπίσκοπος ΕΠΙΣΚΟΠΟΣ II,18/3; 23/1. VI,13/1; 15/2
ἔρημος ΕΡΗΜΟΣ XIII,9/4
ἑρμηνεία ϨΕΡΜΗΝΙΑ XI,18/3
εὐαγγέλιον ΕΓΑΓΓΕΛΙΟΝ II,2/2. IX,2/2. XI,20/4

157

εὐαγγελιστής **εγαγγελιстнс** I,11/1; 12/1; 18/1. VII,9/1. VIII,19/1. IX,24/4

εὐσεβής **εγсεвнс** VI,18/1. — (**μετ**)**εγсεвнс** XI,11/2

εὐφραίνειν **εγφρανε** VIII,1/2

ἐφ᾽ ὅσον **φωсон** XIII,21/1

ζωγραφεῖν **ζωγραφι** II,6/1; 21/2. IV,12/3. V,6/1; 20/1. X,6/1. XI,6/1. XIII,6/1

ἤ **н** VI,7/1. — **γ** XIII,20/1

ἡγεμών **ϩнгεμων** IV,19/3; 23/4

ἡλικία **ϩγλнкιλ** IV,21/1. — **γλнкιλ** XI,20/1

ἡσυχία **εсγχιλ** XII,21/3

θάλασσα **θλλλссλ** VII,9/4. VIII,18/3. X,10/3. XIII,9/3

θεοτόκος **θεωΔωкос** I,1/4; 13/4; 20/1; 24/2. — **θεωΔοкос** I,15/2

θεωρεῖν **θεωρι** I,3/3; 8/1; 9/3. V,15/3. VIII,9/1. IX,8/1. X,8/1; 11/3. XIII,8/1

θεωρία **θεωριλ** I,14/1. VIII,15/1

θλίβειν **θλιвε** XII,11/2

θρόνος **θρονос** IX,8/4

θυσιάζειν **θγсιλζε** II,14/3

θυσιαστήριον **θγсιλстнριон** VIII,7/3

ἱερεύς **ϩιερεγс** IV,4/1. — **ϩιεрос** X,13/4. XII,18/1

ἱστορία **ϩιсτωριλ** II,18/2

ἰώ **ιω** III,9/1

καί γάρ **гεклр** I,3/1. XI,3/1. XII,3/1. — **гεглр** II,3/1. III,3/1. IV,22/1. V,3/1. VI,3/1. VII,3/1. VIII,3/1. IX,3/1. X,3/1. — **кεглр** III,10/1. IV,15/1. VI,10/1. — **клιглр** XI,10/1. XIII,10/1. — **глιглр** XIII,3/1

καινή **кγнн** VII,3/2. XIII,5/3

καλλωπίζειν **клλιωπιζε** VI,23/2

καλῶς **клλωс** I,10/1. II,10/1; 17/2. V,10/1. VI,22/3. VIII,11/1. IX,10/1. X,10/1. XI,23/3

καρπός **клрпос** IV,15/4. — (**ρεϥ†**)**клрпос** IV,15/1

κάστρον (castrum) III,12/2

κατά **клтλ** IV,10/3. VII,11/1. VIII,24/2. X,13/3. XI,1/3; 21/3. XII,10/1. XIII,13/4

καταργεῖν **клτλргι** XII,9/1

κελεύειν **кεлεγε** III,6/4

κελεφός **кεлεφос** IV,18/4

κιβωτός **кιвωтос** I,22/3

κλάδος **клλΔос** IV,15/2

κληρονομία **клнρономιλ** IV,3/3

κλῆρος **клнрос** XII,12/4

κοντάριον **конΔλριон** II,23/3

κοσμεῖν **кωсмι** VI,6/1, /3

κόσμος **космос** I,13/1; 24/1. II,15/1. IV,11/3. V,12/4. VII,17/3; 24/1. VIII,25/1. IX,9/2; 12/4. X,1/1; 2/4; 5/2; 24/1. XI,21/4. XII,15/3

κρίνον **кρινон** X,22/3

κωνώπιον **коновιон** III,2/4; 4/3; 8/2; 9/1. — **коνωвιон** III,3/2

λαός **λλос** I,2/3; 20/3; 24/1. IV,14/1; 20/1. V,15/1. VII,24/1. VIII,12/1; 25/1. IX,11/1. X,11/1; 24/1. XI,4/2; 9/3; 12/3. XIII,9/2; 11/2; 14/4; 22/3

λέξις **λεξιс** XI,13/2

λόγος **λογос** XI,6/4; 8/4; 11/1; 17/3

λογχίζειν **λογχιζε** IV,23/3

λοιπόν **λοιπон** II,11/1. V,11/1. VI,11/1. XII,11/1. — **λιπон** XIII,11/1

λυχνία **λγχνιλ** I,6/3

μαθητής **μλθнтнс** VII,9/3. — (**ερ**)**μλθнтнс** XII,2/2

μαργαρίτης **μλρклριтнс** I,12/4

μαρτύριον **μλρτγριон** II,17/3. — **μλр-тнριон** II,20/3

μάρτυς **μλρτγρос** II,19/3. III,1/3; 19/2. IV,3/1; 13/3; 14/2; 17/3; 18/2; 21/4; 24/3. V,14/1; 23/3; 24/1. VIII,3/3

μελετᾶν **μελετλ** XI,6/3; 17/2

μοναστήριον **μонλсτнριон** VI,21/1. XIII,15/4; 17/2; 23/2

μοναχός (**μnt**)**монлхос** XII,6/4

μυστήριον **μγстнριон** X,15/1

νόμος **номос** XI,12/3. XIII,18/4; 19/1

ξένος **ϫενωс** VI,14/1

οἰκουμένη **ικογμεнн** VI,1/2. IX,10/4. — **οικογμεнн** XI,16/4

ὁμολογία **ϩομολογιλ** XI,8/1

ὄντως **ωnτωс** II,24/1. III,24/1

ὅπλον **ϩοπλон** IV,4/3

ὀρεινή **ωρινн** I,18/3

ὀρθόδοξος **ορθοΔοϫος** XI,24/2

οὐκ **ογк** IV,10/1

παλαιά **πλλελ** VII,3/2. XIII,5/1

χάρισμα ϫⲁⲣⲓⲥⲙⲁ IV,14/3. VIII,23/1.
  XII,22/1
χιών ϫⲓⲱⲛ X,19/4
χλαμύς ϫⲗⲁⲙⲩⲥ IV,18/3
χορεύειν ϫⲱⲣⲉⲅⲉ VII,22/2
χορός ϫⲱⲣⲟⲥ V,24/1. — ϫⲟⲣⲟⲥ V,24/2,
  /3
χρεία (ⲉⲣ)ϫⲣⲓⲁ II,15/3. — (ⲣ)ϫⲣⲓⲁ
  X,9/3
χρῆμα ϫⲣⲏⲙⲁ II,15/2; 22/1
χώρα ϫⲱⲣⲁ IV,16/3; 24/1. V,22/1.
  IX,15/4

ψάλλειν ⲯⲁⲗⲗⲓ I,4/1; 23/1. V,23/2 bis.
  VIII,24/1. IX,23/2. — ⲯⲁⲗⲗⲉⲓ
  I,23/1. VIII,24/1. IX,23/1 bis. —
  ⲯⲁⲗⲓ I,23/2 bis. V,23/1 bis.
  VII,23/1. VIII,24/3. IX,23/2
ψαλτήριον ⲯⲁⲗⲧⲏⲣⲓⲟⲛ I,10/2. II,10/2.
  IV,6/2; 22/2. V,4/2. VII,4/2.
  VIII,11/2. IX,10/2. X,10/2.
  XIII,4/2
ψυχή ⲯⲩϫⲏ I,19/2. IV,22/4. XI,11/4.
  XII,1/2; 23/1. XIII,23/1

ᾠδή ⲱⲇⲏ VII,4/3; 20/2
ὡς ϩⲱⲥ IX,20/3

IV. Index of Literary References

160